DECODING BRANDING

Decoding Branding explains the evolution of branding and how the disrupting factors like digital revolution, technological advancement, changing consumer behavior, and the COVID-19 pandemic have reshaped the marketing landscape. Fundamental principles of fostering strong brands are distilled with illustrations of case studies from various industries. A structured and holistic framework to building and revamping brands is clearly presented for corporations to remain competitive in this constantly changing operating environment. Interviews with branding experts and corporate leaders are featured at the end of each chapter to allow readers to obtain a complete appreciation of brand development from different perspectives.

Royce Yuen is a marketing veteran and has more than thirty years of brand-building experience. He was formerly the Chairman of Ogilvy Southern China / Hong Kong and the HK4As. Royce is a Professor of Practice and has been lecturing on branding and communications for MBA programs across China and Hong Kong for more than two decades. Royce was awarded an Honorary University Fellowship by the Hong Kong Polytechnic University, named Scholar Marketer by the Hong Kong Institute of Marketing, and appointed Justice of the Peace by the Government of the HKSAR. He serves on several advisory committees for the HKSAR and is an advisor to the Our Hong Kong Foundation.

D1089429

DECODING BRANDING

A Complete Guide to Building
and Revamping Brands in
the Age of Disruption

Royce Yuen

Routledge
Taylor & Francis Group

LONDON AND NEW YORK

First published 2021
by Routledge
2 Park Square, Milton Park, Abingdon, Oxon OX14 4RN

and by Routledge
605 Third Avenue, New York, NY 10158

Routledge is an imprint of the Taylor & Francis Group, an informa business

© 2021 Royce Yuen

British Library Cataloguing-in-Publication Data
A catalogue record for this book is available from the British Library

Library of Congress Cataloging-in-Publication Data
A catalog record has been requested for this book

ISBN: 978-1-138-80266-7 (hbk)
ISBN: 978-1-138-80267-4 (pbk)
ISBN: 978-1-315-75407-9 (ebk)

Typeset in Bembo
by Deanta Global Publishing Services, Chennai, India

For Gadys, Hillary, and Sonia
Thank you for being my motivation and inspiration in life

CONTENTS

FIGURES

Figures

Images

FOREWORD

In his career, Dr. Royce Yuen has been a distinguished practitioner of marketing and advertising, a profound academic interpreter, and a much-in-demand consultant. He has experienced first-hand all the great waves of disruption which have broken over the communications landscape as a result of the digital revolution. Now, 20 years or so into that revolution, it is timely to ask whether branding – one of the pillars of business since the nineteenth century – is still a necessary or potent strategy for a business.

Some zealots have argued that in a digital world, branding has become less relevant, even superfluous. I have always found that an extreme view, which conflates two very different points: the role of mass media and the role of media. We have, indeed, seen the end of the supremacy of mass media. But it does not follow that we have seen the end of branding. In fact, I would argue exactly the reverse. The de-massification which Dr. Yuen describes actually makes branding more important. The more fragmented the world of content and the multiplicity of messages that characterize any digital eco-system are, the more you need some principle of editing, and it has always seemed to me that one of the purposes of brands is to act as editors. In the past it was easier (not better) when one had simply to create a 30-second television commercial. Now it is much, much more difficult.

Consumers remain fundamentally unchanged; they just have many more messages to decode, and brands make it easier for them to do that. Nor have they become merely functional end users who depend simply on the provision of information in order to make a purchasing decision. In one of the most important insights in this book, Dr. Yuen points out that "Brands provide rational reasons for consumers to behave irrationally." That was the case, is the case, and always will be the case.

Decoding Branding is an important contribution to business literature today. As Dr. Yuen writes, "A good brand radiates positive energy." I think exactly the same can be said of a good business.

Miles Young
Warden, New College Oxford

PREFACE

In my more than three decades of working with numerous corporations across various sectors, I have come to realize that there are four types of brand-owners:

- Firstly, there are brand-owners who are not aware of and do not understand the importance of branding.
- Then, there are brand-owners who are aware of but do not truly understand the importance of branding.
- There are also brand-owners who are aware of and understand the importance of branding but have chosen not to consistently and adequately invest in brand-building.
- Finally, there are brand-owners who recognize, respect, and commit to brand-building, and eventually become leaders within their categories.

This book is written for the last type of brand-owner and even more so for the former ones. Through the following chapters, I intend to trigger more discourse, thinking, and eventually actions to build more great brands.

Branding is such a dynamic and ever-evolving concept that I hope to update this book periodically to include the latest branding developments. Readers are welcome to share and contribute their views on the *Decoding Branding* website to collectively enrich the domain of branding. The website will serve as a platform for brand enthusiasts to exchange ideas, and some of its content may be selected for incorporation in the next edition of *Decoding Branding*.

www.decodingbranding.com

ACKNOWLEDGMENTS

My sincere gratitude to the following scholars and business leaders who have generously contributed their views on branding:

Edward Bell
Christopher Chan
Michael Chan
Wilson Chan
Arthur Chang
Vincent Cheung
David Fong
Chong Got
Randy Lai
David Lee
William Leung
Terence Ling
David Qing
Kanie Siu
Kim Siu
William Shum
Richard Sun
Philip Tsai
David Tse
Kent Wertime
Eliza Wong
Kent Wong
Mike Wong
Ruthia Wong

Sunny Wong
TK Wong
David Yeung
Anna Yip
Henry Yip

A NOTE FROM MY DAUGHTERS

Dearest Daddy,

Surprise! An early congratulation on your new book. We know it's currently still in the works, but we are already so proud of and excited for you. When you told us you were finally going to write a book, we knew that it would be amazing from the get-go. You are a born teacher, so it is just natural that you would eventually impart your wisdom through the written word.

You have always been a source of inspiration in our lives, a wonderful source of tenacious, fearless, and passionate energy that has constantly reminded us to be persistent, never to give up, and always to pursue what we love. We have no doubt that this book, and the journey of writing it through its highs and lows, will just be another shining example of that. Even though we will be away mostly in Berkeley and Chicago when you are continuing to write, we (and of course mom!) are always here as your biggest, unwavering supporters to cheer you on! We love you very much and we can't wait to read your book!

Love you always,
Your twins
Sonia and Hillary

Picture of the author and his twin daughters

1

WELCOME TO THE AGE
OF "DISRUPTION"

Disruption, as a word, is not new to the dictionary.

But the way it is used to describe the rapid and unprecedented reshaping of the marketplace has given the word novel and profound implications.

According to the *Merriam-Webster Dictionary*, "disruption" is defined as "the act or process of disrupting something: a break or interruption in the normal course or continuation of some activity, process, etc."[1] This definition may suggest that disruption is bad and undesirable because it interrupts a current state of being. Yet if the so-called destruction of the current way of doing things is leading (or forcing) us to come up with more innovative or simply more sensible ways of performing our work, then disruption is not necessarily a dreadfully evil force.

It is interesting to note that the Wikipedia page for "disruption" does not list a single explanation of what the word means. Instead, the site enumerates a range of concepts and phenomena that are associated with disruption, ranging from biological cell disruption to the Disruption of 1843 that divided the Church of Scotland. Of the many disruptions listed on Wikipedia, two are of particular interest to this book:

1. "Disruptive Innovation": a term coined by Clayton Christensen, disruptive innovation is a process by which simple and accessible products that start at the bottom of the market can eventually threaten established companies, moving upmarket relentlessly to meet the needs of mainstream customers.[2]
2. "Creative disruption": introduced in 1992 by TBWA's chairman Jean-Marie Dru, creative disruption is an approach, and more so a mindset, for overturning cultural and market conventions so that future trends can be identified and leveraged in branding.[3]

IMAGE 1.1   Chinese phrase of disruption pointed out the market has been fundamentally transformed.

The Chinese term that is commonly used by businesses today to mean "disruption" is *diǎn fù*, which further emphasizes the business implications behind the word (Image 1.1).

According to Baidu, the most popular search engine in China, "disruption" means to "overthrow" the status quo by causing substantial change to the structural and fundamental nature of things.[4]

Threat or opportunity?

By taking all of the above definitions into account, we can arrive at a more complete assessment of the term "disruption" that helps us think about businesses across culture and time:

- Disruption is likely provoked by market players with the ambition to redefine the category.
- These players may not be, and usually are not, the traditional blue chips but instead more nimble outfits that are free of any baggage or legacy.
- Technology has been a catalyst that empowers these setups to do things drastically differently.
- Creativity fuels this revolution and provides the spark for numerous chain reactions.
- Those who are complacent about their past achievements perceive disruption as a negative force that interrupts existing industry practices or threatens their current market position.
- Yet those who embrace or spearhead change quickly recognize the positive effect of disruption, and see that genuinely "nothing is impossible."

"Change Management" as a concept has been substantially researched and written about over the past few decades. Perhaps Peter Drucker put it best when he said, "If you want something new, you have to stop doing something old."[5] The point is, if we don't do something new, our competitors will. In fact, consumers are constantly, either consciously or subconsciously, looking for something new. To them, "new" does not only mean current or up-to-date. "Being new" is about being "easier to use," "more entertaining," "higher performing," "more understanding," "better valued," and of course more "trendy" and "cool." It is worth revisiting the words of Jack Welch, former chairman and CEO of General Electric, who observed that "if the rate of change on the outside exceeds the rate of change on the inside, the end is near."[6] This book will present cases that illustrate how the changing expectations of Netizens and the current state of competition are influencing the market. Indeed, those who drive disruption do so not only to *disrupt*, but also to *survive*.

Today's millennials may not have seen or heard of the following items that were once popular and even essential in their parents' or grandparents' day – roll film, yellow pages, facsimile, Walkman, Discman, instant camera, electronic translator, voice-recorder, etc. (Image 1.2). All these products were designed to perform one function and have been completely replaced by the smartphone, which can perform all of the above and more. It is brutal when products or even industries are totally wiped out, erased, and forgotten. That's why brands have to step up and be more than just functional brands by offering something more substantial and intimate to consumers.

IMAGE 1.2 List of some products that have been made obsolete in the digital era.

The digital revolution and purpose-driven marketing

The Internet is now, without a doubt, part of our everyday lives. It has changed the way we work, learn, play, shop, and interact. The Internet first emerged in the 1960s and was originally an initiative to enhance military capabilities. It became widely deployed in the commercial sector in the 1980s but didn't initially cause a market disruption. It was not until fiber optics and the increasing penetration of mobile devices enhanced the global network infrastructure that a paradigm shift occurred. Now, massive data can be transmitted at high speed, processed, and stored with cloud computing. A window of opportunity has opened for smaller players to compete with business "goliaths," not by "size and scale" but through "innovation and intelligence."

Yet this is not the first time that something new and revolutionary has happened to mankind. The invention of the radio and television also drastically changed the way we live and perform marketing. So why and how did the digital revolution cause such an unprecedented disruption? The answer is simple. Both radio and television are media that merely serve as carriers of information and commercial messages. Audiences turn on the radio and television to consume news or entertainment but are inevitably and involuntarily exposed to advertisers' sponsored messages. In that sense, radios and televisions are not so different from print media or the billboards we drive past on the road.

The Internet, on the other hand, is much more than a one-way medium. Although it does serve as an advertising medium, people also go online to obtain information, exchange views, shop, and write reviews. Thanks to social networking platforms such as Facebook, YouTube, Pinterest, Instagram, LinkedIn, and TikTok, people can upload posts, photos, and videos anytime and anywhere. These platforms are the tipping points of disruption that enable consumers to truly call the shots. As we will see in later chapters, a trending topic on Twitter or a viral Instagram post can make or break even the most sizable corporation in the world. Netizens are so influential that *Time Magazine* awarded "Person of The Year" in 2006 to "YOU – the users of the Information Age."[7]

If *Time Magazine* is going to give Netizens the same award again, it will have to change the picture on its front page from a PC to a smart device. After all, the first generation of the iPhone was launched one year after the Netizens were named Person of the Year. Nowadays, consumers do not only rely on mobile apps to perform their daily tasks – they themselves are becoming more mobile. As Philip Kotler, Hermawan Kartajaya, and Iwan Setiawan explain in *Marketing 4.0*, new consumers tend to move around often, live life at a faster pace, and prioritize immediacy. To effectively engage these consumers, marketers must transition from the traditional four Ps to the four Cs:[8]

1. *Co-creation*, a process that invites customers into the ideation stage of product development, allowing the target audience to customize services according to individual tastes;

2. *Currency*, whereby retailers use big-data analytics to implement dynamic pricing based on market demand and consumer buying habits;
3. *Communal activation*, in the form of peer-to-peer marketing campaigns that attract new consumers through a wide yet personal distribution network;
4. *Conversation*, encouraged by social media platforms that create a space for brands to communicate with consumers, and for consumers to share their reviews of brands.[9]

The notion of migrating the marketing mindset from the four Ps to the four Cs recognizes and leverages the power of consumers in the digital age. In fact, there is no doubt that being consumer-centric is paramount for any commercial organization or even non-governmental organization (NGO). As Professor Theodore Levitt put it in his classic marketing book *Marketing Imagination* (1983), "the purpose of a business is to get and keep a customer."[10]

The difference is that in today's marketplace, enterprises should focus on much more than customer conversion and retention. They must be aware of and hopefully manage to steer the influence that one customer can have on a possibly uncountable number of customers and prospects. A single person may have a restricted sphere of influence in the physical world yet be hugely influential in the virtual world. Even if their network is limited, a single comment can be seen by someone who can then reach hundreds of thousands of followers.

In September 2004, a blogger posted a video on YouTube demonstrating how quickly and easily Kryptonite's Evolution 2000 bicycle lock could be compromised by only a few twists of a Bic pen. This revelation cost the company an estimated USD 10 million in just 10 days as Kryptonite scrambled to replace bicycle locks through a free exchange program.[11] The damage could have been far more severe, however, since the video directly challenged Kryptonite's brand promise of providing "the unbreakable bond." A simple pen could have led to the total collapse of Kryptonite's brand equity, breaking not only the lock but also the trust between the company and its customers.

Such incidents can happen at any time and to any corporation. It is therefore essential for marketers to remain alert and be prepared to respond swiftly and appropriately to any critical comments directed towards their brands. The good news is that the digital era's "word of mouse" can also spread positive news with the potential to shake up the whole world. Take the Ice Bucket Challenge for instance, a global phenomenon from the summer of 2014. Those who accepted the challenge dumped a bucket of ice water over their heads in order to solicit donations for the ALS Association (Image 1.3), an American NGO that raises awareness on amyotrophic lateral sclerosis (ALS). Although the challenge was criticized for wasting water and being used by celebrities as a publicity stunt, the campaign was nonetheless able to raise over USD 115 million within a short period of time for ALS organizations.[12]

As such, the world's most famous equation may have another meaning in the context of marketing (Figure 1.1):

IMAGE 1.3 Business leaders (Allan Zeman, Group Chairman of Lan Kwai Fong Group), second on the left and government officials (Greg So, Former Secretary of CEDB, middle) joining the Ice Bucket Challenge in Hong Kong. Credit: am730.

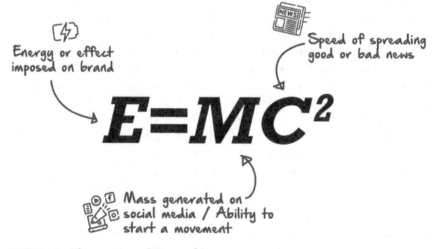

Energy or effect imposed on brand

Speed of spreading good or bad news

$$E = MC^2$$

Mass generated on social media / Ability to start a movement

FIGURE 1.1 The equation of $E = mc^2$ has a new meaning.

M = The massive online communities that populate social networking sites. These users often share the same interests and can be easily mobilized.

C = These Netizens can communicate across borders using text, photos, videos, and more at the speed of light through hand-held devices.

E = The unrivaled energy or effect that spreading news can impose on any brand or organization is tremendous or even lethal.

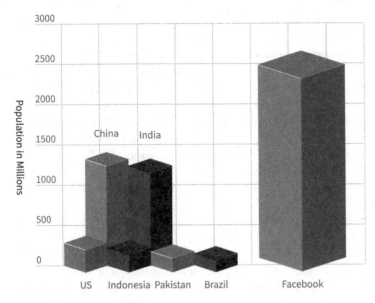

FIGURE 1.2 Comparison of population by countries (2020).

The equation above shows that technology has allowed individuals to form a group so large that it cannot be ignored. This is indeed the power of social networking. According to official statistics published on Facebook, the social media site boasted 2.6 billion monthly active users in the first quarter of 2020.[13] In other words, if Facebook were a country, it would be bigger than China, India, and the US in terms of population size (see Figure 1.2).

As consumers spend more time online, they are becoming increasingly tech-savvy. Aside from mastering different mobile apps that are usually free to download, they have also shifted their purchases from offline to online, first for everyday items such as groceries, then for high-ticket items such as luxury goods. In 2019, retail e-commerce sales worldwide amounted to 3.53 trillion while e-retail revenues are projected to grow to 5 trillion in 2021.[14] The extensive period of global lockdown due to COVID-19 has also migrated considerable consumer behavior to the online environment (there will be further discussion of COVID-19 later in this chapter).

E-commerce × China = Ultimate disruption

Since the early 1990s, China has consistently been the world's fastest-growing economy. It opened its economy and population to the outside world with a degree of speed and success that was unprecedented not only for China, but also for any country. China is the only country with the economic scale and activity to match the United States. Because of the size of China's market, the success of any global brand will largely depend on its performance in China. It is also the only market that may produce a rival to Google, Facebook, Twitter, or Amazon simply by building on businesses established locally.[15]

Praised by Forbes as one of the world's most powerful apps,[16] Tencent's WeChat is a social networking tool similar to the US-based messaging service WhatsApp. And yet, WeChat has evolved into much more than an instant messaging service. Apart from allowing users to communicate through text messages, voice recordings, pictures, "stickers," video calls, Bluetooth, and more, WeChat is known as China's "app for everything" or "super app" because of its extensive range of functions and platforms. Users can read articles, share their GPS location, play games, and wire money. WeChat also allows companies and organizations to register official accounts, enabling users to book doctor appointments, pay utility bills, order takeout, call a cab … the list goes on.[17]

WeChat hit its milestone of 1 billion monthly active users during the Lunar New Year in February 2018. More than 688 million users sent or received monetary gifts through WeChat's "red envelope" application, a function based on the traditional Chinese red packet given as a gift during special occasions.[18]

The other Internet giant in China is the Alibaba Group. When it was listed in the United States, its astonishing initial public offering (IPO) of USD 25 billion broke all records to become the largest IPO in history (Image 1.4).[19]

After starting off as a pure business-to-business (B2B) platform in 1999, Alibaba rapidly extended to business-to-consumer (B2C) and consumer-to-consumer (C2C) in 2003 by launching Taobao, a platform where small businesses and individual entrepreneurs can open online stores that sell almost anything you can imagine.

IMAGE 1.4 Will Alibaba Group founder Jack Ma be able to see the future of e-commerce with his invisible binoculars? Credit: am730.

Moreover, while Alibaba did not invent "Singles' Day," an unofficial Chinese holiday that celebrates bachelors (the four "1"s in 11/11 make it an apt day for recognizing singledom), it seized the opportunity to transform the day into a one-day shopping spree. The sheer magnitude of the sales turnover on Singles' Day alone shocked the world by generating more sales than Black Friday, Thanksgiving, and Cyber Monday combined.[20]

According to Alibaba, over 15 million products from more than 200,000 brands, including over 22,000 international brands, offered special discounts on Tmall.com for the 2019 Singles' Day, jointly contributing to a record-breaking sales turnover of USD 38.4 billion—selling more than half of what Amazon sells in an entire quarter.[21] A spin-off from Taobao, Tmall.com is an open B2C platform that enables businesses worldwide to reach China's vast and growing consumer market. Tmall.com has established itself as the destination for quality, branded goods. Catering to increasingly sophisticated Chinese consumers, Tmall .com is the most visited B2C online retail website in China.

After ten years of operating Singles Day, Alibaba is fully aware that November 11 cannot just be a day for brands to slash prices and clear their inventory. Alibaba also amplified the event's entertainment value by inviting international stars such as Daniel Craig, Mariah Carey, Pharrell Williams, and Taylor Swift to the Singles' Day Countdown Gala. Marketers also seize this opportunity to test new ideas and product concepts, knowing that tens of millions of online shoppers have their credit cards in hand on November 11. As such, Singles Day also spotlights innovation in the market, and a total of one million new products were launched during the event in 2019.[22]

Gigantic numbers and rapid change are characteristics of the cyber marketplace, which can be especially intimidating to brand owners who still operate under a production-centric or sales-centric philosophy. The next few chapters will further examine the changing market dynamics in the age of disruption so that marketers can thoroughly understand these new waves and rethink, refine, or redefine their branding strategies.

Many international brands that do not primarily rely on online activity to achieve their sales goals (such as luxury or premium goods) have long recognized that their presence and performance in the China market will have a major bearing on their future sustainable growth. According to McKinsey, the value of the global luxury goods market is expected to reach USD 405 billion by 2025, while Chinese consumers will account for 44% of the total global market.[23]

The German luxury brand Montblanc is one such brand that is determined to continue its investment in China. In 2012, Montblanc opened its largest flagship store in Beijing's Sanlitun district, occupying four stories with a total area of 19,375 square feet.[24] The concept store is more than just a place for making transactions; it is a mini museum that showcases iconic Montblanc creations from the past century and allows visitors to immerse themselves in the brand world of Montblanc via technology and virtual reality experiences.

Five years later, another international brand made headlines by establishing itself in China: Starbucks opened its then-largest store in Shanghai in December 2017. Located in Reserve Roastery Shanghai, the giant Starbucks boasted 30,000 square feet of space featuring in-house roasting, three coffee bars, and a special Teavana tea bar.[25] Although Chicago has since overtaken Shanghai as housing the largest Starbucks in the world, the brand is committed to opening one new store in China every 15 hours through 2022, reaching its goal of having 6,000 stores in the mainland.[26]

What made the Starbucks in Shanghai so "disruptive" was not merely its size but also the fact that it teamed up with Alibaba to create the "first fully immersive coffee experience in Asia" using augmented reality and a delivery service that could reach almost every corner in China.[27]

Car manufacturers such as BMW also pinpointed China as the market that will take the lion's share of its electric car supply. In 2019, BMW increased its manufacturing capacity by boosting the number of cars it produced annually at two facilities in China to 520,000.[28] The breadth of the market is a positive sign that China may be able to consume BMW's full product range, from entry-level vehicles to high-end electric sports car like the i8.

Another forerunner in China's electric car market is Tesla, which began building its Gigafactory 3 in Shanghai in December 2018. The factory aims to produce 500,000 electric vehicles annually and may surpass the USD 5.5 billion Shanghai Disney Resort as the largest foreign manufacturing investment in Shanghai (Image 1.5).[29]

So why is China a desirable destination for disruptive innovation? Its appeal has much to do with its scale and intensity. Apart from having a huge market, Chinese consumers, especially the booming middle class, are adventurous spenders and will be a major force to fuel the growth of this second largest economy in the world. In fact, the central government's 13th Five-Year Plan (2016–2020) makes it clear that domestic spending will continue to drive the sustainable momentum of its GDP. The plan also prioritizes the development of green and sustainable energy initiatives, reflecting the government's determination to combat the drastic deterioration of air quality that has been a side effect of tremendous economic growth, particularly in northern China.

In just 40 years since the launch of its market reforms and open-door policy, China has quickly transformed itself from the world's factory to the world's market, and now the world's research and development center. International brands are prepared to use China's huge domestic market as a test bed for launching new products and their initial investment can be justified. When proven workable in China, the new products will then be transported to other Asian markets that share some cultural proximity. Businesses that successfully launched in the Chinese market include Kraft's Oreo wafers (Image 1.6) and Coca-Cola's Minute Maid Pulpy, a juice that debuted in China in 2005. In just five years, Minute Maid Pulpy became Coca-Cola's first brand developed and launched in an emerging market to reach USD 1 billion in global retail sales.[30] It is now one

IMAGE 1.5 Tesla is eyeing the largest electric car market on the planet to preempt the erosion when traditional car manufacturers around the world shift gear to electric cars. Credit: am730.

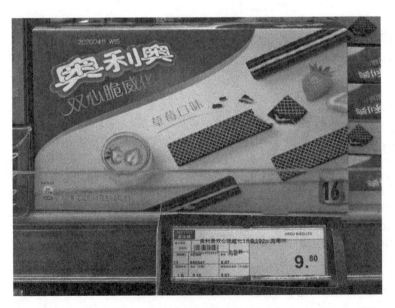

IMAGE 1.6 The first Oreo in wafer format is one of the best sellers in China.

IMAGE 1.7 Created for the China market, Minute Maid is now available in over 15 countries.

of the premier juice brands in more than 15 countries and regions, including Indonesia, the Philippines, Thailand, and India. To cater to Chinese people's preference for healthier drinks, Minute Maid even launched a line extension that featured a Pulpy Super Milky drink with chewable fruit dice (Image 1.7).

The successful cases listed above should remind brand owners that the most sensible strategy is not to treat China as a standalone market, but as an integral part of a global strategy. Instead of distancing oneself from China because of its intimidating scale and rapid growth, brands should aim to truly understand its market dynamics and achieve synergy.

Post-COVID-19: Brand revival

COVID-19 has resulted in an unprecedented global lockdown. Different reports have analyzed the impact of COVID-19 on various aspects of the global economy. Although these reports have different angles when analyzing the situation, they all share one common conclusion – the world will never be the same. From a marketing perspective, the market will undoubtedly be further disrupted and have a lasting effect on all the different sectors.

COVID-19 was, in fact, an acid test of brand equity, one that resulted in polarized outcomes for brands. One common question found in a typical brand assessment is "Imagine what will happen to you (i.e., the respondent) if the brand ceases to exist in the world one day?" The intention of this question is to gauge brand resilience and the level of consumers' reliance on the brand. COVID-19 has forced people to stay home, which has allowed people to realize that their lives are totally unaffected by the absence of certain brands. They also realize that there are brands that play an essential role in their lives. We are not merely talking about the need for daily supplies, which is rather inelastic in terms of market demand. Brand-owners have to confront themselves on how their brands and the setup of their business genuinely add value to people's lives.

This section outlines several changes in consumer behavior that brand-owners can anticipate as a result of the pandemic. Brand-owners should factor in these ideas when adjusting their branding strategy for the post-COVID-19 period.

1. **Home as a marketplace**

    Logically, one can anticipate that consumers will migrate their behavior online, which will further drive the growth of e-commerce or mobile commerce. Enterprises should therefore focus on digital growth and shift their business as much as possible to the virtual environment. After all, having a digital presence is a prerequisite in today's world, and many operators already sell their merchandise online.

    Yet simply moving a significant portion of one's business online may not be a strategic response to changing dynamics. Take the gym, for example. Although many people lost gym access during the lockdown, they still want to exercise and perhaps want to do so even more since they have idle time at home. Gym operators can continue to engage their members by providing a mobile app that guides members on how to complete home workouts. A progressive operator can even offer to lease exercise equipment to customers who are prepared to pay a reasonable rental fee. For those who do not want to pay, the gym should come up with smart ways to adapt resources already available in homes, such as couch and chairs, into makeshift workout equipment.

    To engage customers effectively, brands have to rethink their brand promise and re-organize their service delivery so that the compromise of brand experience will be minimal.

2. **A new global perspective**

    Although people around the world were forced to stay at home, they quickly found other ways to connect with their friends and families. Thanks to the connectivity enabled by social media, people from different corners of the world supported each other by showing their care and compassion virtually. We realize that we speak different languages and live in different continents, and yet we have never felt so close to each other. When consumers adopt a new global view, brands will also have to become borderless and expand their responsibility to address the needs of a more united global community.

3. **The importance of empathy**

Ogilvy conducted an extensive review during the 2008 financial crisis and came up with some practical advice on how marketers can manage brands during the recession. A key point is the importance of developing creative ways to support consumers who are under a lot of stress, both financially and emotionally.

Some people believe that COVID-19 is likely the worst catastrophe since the Great Depression of 1929. Brands have to walk the talk and demonstrate their care and support so that the users can offload some of their pressure through innovative brand engagement.

4. **Health and safety to the forefront**

Depending on the product category, health and safety are likely to form the choice criteria for brand selection. This is more imminent for categories like food and beverages. Although consumers are unlikely to change their diet completely, they will pay more attention subconsciously to the health implications when consuming any brand. Stakeholders will expect most categories, especially the travel industry or education sector, to prioritize infection prevention and sanitation.

5. **Catering to conscious spending**

One unfortunate outcome of COVID-19 is the loss of countless jobs due to the economic challenges faced by all businesses. Even those who can keep their jobs may still have a sense of financial insecurity that deters them from spending. The aforementioned Ogilvy report states that the propensity of people to spend has more to do with their expected future earnings than their current financial condition. Inevitably, people will trade down for certain categories, and be much more conscious or conservative when it comes to purchasing big-ticket items.

To cope with changing spending patterns and consumer mindsets, brand-owners may want to review their product assortment and offer stock-keeping unit (SKUs) that are more palatable to new customers. Offers such as free trials, discounted memberships, and hassle-free returns will be attractive to consumers who do not want to immediately commit to spending.

6. **Expecting the unexpected**

In April 2020, the *South China Morning Post* reported that around 460,000 Chinese firms had already closed due to the instability caused by the pandemic.[31] In the same month, CNBC estimated that around 7.5 million small businesses in North America would shutter if the pandemic worsened.[32] Knowing that enterprises of any size are taking a hit, governments around the world are increasing funding substantially to sustain the regular economic activities.

The Chinese word for "crisis" is a combination of two characters – "danger" and "opportunity." Some of the enterprises that have been forced to close their previous businesses may bounce back by offering something out-of-the-box that fulfills the need of a particular market segment. This is especially possible in the sharing economy, where people can collaborate and provide new business offerings together. Brand-owners have to expect the unexpected because new competitors may take any shape and form, and can stealthily nibble away at the market share. For instance, a small digital outfit with only two or three staff can compete with a large 4As agency by specializing in certain marketing services.

7. **Caring for internal customers**

    When companies start to panic, some of them will immediately think about cost-cutting and downsizing. This will cause a lot of internal distress and insecurity that can affect the company's performance in many ways. Brand-owners are advised to keep up a dialogue with their employees and maintain a high level of transparency regarding the critical issues faced by the corporation. Coming up with a new mode of operation that is viable for both business owners and employees will keep the company afloat. Once the economy bounces back, these companies will be more prepared to seize the opportunity.

8. **Smart branding and customized solutions**

    As people spend more time buying and browsing online, they leave behind significant traces of their digital footprints – important traits that corporations can use to come up with customized solutions for every individual. Smart branding is about fully leveraging the power of data and artificial intelligence (AI) to understand and predict consumer needs so that the company can secure their relationship and maximize revenue opportunities.

A brand-builder's perspective

At the end of each chapter, this book will present an interview with a renowned brand-builder alongside a case study in branding. These interviews and case studies are arranged based on their relevance to the content of the respective chapters. Their purpose is to examine the topics covered in each chapter from the perspective of an experienced practitioner. The case studies depict real-life applications of market observations and show how some marketers have successfully weathered the storm to emerge as winners.

Interview with Terence Ling, Head of Strategy, TBWA Hong Kong

Mr. Terence Ling has over 20 years of marketing and agency experience, and is a chief architect of customer and marketing strategy for brands across diverse industries and regions. He is currently the Head of Strategy of TBWA in Hong Kong, overseeing a team of brand, social, PR, integrated, data, and media strategists.

Royce Yuen: Since TBWA is an agency that has been pioneering "disruption," what's your view on "disruption" as a market phenomenon?

Terence Ling: TBWA defines disruption as convention-breaking strategies that help brands seize a larger share of the market and future. A good example is the way FedEx disrupted the supply chain business by introducing multiple forms of shipping: the first PC-based automated shipping system, later named FedEx PowerShip; FedEx Tracking, which allows customers to keep tabs on the status of packages in transit; the first all-electric trucks to be used in the US parcel delivery business; etc.

Disruption is never meant for only technology or start-up companies. Many big and traditional companies are becoming the prey in the age of disruption when they could have been the hunter or predator. There are many opportunities for those who are gradually waking up to the benefits of disruption.

RY: Is the digital revolution and e-commerce causing any "disruption" to brand owners?

TL: Empowered by technology, brands are learning that the speed to launch, test, and optimize a new idea is much faster than ever before. Furthermore, as products become trackable, their results are also measurable. Companies that still operate with a traditional R&D mindset will be challenged by the new way of thinking and doing things.

At the same time, precisely because of the aforementioned speed, many established companies will also be challenged and disrupted by smaller players who move swiftly and are better at leveraging technology.

Consumers these days embrace technology in their daily lives. They demand and expect companies and service providers to deliver goods and services according to their needs and habits. Corporations who fail to comply with the new norm will face the danger of becoming obsolete.

RY: How do some brands embrace this disruption and turn it into an opportunity?

TL: I wish there were more [disruption] ... the current transformation is not fast enough.

We are fortunate that some of our clients are willing to adapt, or at least try new things.

Our partnership with Standard Chartered is a good example. The conventional way to market a credit card is to use an enormous media budget to blast the same message all over town, usually featuring a celebrity. Roadshow agents also randomly intercept pedestrians, possibly including existing customers.

Our idea is to launch an acquisition engine to counter this "one size fits all" approach. We'll use trending signals alongside lifestyle and platform data to communicate one-on-one with customers with a thousand different types of interests. By offering a personalized piece of content followed by a personal tracking mechanism that helps us follow through the entire funnel of marketing, we are able to create deeper engagement based on individuals' relevant interests and then finally convert them at the right moment.

We are working with Google and other technology partners to create over 200 different types of ads in real-time, matching individuals with the right content based on their YouTube search history. This is becoming the new strategy and marketing approach as we are seeing a substantial increase in customer interest throughout the entire marketing funnel that finally leads to the subscription of credit cards.

We're still learning what are better signals and topics across a number of categories that can help us achieve a higher return on investment (ROI) at a lower marketing cost.

RY: Is the agency world being disrupted as well?

TL: Absolutely. The shrinking of the entire market in recent years has been quite apparent.

Some agencies have been slow in realizing that there are so many different types of solution-providers today, such as online platforms, content providers, networks of key opinion leaders (KOL), and bloggers. These disruptors can be your best ally or worst enemy.

I think most traditional creative agencies do not see this change coming, which is why most of them have suffered drastically. They are slowly waking up … no one sees integration as a luxury anymore. But at the same time, frankly, if you're not good at one thing, linking all the good things together doesn't mean you're good at anything.

For too long, creative agencies have claimed to be the master of the business relationship and promised to deliver effective communications to solve business problems. Ironically, these agencies have not held onto reliable business data, and many of this valuable information has been with the media side. This is probably due to the separation of the media component from the advertising creation process, which has restricted the agency to offer a complete and holistic solution to the client..

RY: Is the role of the agency changing, and how does it add value to its client's business these days?

TL: Clients are still looking for strategic inputs from their agency partners. However, what they seek is no longer confined to the brand or campaign strategy but a total marketing strategy across everything you do, including how you figure out the right segmentation in the first place. They should ask questions like, "What is supposed to be the right pricing strategy, and what is the product roadmap?" "How to work with and add value to clients by leveraging your deep level of consumer insight and behavioral insight?" " Before we even talk about the communication plan, what is the most disruptive product strategy?"

I genuinely believe that agencies can step up and play an even more prominent role in collaborating with clients.

RY: Are brands expressing themselves differently in this day and age?

TL: There are some brands whose business nature rides precisely on the whole digital revolution. One of the best examples is online travel agencies. The Expedia group is the number one spender for both AOL and performance-based marketing. It gains substantial top-of-mind awareness as well as market interest.

This new breed of brands may be better at understanding and using digital technology, but the meaning of brands remains the same. It goes back to the classic marketing principle – how to deliver an exceptional experience to your customers.

Brands have to offer exceptional customer experience, including but not restricted to the digital experience. This holds true for all brands, including the "bricks and mortar" type of companies.

RY: How does brand-building differ from before?

TL: Building a brand is no longer about producing a big (TV commercial) TVC. These days, people are being influenced and they judge a brand based on the actual experience it provides instead of merely the communication provided by the brand.

In the past, we had a monoculture where everyone sat in front of a TV consuming the same content together. The TVC could have commanded a lot of cultural capital at that time. Now, people have so many screens and split their time between different screens, possibly building a disconnected picture of the world.

Customers today are able to collect thousands of opinions that may influence their perception of the brand, including but not limited to the perception or real experience of others.

The job of marketing is to influence consumer perception, which is partly rational and partly irrational. We have to help customers to see things in a fairer light by all means, and then steer them to the conclusion that aligns more with our objective.

Using data to win over unique prospects in real-time

Standard Chartered's "Simply Cash" credit card provides 1.5% cash-back with no conditions attached to any transaction. However, in Hong Kong's highly saturated market, many credit cards already offer higher cash-back rates on designated spending categories. Standard Chartered needed to demonstrate that Simply Cash was the only cash-back card that could appeal to millenials' diverse interests by offering unlimited cash back on all purchases.

A task force led by TBWA Hong Kong and including Carat, iProspect, and Google developed a data-driven, real-time, and personalized acquisition approach that converted leads based on personal spending interests.

By triangulating search, social, behavioral, and first-party data, the team could uncover the long-tail of personal interests amongst the millennial audience. Within broad lifestyle categories such as dining and shopping, the team found over 1,200 micro-interests, such as trending beverage products or upcoming fashion labels.

Using this data, over 240 lines of copy script and eight base videos were created as "ingredients" to feed into Google's Director Mix advertising solution. The technology spotted audiences who were looking for YouTube video content related to the micro-interests. Once such audiences were found, it "mixed" personalized pre-roll video ads for them using the pre-developed creative material and served them before the sought-after content. Over 16 million ads were personalized during the campaign.

This flock content was a key "hook" at the start of a content journey that followed through with such leads. They were re-targeted with longer branded content, and those who were identified as having higher product intent were then re-targeted with conversion content. The seamless experience connected them with the sign-up portal that made card applications easy to complete.

The campaign was able to reverse a sustained decline in card applications and achieved a 62% increase in card applications at a 23% lower cost per application. It was highly recognized both at local and international institutions. It won the Grand Effie at the 2019 Hong Kong Effie Awards and was ranked 68th on WARC Effective 100 – a ranking of the world's most awarded campaigns for effectiveness.

This is how the campaign was designed to enable a natural and effortless experience. When an audience looked for YouTube content that matched one of the pre-identified interests, they were served with a customized pre-roll video ad relevant to the exact content they were searching. They were then re-targeted with a more extended version of the video that explained more about the product – those who did not skip this were identified as having higher product intent. They were further re-targeted with display ads that drove them to the product sign-up page (Figure 1.3).

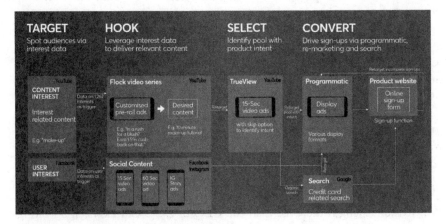

FIGURE 1.3 The seamless acquisition journey.

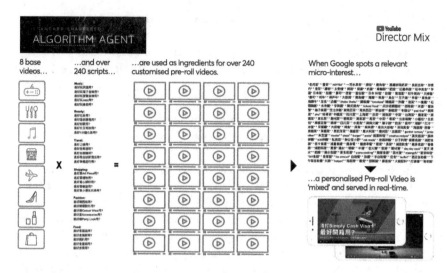

FIGURE 1.4 The real-time advertising engine.

After the set of over 1,200 micro-interests were identified, they were used to create eight base videos representing eight lifestyle categories and over 240 copy scripts to relate with the individual micro-interests. Once Google spotted an audience with a matching interest on YouTube, it "mixed" a personalized pre-roll video ad using the pre-made creative material and served it in real-time (Figure 1.4).

Case study – UCO

Finding a strategic position in the new ecosystem

Headquartered in Hangzhou, UCO is a multi-platform e-commerce distributor for cosmetics brands in China. It provides digital and market-entry support, omni-channel retail operation, social media content creation, and more services to over 40 international brands in China such as Estée Lauder, L'Oréal, L'Occitane, and Clarins. UCO operates on Tmall/Tmall Global and other leading Chinese e-commerce platforms including JD.com, VIP.com, Kaola, and RED (XiaoHongShu). It also hosts WeChat stores and sites for brands. In addition to e-commerce retail, UCO offers online-to-offline commerce to help beauty brands broaden their distribution networks and provide better customer experiences. Its gross merchandise value (GMV) sales exceeded USD 1.4 billion in 2019.[33]

Interview with Arthur Chang, Chairman and CEO of UCO

Mr. Arthur Chang is the Chairman and CEO of UCO and has been operating the business for almost 10 years. Previously, he was the Vice President of Global

IMAGE 1.8   A brand that emerged in the digital era, UCO is going from strength to strength. Credit: UCO.com.

Sales at Alibaba from 2007 to 2010. UCO was one of the few e-commerce operators that identified the retail opportunity presented by Singles Day, and Mr. Chang understood the potential of this flagship marketing initiative through the Alibaba Group. UCO is able to take full advantage of the growth of e-commerce in China by genuinely understanding what, how, and why Chinese consumers purchase cosmetics products online.

Royce Yuen: What role does e-commerce play in the total ecosystem and customer journey for the cosmetics and skincare market globally?

Arthur Chang: E-commerce is a catalyst for global market consolidation, not only because it is unrestricted by geographic boundaries and therefore capable of reaching a phenomenal scale, but also because it is a more effective way of managing a business in real-time. Smart and efficient operators integrate both online and offline businesses to maximize business opportunities. They are able to kick out the less efficient players who fail to cope with the changes in technology and consumer behavior.

RY: To what extent has e-commerce "disrupted" the cosmetics and skincare market in China?

AC: It is indeed a disruption, as 30% of industry sales currently come from online activity and continue to grow. This represents a fundamental change in consumers' buying behavior. This behavioral change is driven by technology, due to the penetration of mobile Internet and smartphone supported by wider bandwidth, which allows the streaming of videos and other forms of communication. In fact, the way e-commerce is performed is also evolving with an increasing dependence on social content marketing. The roles that friends and KOL play are also instrumental to the advancement of e-commerce, making it totally different than browsing in a traditional department store.

RY: Is the China market quite different from other major markets in the world for the same category?

AC: Like the United States, China is a big market and yet quite homogeneous in terms of language and culture. By contrast, India is quite a different market. It is big but also very diverse. Chinese consumers in general are adventurous and open-minded. They welcome new product forms and ideas and are willing to try out new things even if they are not perfect yet. The speed of market adoption in China is extremely fast, and the per capita ownership of smartphones is one of the highest in the world. Most people in China do not use paper currency anymore these days. Even street hawkers and buskers can accept e-payment. All these factors combined creates the perfect environment for market development and transformation.

Moreover, China has a vast geography and consists of different tiers of cities. The cities from tier one to tier five represent a wide spectrum, which is why the market can be quite fragmented with many different sub-segments.

For example, consumers in tier one cities may move on to niche brands while consumers in the lower-tier cities are still moving up the value chain to try out mainstream brands. Marketers must understand that the life cycle of a brand is not linear in China; brands can operate at various stages of the cycle at the same time depending on their location in China.

RY: Is Singles Day (November 11) just another mega sales promotion? What are the other possible strategic implications it may have on both the buy and sell sides?

AC: Singles Day is an open platform, and it is up to each brand to decide what it wants to get out of it. To the savvier operators, it is much more than a sales promotion. When else can you reach possibly millions of unique visitors in a single day? It is a rare market opportunity for gaining exposure and interacting with many potential customers of different natures. Many foreign brands and companies are tapping this platform to enter the China market. From a consumer's perspective, they are joining an online carnival on top of their usual treasure-hunting. Some of them actually do pre-festival planning to ensure they are getting the most out of every minute they spend online during Singles Day.

RY: How are physical retail stores responding to this paradigm shift? Are retailers responding fast enough?

AC: Those who are not responding fast enough will soon or already be out of the market. Even restaurants that provide on-premise dining will not miss the opportunity to use online tools to tap the delivery or takeout market. Not to mention that many consumers rely on the comments other people post online to decide where to patronize. Managing your brand's presence in the digital space will have a direct impact on the sales performance of your physical store.

RY: What is the role of "brands" in this digital revolution? Has its role been diminished? Why?

AC: Consumers still believe in brands. Brands that are able to build emotional connections with consumers will stand a higher chance. People do browse and check out new products, but a large portion of consumer behavior can be categorized as habitual buying. Consumers do look for the specific brands they have in mind or are more familiar with. Of course, this will depend on the product category and the market segment, but the rules of building brand loyalty in the virtual world are just as important as they are in the physical world.

Notes

1 "Disruption." *Merriam-Webster.com*. Accessed September 22, 2020. https://www.merriam-webster.com/dictionary/disruption.
2 Christensen Institute. "Disruptive Innovations," 2020. https://www.christenseninstitute.org/disruptive-innovations/.
3 Dru, Jean-Marie. *Disruption: Overturning Conventions and Shaking Up the Marketplace.* Wiley, 1996.
4 Baidu. "Dian Fu," March 16, 2016. https://baike.baidu.com/item/%E9%A2%A0%E8%A6%86/33747.
5 Drucker, Peter F. "Quotes." *Goodreads*. Accessed September 23, 2020. https://www.goodreads.com/author/quotes/12008.Peter_F_Drucker.
6 Allison, Scott. "The Responsive Organization: Coping with New Technology and Disruption." *Forbes*, February 10, 2014. https://www.forbes.com/sites/scottallison/2014/02/10/the-responsive-organization-how-to-cope-with-technology-and-disruption/#56e9b0963cdd.
7 Grossman, Lev. "You – Yes, You – Are TIME's Person of the Year." *Time Magazine*, December 25, 2006. http://content.time.com/time/magazine/article/0,9171,1570810,00.html.
8 Kotler, Philip, Hermawan Kartajaya, and Iwan Setiawan. *Marketing 4.0: Moving from Traditional to Digital*. John Wiley & Sons, 2016.
9 Ibid., 50–51.

10 Levitt, Theodore. "The Globalization of Markets." In *Marketing Imagination, New, Expanded.*, 48. New York: Free Press, 1986.

11 Levick, Richard S., and Larry Smith. "A Whole New Ballgame." In *Stop the Presses: The Crisis and Litigation PR Desk Reference*, 93. Washington, DC: Watershed Press, 2007.

12 The ALS Association. "Ice Bucket Challenge Dramatically Accelerated the Fight against ALS," June 4, 2019. https://www.als.org/stories-news/ice-bucket-challenge-dramatically-accelerated-fight-against-als.

13 Spangler, Todd. "Facebook Hits 2.6B Users, Cites Big Q1 Ad Sales Drop from COVID-19." *Variety*, April 29, 2020. https://variety.com/2020/digital/news/facebook-q1-2020-2-6-billion-users-ad-drop-coronavirus-1234593395/.

14 Lipsman, Andrew. "Global Ecommerce 2019." *eMarketer*, June 27, 2019. https://www.emarketer.com/content/global-ecommerce-2019.

15 Tse, Edward. *China's Disruptors: How Alibaba, Xiaomi, Tencent, and Other Companies Are Changing the Rules of Business*. Penguin, 2015.

16 Lim, Jason. "WeChat, One of the World's Most Powerful Apps," May 19, 2014. https://www.forbes.com/sites/jlim/2014/05/19/wechat-one-of-the-worlds-most-powerful-apps/#663619e774f1.

17 Shakhnazarova, Nika. "Here's Everything to Know about WeChat – China's Billion-User Answer to WhatsApp." *The Sun*, February 4, 2019. https://www.thesun.co.uk/tech/8349991/heres-everything-to-know-about-wechat-chinas-billion-user-answer-to-whatsapp/.

18 Deng, Iris. "Tencent's WeChat Hits 1 Billion Milestone as Lunar New Year Boosts Monthly Active Users." *South China Morning Post*, March 5, 2018, sec. Tech. https://www.scmp.com/tech/apps-gaming/article/2135690/tencents-wechat-hits-1-billion-milestone-lunar-new-year-boosts.

19 Mac, Ryan. "Alibaba Claims Title for Largest Global IPO Ever with Extra Share Sales." *Forbes*, September 22, 2014. https://www.forbes.com/sites/ryanmac/2014/09/22/alibaba-claims-title-for-largest-global-ipo-ever-with-extra-share-sales/.

20 Taylor, Kate. "Black Friday and Cyber Monday Set Records – But Combined, They Still Only Made Up Half of Alibaba's Singles Day Online Sales." *Business Insider*, December 1, 2018. https://www.businessinsider.com/black-friday-cyber-monday-vs-singles-day-sales-2018-12.

21 Klebnikov, Sergei. "Alibaba's 11/11 Singles' Day by the Numbers: A Record $38 Billion Haul." *Forbes*, November 11, 2019. https://www.forbes.com/sites/sergeiklebnikov/2019/11/11/alibabas-1111-singles-day-by-the-numbers-a-record-38-billion-haul/.

22 Bu, Lambert, Lei Xu, and Daniel Zipser. "The Innovations behind China's Singles Day Shopping Phenomenon." *McKinsey & Company*, December 3, 2019. https://www.mckinsey.com/featured-insights/china/the-innovations-behind-chinas-singles-day-shopping-phenomenon.

23 Bu, Lambert, Benjamin Durand-Servoingt, Aimee Kim, and Naomi Yamakawa. "Chinese Luxury Consumers: The 1 Trillion Renminbi Opportunity." *Marketing & Sales Practice*. McKinsey & Company, May 2017.

24 Wheeler, Carolynne. "Montblanc Opens Beijing Flagship." *WWD*, June 3, 2012. https://wwd.com/fashion-news/designer-luxury/montblanc-brings-monte-carlo-glamour-to-china-5939980/.

25 Jacobs, Harrison. "Starbucks Reserve Roastery Shanghai is World's Biggest Starbucks." *Business Insider*, April 22, 2018. https://www.businessinsider.com/starbucks-reserve-roastery-shanghai-china-is-worlds-biggest-2018-4.

26 Bird, Jon. "Roasted: How China is Showing the Way for Starbucks in the U.S." *Forbes*. Accessed August 28, 2020. https://www.forbes.com/sites/jonbird1/2019/01/15/roasted-how-china-is-showing-the-way-for-starbucks-u-s/.

27 Koman, Tess. "Honestly, Let's all Just Go Live in the Brand New Biggest Starbucks in the World." *Cosmopolitan*, December 5, 2017. https://www.cosmopolitan.com/food-cocktails/a14105460/starbucks-shanghai-roastery/.

28 Sachgau, Oliver. "BMW Unveils Plan to Boost Production in China." *Bloomberg*, July 9, 2018. https://www.bloomberg.com/news/articles/2018-07-09/bmw-unveils -plan-to-boost-production-in-china-amid-trade-war.

29 Ren, Daniel, and Maggie Zhang. "Tesla to Make Electric Cars in China Even as Trade War Simmers." *South China Morning Post*, July 10, 2018. https://www.scmp .com/business/companies/article/2154674/tesla-build-its-gigafactory-shanghai-ca pacity-produce-500000-cars.

30 Yuwei, Zhang. "Coke's China Plan on Right Track." *China Daily USA*, August 5, 2011. http://usa.chinadaily.com.cn/epaper/2011-08/05/content_13058043.htm.

31 Leng, Sidney. "Nearly Half a Million Chinese Companies Close as Pandemic Batters Economy." *South China Morning Post*, April 6, 2020. https://www.scmp.com/econ omy/china-economy/article/3078581/coronavirus-nearly-half-million-chinese-c ompanies-close-first.

32 Iacurci, Greg. "7.5 Million Small Businesses Are at Risk of Closing, Report Finds." *CNBC*, April 14, 2020. https://www.cnbc.com/2020/04/14/7point5-million-small -businesses-are-at-risk-of-closing-report-finds.html.

33 LinkedIn. "UCO.Com Overview." Accessed September 23, 2020. https://www.lin kedin.com/company/%E6%9D%AD%E5%B7%9E%E6%82%A0%E5%8F%AF% E5%8C%96%E5%A6%86%E5%93%81%E6%9C%89%E9%99%90%E5%85%AC %E5%8F%B8/about/.

2

CONNECTING A DISCONNECTED WORLD

To some, if not many, corporations, the function of marketing is to generate sales. The entire organization is geared towards delivering the target revenue and their focus throughout the year is on hitting the numbers. Some may argue that this is not the case since companies also set other key performance indicators (KPIs). Needless to say, corporations these days should be fully aware that their *raison d'être* is more than just selling more units. However, the reality is that the year-end bonus for most executives, no matter how senior or junior they are, is often tied to the sales performance at a corporate or individual level. Many corporations offer a compensation package that consists of a base salary plus a sales commission, hoping that their staff will put in their utmost effort into selling more in return for a higher commission.

Profit maximization has thus become the biggest motivation for many corporations, gradually nurturing a corporate culture that focuses on closing deals rather than delighting customers. Keeping customers happy is not unimportant, but companies might just see it as a function of driving more sales. Marketers these days may not repeat Henry Ford's famous saying that "you can have the car in any color you want as long as it is black," but they are nonetheless not operating their business with the customers' preferences or best interests in mind. Even large companies do not always meet their own customer service guarantees; on April 9, 2017, United Airlines security officers injured and forcibly dragged a 69-year-old Vietnamese-American man, Dr. David Dao, out of his seat because his flight was overbooked. This incident exposed the controversial industry practice of overbooking, which optimizes airline sales while allowing them to legitimately "bump" any passenger according to the fine print of their terms and conditions. Hong Kong newspaper *The Standard* described it as "pathetic" and "unethical for a service provider to knowingly sell tickets to more customers than they can entertain."[1]

In the old days, Dr. Dao's misfortune might have been just another unpleasant incident that consumers had to swallow and accept. But in the age of disruption, consumers were willing to demand justice on his behalf by posting the uncut video of the encounter online. Once the video went viral, United found that it needed to deal with not only Dr. Dao alone, but also the existing and future customers of United.

Although United and Dr. Dao resolved the issue by reaching an undisclosed settlement agreement, the airline's brand image has been forever tainted as consumers can always dig up any historical information or data easily on the Internet.

The new market equilibrium

The United case highlights perhaps the most important aspect of the age of the disruption that has already been mentioned multiple times in this book so far – the evolving role of consumers and their amplified power of influence. If we apply Michael Porter's Five Competitive Forces to the case, it is apparent that the "bargaining power of the buyers" increases exponentially when tens of millions of consumers are unanimously making the same demand. Their bargaining power directly intensifies the competition in the industry to the extent that some analysts describe corporations as totally "naked" in the digital world; the design, functionality, and worth of their products are thoroughly discussed online for anyone to see.

Henry Ford's one-color sales pitch could never be accepted under today's paradigm shift. On the contrary, manufacturers finally have to answer to consumer demands. As a result, mass production has been replaced by more "customized" and "personalized" versions of the same product to suit the different needs and desires of consumers. This new means of production has drastically shortened the product life cycle and reduced the capacity of each production run. It has forced some marketers to operate in survival mode and inevitably triggered some players' attempt to maintain their market shares through price promotions that ironically put them in an even more vulnerable position.

Now that consumers are empowered by all the information they need to buy anything, anytime, and anywhere, they will concentrate their energies on locating the best deals. This task is streamlined by sites such as trivago that are dedicated to helping consumers hunt for the best price. It is not uncommon for consumers these days to visit retail stores operated by brands to physically try out an item and then go online to find the same merchandise at a lower price point.

Although we are witnessing the evolution of the market, with power being shifted from the sellers to the buyers, the end result is actually not so different – a disconnected world. This disconnection is the result of each side trying to maximize its own gain during sales transactions. This is why branding is so paramount in the digital era; it can bring order to a disrupted marketplace by genuinely fulfilling the different levels of consumer desire, and in turn leading to the sustainable viability of businesses operated by sellers. An "intelligent" brand, empowered by data and real-time insights, can harmonize the two sides, and contribute growth-momentum to an industry.

An intelligent brand is much more than a strategically positioned and well-crafted brand in the old-fashioned sense. In conventional marketing, a brand is strictly defined to fulfill the unfulfilled needs of its target customers. In the past, the role of the brand was to notify audiences that its products were the right solutions to their problems. In a sense, the brand served as an important bridge between customers and products. In the future, branding will be a dynamic and organic concept empowered by data. Of course, the brand will continue to represent the "promise" made by the manufacturer or service provider, but the breadth and depth of the insights derived from data will allow the seller to produce the right amount of goods in the right format without insufficient or excessive inventory. Brands will no longer require ad hoc customer satisfaction surveys, since buyers constantly give away substantial feedback on what they like and dislike on social media. The key will be to organize the unstructured data coming from various sources and distill the elements that are most critical to production and operation. As such, a new market equilibrium can be reached that satisfies both sellers and buyers through ongoing market self-regulation. Chapter Five of this book will further elaborate on how to build big brands with big data. For now, it will be useful to examine the evolution of brands and other marketing components that lay the foundation for this new marketing practice.

Evolution of media

Paid media

Many great brands of the past, including leading FMCG brands owned by industry leaders such as Procter & Gamble and Unilever, were created by advertising achievements. They had marketing budgets that allowed them to dominate the share of voice in "paid media," predominantly represented by TV, print, and outdoor advertising.

Following the increasing pervasion of the Internet and smartphones, consumers are moving away from the big and shared screen to smaller but more individual screens. eMarketer predicts that 43% of media ad spending in the US will go towards mobile advertising by 2020, surpassing the total spending allocated to other traditional media.[2] As a result, the paid media scene is becoming more and more fragmented; any website with a reasonable traffic count can join the ad network and automatically distribute sponsored content through programmatic advertising. Agencies that used to produce expensive TV commercials with a big production budget now need to re-evaluate how they can continue to disseminate brand messages in today's disrupted media environment.

To prevent audiences from skipping or blocking ads, product placement in movies is becoming more common, and some brand integrations are better orchestrated than others. It is interesting to compare the product placement of Coke in the first *Independence Day* movie (1996) and MengNiu Dairy in

Independence Day: Resurgence (2016). Many audiences found the Coke placement more acceptable because the product had a part to play in the plot, whereas MengNiu seemed like an afterthought to the script.[3] It exists literally as a "placement" in the movie, adding little if no value to the story. Whether or not its inclusion generated positive or negative impact on the brand is thus debatable.

The all-time master of product placement is probably Audi. In most of the movies it sponsors, such as *Agent 47* and *The Transporter Refueled*, the vehicle itself plays a crucial role through a thrilling action scene. The product not only becomes an integral part of the story, but also allows the Audi brand to manifest its unique personality and superior product performance by adding tremendous entertainment value to the movie itself. The effectiveness of Audi's product placement is rooted in the brand's ability to understand and capitalize on the reason people go to the movies – to be entertained.

Earned media

Consumers always approach editorial content with a more open-minded attitude. As the content is typically not paid by advertisers, consumers normally find its information more credible and are therefore are prepared to spend more time digesting its contents. Like "advertorials" from the old days, "native ads" are meant to replicate the online media format and disguise themselves as editorial content. Nonetheless, consumers these days are very smart and can often to tell eventually, if not at once, whether what they are reading is actually a piece of sponsored content.

The proper way to maximize the mileage of earned media, as the name implies, is to devise a fascinating story that has a strong human-interest factor and complements the media it appears in, be it online or offline. This has been a golden rule ever since marketers started to leverage public relations and media partnerships to get their message across. What makes digital influence different and perhaps more powerful than the traditional press release is the fact that in the digital world, brand messages can be crafted according to each media platform and even include interactive elements for communicating with consumers.

Owned media

Owned media is possibly the least costly channel for advertising, and also the format that gives the brand owner the most control. And yet, its results are often far from satisfactory. The most common types of owned media are the corporate website, the retail outlet, and the frontline staff. One of the most common pitfalls of corporate websites is the inclusion of information that is important to corporate stakeholders but not to generic viewers. It is not unusual to find websites that contain a section featuring its advertising show reel. But if their viewers are skipping ads on YouTube, why do corporations think viewers will bother watching the ads on their sites? Their other apparent mistake is treating their website as an electronic brochure with static and dated information. In the digital age, people expect to access the most current and relevant information at all times. This is also an important principle of search engine optimization (SEO); if a website's content has significant market appeal and is often referenced or cited, it will rank higher in search engine results.

While the website is the brand's online destination, the retail outlet is the offline or onsite destination where the brand and its customers meet. The reason why physical stores still exist although e-commerce has already disrupted the entire retail sector is that stores communicate directly with the audience by appealing to their five senses. People can "experience" the brand essence in person by seeing, hearing, feeling, touching, and even tasting the brand. Abercrombie and Fitch (A&F) was famous for positioning shirtless male models with six-pack abs outside its stores, and for spraying its unique FIERCE cologne throughout its shop, detectable even from a few blocks away. Customers bought the style and personality of the brand rather than its polo shirts. Although A&F eventually stopped using male models in 2015 and toned down its cologne campaign, the high visibility of its retail stores nonetheless allowed it to attract much consumer attention. Its decision to rebrand itself, highly motivated by feedback from the public, also goes to show that consumers have the ability to make powerful demands in today's digital era.[4]

Business operators have come to realize that Online to offline (O2O) is the way to manage a business these days. Yet many of them see online and offline as two stand-alone parts of business operations, with independent emphases and values, when technologies have demolished the boundaries. Now, consumers already embrace online and offline in a smart and seamless way. It is much more than searching for the merchandise online, trying it on at the physical store, and then purchasing it online at a cheaper online outlet. Consumers are continuously operating their smartphones even when they are inside the store, checking not just the price but also the reviews and popularity of the product. Serious buyers may browse further in terms of product features and performance online before they hand over the item to the cashier, not to mention that they may share the item to solicit comments from friends before deciding whether to buy or not. O2O, therefore, needs to be redefined. It is no longer about "O + O" but rather "O × O" as the line between online and offline is harmoniously blurred, and consumers are opting for a total and smart shopping experience. Hence, cosmetics brands like MAC in Shanghai offer consumers interesting tools and encourage them to try out their products in augmented reality when they visit the store.

A brand is not a brand if it lacks emotion, and the best way to communicate emotion is through people. We go to a restaurant for its food, but whether we return to the same restaurant usually has to do with the quality of the service rather than the food. The importance of "people" in the process of brand-building cannot be emphasized enough. In truth, the fate of our brand actually lies in the hands of frontline staff who are usually the most junior and least compensated employees under the corporate structure. The issues of "internal branding" will be explored at greater length in the subsequent chapters of this book.

Shared media

It is almost a given that people with spending power will be members of several social networking sites. *Brandwatch* estimates that 3.725 billion people are active on social media, and that each person has an average of 7.6 social media accounts and spends 142 minutes social networking every day.[5] The most popular social media channels are usually available in multiple languages and enable users to connect with people across geographical, political, and economic borders. Creating an account is typically free, but platforms such as LinkedIn offer premium memberships that include upgrades and exclusive features for a fee.

Due to its constant presence in our daily lives, social media has an undeniably strong social impact. Social networks are so influential not just because of their reach and scale, but also because of the massive amount of user-generated content (UGC) they house. Needless to say, people will be more likely to read and trust comments made by their peers than the advertisers' official party lines. Social media has given rise to a new species of KOL who may not be associated with any publishing or professional groups but are able to command the respect and ongoing support of many followers. Their huge fan base has become their bargaining chip when negotiating deals with brand owners. Unlike traditional celebrities who may just be distant endorsers, KOLs often come across as more authentic and credible. They are likely to possess more knowledge and expertise than celebrities do for certain product categories. Their followers enjoy a more personal relationship with them and may even interact with them directly. It is a known fact that the number of followers a social media influencer has may be inflated by bots or other fake accounts. In fact, there are now tools for helping marketers verify the popularity of these KOLs. Nevertheless, working with various KOLs or key opinion consumers (KOC) in a highly customized way has become a regular duty for marketers. The process involves more than scouting the right mix of KOL and KOC and negotiating the price with them individually. It also necessitates educating or coaching them so that they have sufficient product knowledge to talk about what they are using. It will be much more ideal if their endorsement comes from a genuine understanding of and preference for a brand rather than purely commercial motivations (Figure 2.1).

Marketers these days recognize the importance of social media, but there are still a number of important principles to remember:

1. Social media can be more "mass" than "mass media." The barrier to entry for rolling out a new social site is low. The combined number of social networking sites and mobile apps worldwide is quite phenomenal; by the end of March 2019, 2.6 million and 2.2. million apps were available to download on Android and iOS platforms, respectively.[6]

FIGURE 2.1   The ability and skills in managing all four types of media are critical to the success of any marketing campaign.

2. Social media isn't free.
3. Social media is an important piece of the puzzle, but not the entire thing.
4. Social media is pointless unless you use it to track performance.
5. Social media requires active and strategic management. Some marketers are too scared to dive headfirst into social media because they are concerned about the resources and commitment required to do a good job. Others adopt a "laissez faire" approach, expecting to operate social media on "auto-pilot" and allow users to take the lead. Neither of these approaches is desirable.

To maximize the value of social media, marketers should adopt a more active and strategic approach in assessing the brand's market position and the intensity of consumers' brand engagement. Marketers can then fine-tune their social media strategy according to real-time insights through the following steps:

Monitor

Brand-owners can use different social listening tools to find out consumers' priorities and concerns throughout the different stages of their purchase journey.

They can also gauge the overall market sentiments and trends for their category, plus how well their brands perform compared to competitors. Content analysis tools can use AI to detect the nature of user comments which will allow brand owners to continuously understand their brand positions. Customized communication or action can be tailor-made for different target groups to increase the final conversion rate.

Defend

If misperceptions, negative comments, or even false accusations are detected, brand owners can take prompt action to rectify the situation or provide clarification so that the brands will be judged in a fair light. Safeguarding the brand's reputation or key personnel should always be considered an ongoing priority.

Steer

During normal times, brands can perform customer service by engaging customers on social media platforms such as their Facebook page. Brand owners can also design marketing activities with an inherently social motivator that spurs broader engagement and sharing. They can collaborate with influencers and leverage their endorsement to deepen consumers' conviction in the brand, eventually turning them into brand advocates.

Commerce

Social media is no longer just about sharing funny pictures, interesting experiences, or useful product information. Social commerce is becoming a trend, particularly during festive seasons or special shopping events such as (618) Shopping Festival and Singles' Day in China. KOLs are staged to livestream to their fans and share personal comments about products which often lead to tremendous sales that are unmatched by any traditional means, especially for more emotional product categories such as cosmetics, fashion, and jewelry.

Initiate

Since consumers actively engage in all the latest news and happenings through social media, brand-owners can proactively lead consumers towards long-term behavioral changes with different deals or consumer education. They can also solicit input from the end-user's perspective on how to further improve the product and services. This will encourage a continuous refinement of the brand strategy to generate desirable business results.

Evolution of marketing

Mass marketing

In the mass production era, when manufacturers had the upper hand and could dictate the entire sales process, they possessed information that was inaccessible to consumers. The primary interest of factory owners was maximizing the production capacity of their plants. The way to prosper was to achieve economies of scale by producing more of the same goods. Production was supported by domestic mass distribution channels, and if there was excess capacity, goods could be sold abroad. Mass marketing was the instrument for promoting brand awareness and sales. By pushing one-way information via mass communication, manufacturers could effectively reach most buyers. Customer satisfaction was achieved by selling better and cheaper products (as manufacturers progressed along the learning curve), but the types of products sold were largely determined by the manufacturers.

Direct marketing

As the market developed, manufacturers had to accept that not all the consumers wanted the same thing; in other words, "one size doesn't fit all." Moreover, media placement was becoming more costly, raising concerns about the return on investment with mass advertising. Compounded by the emergence of niche players focusing on serving specific customer segments, mass marketing started moving in the direction of direct marketing. Marketers began to realize that it might be more effective to combine conventional advertising with other promotional vehicles. With the absence of advanced technology in the early 1980s, most direct marketing campaigns were in the form of direct mailing. Unlike traditional advertising, which was restricted by media space or duration, direct mail gave marketers the flexibility to expand their content and provide more details of the subject to aim at customer conversion, supported by a more customized offer. Even for advertising, marketers would try to include response devices in the form of discount coupons or hotlines, whenever possible, to drive desired consumer action and to measure the effectiveness of the campaign.

The effectiveness of a direct marketing campaign will largely depend on the quality of its mailing list. Due to privacy issues and factors such as inconsistent quality, renting or buying a list to facilitate direct marketing is rarely practiced these days. Instead, corporations now prefer to build their own customer or prospect database via events or promotions to better understand the individuals before communicating with them. Email marketing has gradually replaced direct mail because of its speed, lower cost, and interactivity. Nonetheless, the golden rule for any kind of direct marketing remains the same: avoid becoming junk mail, i.e. sending out communications too often and pushing content that is not relevant to the receiving end.

Integrated marketing

One of David Ogilvy's most profound sayings is "we sell or else," which can be traced to the roots of what we call "integrated marketing communications" (IMC) today.

Owing to his background in research, David was a true believer in data and evidence, and was committed to advancing the concept of advertising not only on the creative side but also for the outcome of the campaign. Ogilvy & Mather was one of the 4As agency networks that diversified into other areas of the communication spectrum, including direct marketing, public relations, sales promotions, etc. These categories were regarded as "channels" by the industry because the emphasis at that time was on how to effectively reach the defined target audience.

Plenty of literature was published in the 1980s to promote these newer channels, pointing out gaps in the communication world that conventional advertising could not fulfill. The argument was that "a good PR story is infinitely more effective than a front-page ad," not to mention more affordable (earned media is largely free).[7] There was a famous saying among PR practitioners that "you can pay to publish an ad on the back cover of a magazine but PR can put you as the story on the front cover … for free." It was not hard to realize that these debates could work in the favor of more progressive ad agencies like Ogilvy & Mather who had their own arms for PR, direct marketing, sales promotion, etc.

In May of 1985, Ogilvy & Mather International Inc. became The Ogilvy Group. The name change reflected the agency's increasing emphasis on expanding its services and rolling out a more integrated communications approach. Its "Ogilvy Orchestration" initiative intended to bring together Ogilvy & Mather's "many instruments and voices to form one big and impactful sound."[8]

The purpose of the program was to provide existing and prospective clients with complete agency services through seamlessly coordinating the services offered by the agency. Although the initiative could be considered a move to acquire more clients (that may demand more than just advertising services) and secure a larger share of existing clients looking for new ways to connect with customers, Ogilvy Orchestration laid down the foundation for the research and development of IMC, which helped advertisers generate better return on investment (ROI).

Once a brand is defined by its relationship with the consumer, then everything that touches the consumer, everything that affects their relationship, and everything that communicates the brand at every point of contact becomes important. This is what Ogilvy's 360 Degree Branding is all about.

360 Degree Brand Stewardship is the day-to-day practice of understanding and nurturing the brands that have made significant differences in the lives of the people who buy or use them. It is about anticipating any and every encounter a customer or potential customer is going to have with the brand – and making sure every encounter enriches the consumer's overall experience of the brand.

360 Degree Brand Stewardship allows the creation of a brand idea that it builds at every point of contact.

To generate the best results, the campaign must focus its marketing efforts on the highest points of customer involvement. It also demands the use of customized messages for each moment and medium. The strategic intent is to improve the relationship between the clients and their customers, eventually leading to an increase in client value – market share, profit, share price. In short, it drives new opportunities.

IMC has gone through continuous refinement over the years. Don Schultz is one of the most influential scholars in the domain of IMC. He and other researchers advocate for the advancement of IMC to focus not only on the channels but also on the process as well as the customers.[9] The key is to ensure that the combined effect of multiple activities exceeds the sum of their individual effects.

Digital marketing

The obvious shift of the marketing budget from conventional advertising to digital marketing is a clear indication of marketers' increasing reliance on digital means for sustaining their business viability. This is a logical move, since consumers also rely more on digital devices and spend more time searching, interacting, and engaging with brands virtually. Their digital footprints are a window into their personality, which is critical information for marketers when developing effective targeted communication.

The digital world is more than just a promotional vehicle or channel. It is an ecosystem of its own. A brand can strategically promote its awareness on social platforms by targeting users who are more likely to be interested in their product offerings, based on behavioral analysis. To ensure that the brand is searchable online is another important parameter as consumers are actively searching for information. This need-based consumer behavior can promote more effective brand engagement. To further convince consumers, the brand must uphold its credibility not only by publicizing its accomplishments, but also by partnering with third parties so that positive comments about its products can appear in different online platforms. Digital marketing is thus a multi-way marketing model in which the consumer's decision may be the result of the interaction among consumers themselves or the interaction between consumers and influencers. Customer conversion is a key milestone, but it is not the end of the customer journey. The brand must ensure that its consumers are satisfied with the purchase and solicit their feedback through follow-up services. If customers endorse the brand publicly, they may influence peers who are still deciding on which brand to select.

Technology is an integral part of digital marketing and also an important empowerment to marketing practice. To start, the compensation model can be performance-based, such as pay by click or conversion. The programmatic advertising can re-target the same customer who has shown interest in certain

MARKETING EVOLUTION

FIGURE 2.2 Marketing as a discipline has evolved over time due to changes in the media landscape, technological advancements, and other factors.

categories or specific products based on their browsing behavior. Some leading industry players use artificial intelligence (AI) to refine their content marketing strategy or even match different customer profiles to provide marketers with a turnkey solution (Figure 2.2).

Evolution of consumers

Consumer as customer

Peter Drucker once claimed that "the purpose of an enterprise is to create and keep a customer."[10] His point is rather straightforward – if you have more customers, you have more business. If you do not have any customers, you do not have any business. He also points out that the goal of an enterprise is not just to acquire but also to retain its customers.

Consumers purchase products and services. They may buy the goods for their personal consumption or for shared use with families or friends. They may or may not be the end users; in some cases, they buy the product as a gift for others, such as toddlers and seniors.

What has been described so far is the most basic role of a consumer and its only role in the past. Today, the value of a consumer extends way beyond their propensity to spend. A consumer can have a major impact on other people's decisions about brands.

Consumer as director

With a smartphone in hand, any consumer can play the role of a director because they can capture the appearance, service, and even delivery of a brand on camera.

Social platforms such as YouTube, Facebook, Instagram, Pinterest, and TikTok have provided consumers with a free stage for publishing and distributing content in a timely manner. Today's online viewers have a huge appetite for consuming UGC and are eager to share trending stories within their circles. Depending on the nature of the content, the online audience is much more accommodating when viewing UGC as far as production quality is concerned. They prefer content that is more authentic than too dressed-up.

Consumer as reporter

Aside from uploading pictures and videos, the consumer can also report on products in a direct and blunt manner that a professional reporter would never dare to adopt. As long as the content and language used does not violate the rules of the social platform, one can upload almost anything without censorship. Since everyone has a smartphone these days and can spontaneously record anything that piques their curiosity, no incident is shielded from the public eye. These days, it is highly likely that a consumer can publish a story faster than the press.

Consumer as judge

Finally, consumers are not only the producers and viewers of stories, but also the judges that decide the fate of a brand (Figure 2.3). First, consumers trust other consumers more than they trust corporate spokespersons. They may jump to a conclusion simply based on another user's comments without fact-checking it first. Secondly, the consumers may themselves be the users, so their comments carry weight. They may be able to focus on the issues that matter most to other consumers. Thirdly, the consumers can form an unspoken union and act in a highly orchestrated manner to either support or boycott a brand.

We already learned from the Kryptonite lock incident mentioned in Chapter One that one video from a frustrated user can trigger a chain effect and ultimately an explosion of consumer demand that the business operator cannot ignore.

CONSUMER **REPORTER**

JUDGE **DIRECTOR**

FIGURE 2.3 Consumers play different roles when interacting with brands.

Evolution of brands

Functional brand

There are brands that we purchase and possess for one reason and one reason only – their functional benefit. We need them to perform certain tasks. When we do not have the need, they will be out of our sight and mind completely. Peter Drucker reminds us that we never buy a product, anyway; we only buy what the product can do for us.[11] A drill is a perfect example. We buy a drill because of its functionality, and we want to pick a brand that can perform the job properly. This may be a high-involvement process as we do not want to buy the wrong tool. It may also be the case that we are not that familiar with the brands of this category as we seldom spend time researching these brands before we have a particular need. This is what is referred to as "dissonance reducing buying behavior."

There is also a famous saying in the marketing world that we never want to buy a drill. What we want is the hole on the wall. This idea precisely highlights the role of a functional brand in our lives. Command is a brand under 3M that produces a full range of hooks and hangers, from picture-hanging strips to jumbo coat hangers. Command strips are easy to use and remove, and allow for damage-free hanging by leaving no mark on the wall. When I helped my daughters move into their dormitories, we never needed a drill. A bunch of Command products were able to do the trick for hanging their personal belongings.

The above example shows that a functional brand is quite vulnerable as consumers who are not emotionally attached to any particular brand can easily replace it with another product. We will not hesitate to find another method that can tackle our problem or serve the desired purpose. Our decision will be based on simple cost and benefit considerations. Of course, professional carpenters will always need "a drill." But it is worth noting that hassle-free and simple products provide significant benefits that justify premium pricing to some consumers.

Aspirational brand

In contrast to functional brands, there is another category of brands that we think of quite often because we are emotionally invested in them. They possess a magical element that makes them appealing to us, such that we want them even before we can afford them. We use the terms "dream car," "dream watch," or "dream bag" to describe these brands because they exist in our dreams before they become a reality. We use the same logic to describe the "ultimate" goal in other aspects of our lives, such as "dream job," "dream vacation," "dream home," or even "dream girl." The word "dream" represents the critical role that an aspirational brand can play in our lives. It adds value to us that is way beyond functional. That said, an aspirational brand is more than its aesthetic look and design. It is usually able to command superior product performance and fulfill consumer needs. A dream watch will possess sophisticated movement with high precision. A dream car, whether it is a supercar or classic car, will possess certain iconic elements that make it special. An aspirational brand tends to be made with higher craftmanship and better materials but is not necessarily a luxury brand. Still, most aspirational brands can be priced higher than their competitors because consumers are prepared to pay a premium for them.

Moreover, owning an aspirational brand is not about showing off, although it may draw the attention of other people who also consider it their "dream" brand. Rather, aspiring towards a brand gives us the motivation to move onward and upward. It pushes us to not only work harder so we can save up enough money to buy our dream brand, but to also appreciate the finer things in life. Since most, if not all dream brands possess a strong heritage and culture, they enrich our lives as well as our knowledge. In other words, the aspiration derives not from the brand's face value, but from the exceptional story and substance behind it.

Lifestyle brand

A lifestyle brand is a brand that matches our life philosophy. We do not carry these brands to project a certain image. We identify with them because they allow us to pursue the style of living we desire. For instance, minimalism is a type of lifestyle embraced by people who believe that simplicity is beauty. They never wear something that is showy or flashy, but this does not mean they prefer the bland or tasteless; rather, they search for brands that are natural and genuine.

Branding is a dynamic concept. The same brand can mean different things to different people, depending on their relationship with the brand. A brand may therefore manifest itself in different ways and play different roles in the user's life. For example, an Apple Watch may be a functional brand for a user who wants a watch that tells the time and also measures heart rate. Yet to some other people, the Apple Watch may be an aspirational purchase because they are "Apple disciples" who are drawn to the values of Apple as a corporation and a brand. Going one step further, an Apple Watch can also be a lifestyle brand for someone who believes in "connectivity" and thinks the watch would allow them to better manage and enjoy life. As a watch with many functions, the Apple Watch would complement the lifestyle of a user who likes to have multiple aspects of their life at their fingertips.

Responsible brand

A responsible brand is concerned with more than just its own commercial interest. It will not compromise on its ethical values during its pursuit of profit. But for a brand to present itself as responsible, it cannot do so as a marketing gimmick or publicity stunt. Consumers can tell almost right away if a brand is pretending to do good while keeping a hidden agenda of its own.

Indeed, a brand does not become responsible simply by donating to charity. Some skeptical consumers may even see this act of philanthropy as compensation for some other misdoing. If a brand has the courage and persistence to uphold certain ethical values, even if they must take a profit cut or sacrifice a part of their

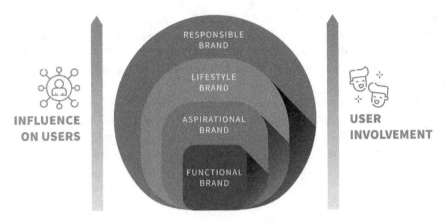

INFLUENCE
ON USERS

USER
INVOLVEMENT

FIGURE 2.4 The different types of brands command different levels of user involvement and influence on users.

production process, it will win the respect and empathy of many stakeholders. There are also brands that are innovative enough to make their social values an integral part of their product and service delivery.

For example, The Body Shop is a cruelty-free brand that is committed to not perform any testing on animals for its ingredients or finished products. The brand even withdrew itself from some markets that legally require animal testing for cosmetics products. The brand particularly appeals to customers who share their views on animal rights – especially women, who are already the target audience of cosmetics brands and tend to be generally fond of animals.

If we examine the relationship between the different types of brands and their consumers, a functional brand will rank the lowest in terms of the "user's involvement with the brand" and the "influence of the brand on users." An aspirational brand will rank higher than the functional brand but lower than a lifestyle brand, which a consumer may use every day. Finally, a responsible brand takes the lead in terms of user influence and involvement, for those who subscribe to the responsible brand are ultimately more than just consumers. They are advocates who share the brand's values and will support and adhere to the brand's mission even when they do not use its products (Figure 2.4).

A brand-builder's perspective

Interview with Prof. David Tse, Chair Professor of International Marketing at the Faculty of Business and Economics at The University of Hong Kong

Professor David K. Tse is the Chair Professor of International Marketing at the Faculty of Business and Economics at The University of Hong Kong. He taught for ten years at the University of British Columbia (1984–1993) after he received his BBA (Chinese Univ.), MBA, and PhD (Univ. of California, Berkeley, 1984).

He returned to Hong Kong in 1993 and joined the University of Hong Kong in 1998. He has taught at universities in the US, Canada, Europe, Hong Kong, and Mainland China. Since 2002, Prof. Tse has served as an Honorary Professor of Marketing at Guanghua School of Management, Peking University, and at Fudan University.

Prof. Tse serves as an academic trustee in the Marketing Science Institute and as a board member of the Sheth Foundation. He is a board member at the Institute of India, China, and America (Emory University); a research fellow for the William Davidson Institute (University of Michigan); and a fellow for the Center for Service Leadership (Arizona State University).

On the professional side, Prof. Tse serves as a non-executive director in medical technology startups.

Royce Yuen: The word "disruption" is frequently mentioned in marketing discourse. What's your view on the market phenomenon of disruption?

David Tse: The current ideas about disruption may come from the root of disruptive innovation. Indeed, with so many changes in terms of how business is done, including but not limited to e-commerce, e-payment, AI, etc., this is undoubtedly an era where disruptive innovation in everything becomes common.

Thus, the era of disruption may indeed be true. When extended to the market – shopping malls and physical banks will disappear, roles like tellers and receptionists will be replaced by AI, and the conventional way of doing advertising will fade away.

The conventional 4Ps are also changing: Product (from owning to sharing or experiencing); Price (highly competitive, real-time bidding), Promotion (content marketing is replacing traditional advertising), Place (e-commerce causes many shopping centers to close). All these changes will urge corporations to understand and approach the market differently.

RY: Is the digital revolution and e-commerce causing any "disruption" to brand-owners? How are they reacting to or coping with it?

DT: Brand-owners are inevitably affected by all the market transformations. They need to cope with diminishing distribution channels, possibly fewer or no retailers supporting their sales activities, and more and more businesses shifting online. Many are struggling and hanging on to consumers that are slowly adapting to this e-payment, e-commerce, and e-advertising environment. Highly competitive pricing is also putting extra pressure on business operators. That said, some are finding new ways to cope with or even prosper in the reshaping marketplace.

RY: Will branding play a different role in this day and age?

DT: Whatever the future holds, branding will be redefined. The extent of its changes will depend on the product category and its specific segment. The high-end market, which is highly sensory-driven, will count on brands to offer more enriched experiences; the mass market will rely on brands to refrain from becoming commodity products.

RY: Is branding becoming more of a science than an art?

DT: The future will be highly data-driven and metrics-crazed. I believe that the science aspect of branding will become more prominent, but the art side of branding will remain equally crucial for the crafting of a great brand. In sum, it may be a world of singularity. Nothing like that has happened before.

RY: What is the definition of "brand" in the most current context?

DT: Branding has always been a dynamic concept. It will be more so in the digital age when things are more transparent and information is more accessible. For low-involvement categories such as fast-food restaurants, a familiar brand provides more assurance. For categories that people pay more attention to but not overwhelmingly so, such as smartphone, automobile, or traveling services, branding adds "meaning" and "lifestyle" to the customer experience. Finally, for high-involvement categories that demand more active engagement, such as education for children or religion, branding connotes a highly emotional relationship.

Case study – Chow Tai Fook Jewellery Group

Multi-brand strategy for offensive and defensive marketing

Founded in 1929, Chow Tai Fook is the group's iconic brand and is widely recognized for its trustworthiness and authenticity. The jewelry brand is renowned for its product design, quality, and value (Image 2.1). A long-standing commitment to innovation and craftsmanship has contributed to the group's success, along with the reputation of its iconic retail brand. It has been embodied in its rich 90-year heritage. Underpinning this success are the group's long-held core values – sincerity and eternity.

With an extensive retail network of close to 4,000 shops in Greater China, Japan, Korea, Southeast Asia, and the United States, and a fast-growing e-commerce business, the group is implementing effective online-to-offline strategies to succeed in today's omnichannel environment.

The group's commitment to sustainable growth is anchored in its "Smart+" strategy, which is in place to promote long-term innovation in business, people, and culture. Another asset underpinning sustainable growth is a sophisticated and agile business model. This supports the group by fostering excellence and extending opportunities along the entire value chain to communities and industry partners across the world.[12]

IMAGE 2.1 A 90-year-old brand is striving to be the preferred choice for jewelry. Credit: ctfjewellerygroup.com.

Interview with Kent Wong, Managing Director of Chow Tai Fook

Mr. Kent Wong joined the Chow Tai Fook Jewellery Group in 1977. Appointed as Managing Director of the company in July 2011, Mr. Wong is responsible for the strategic planning and overall management of the group. With his diverse experience in business development as well as in operations and management, Mr. Wong is Chairman of the Jewellery Advisory Committee of the Hong Kong Trade Development Council (HKTDC) and was named "CEO of the Year/Luxury/Asia" at the 2016 IAIR Awards presentation ceremony held by International Alternative Investment Review. He was also named as "Asia's Best CEO (Investor Relations)" by Corporate Governance Asia, an authoritative regional journal on corporate governance, at its Asian Excellence Awards in 2017, 2018, and 2019 consecutively.

Royce Yuen: How do you ensure there is sustainable growth for an already very well-established business given the uncertain economic outlook?

Kent Wong: We have three long-term goals, namely market share expansion, customer experience improvement, and stable returns to our shareholders. We have strategies and plans in place across the group to ensure that we achieve these objectives. Our "Smart+ 2020" strategic framework, a three-year strategic plan focused on enhancing customer experience, launched in FY2018 and has provided us with a powerful impetus for growth (Image 2.2). Over the last year, we have achieved several exciting strategic milestones as a result. Through the relentless and diligent execution of our "Smart+ 2020" strategic framework, we

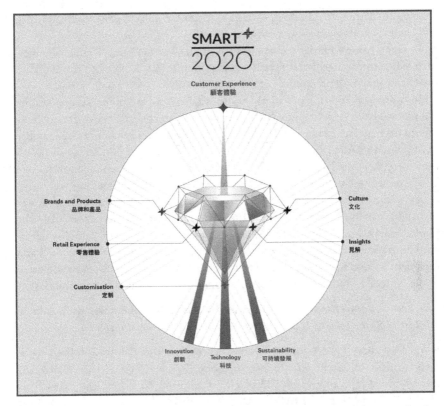

IMAGE 2.2 "Smart+ 2020" strategic framework is a three-year strategic work plan supported by the group's dedicated Smart working teams, which are tasked with the delivery of each strategy from conception through to execution. Credit: Chow Tai Fook Jewelry Group Annual Report 2019.

are confident that we can deliver a seamless and compelling customer experience that ensures we create long-term shareholder value.

RY: Are you witnessing a change in consumer behavior across different markets, and how do you manage the more informed and increasingly demanding consumers of today?

KW: Customers' preference in our key markets has changed rapidly over the last five years. Some themes are common, and some are specific to their particular needs. Nowadays, consumers are increasingly sophisticated in seeking more personalized products and exclusive experiences. This phenomenon is particularly true for relatively affluent groups. Younger customers, on the other hand, focus on mobile, social media, and online experiences as crucial benchmarks for evaluating their selection of brands. These two common themes are generally applicable across all of our key markets.

Mainland China shares these common themes and has the additional challenge of being a vast and geographically diverse market with dispersed retail channels that are forcing brand-owners and retailers to reposition their network and channel strategies to stay relevant.

In Hong Kong and Macau, retailers have to deal with longer-term challenges, such as incremental growth in relatively mature markets, along with the evolving travel and spending preferences of inbound visitors.

In overseas markets, particularly Southeast Asia, we see potential opportunities that we have yet to explore fully. Southeast Asian countries have greatly benefitted from globalization trends. Their production capacity has increased rapidly in response to rising labor costs in Mainland China over the past few years. With the emergence of a larger and richer middle class in those Asian economies, we believe that there will be a huge demand for quality products and services.

As for the scale of the global diamond jewelry market, it stood at a sheering size of 82 billion in 2017, according to De Beers' Diamond Insight Report of 2018. The United States alone has captured 50% of the global market share. Looking across the United States diamond market's value chain, which is highly fragmented and organized around functions, we believe that there is ample room for us to add value to the upstream, midstream, and downstream through our built-in capabilities.

RY: Chow Tai Fook has successfully launched multiple sub-brands in recent years. Is this a defensive or offensive move? Is this multi-brand strategy generating desirable business results?

KW: The group's multi-brand strategy comprises the Chow Tai Fook core brand with its different retail experience offerings. ARTRIUM, JEWELRIA, Experience Shop, and CTF WATCH, in addition to other brands such as HEARTS ON FIRE, T MARK, ENZO, SOINLOVE, and MONOLOGUE, address the diversifying needs of different customers (Image 2.3).

IMAGE 2.3 ARTRIUM is one of the multi-brands that offer a new way to appreciate jewelry. Credit: ctfjewellerygroup.com.

The multi-brand strategy was launched as an initiative to sustain the business growth of Chow Tai Fook due to changing consumer attitudes and behaviors. It also intended to minimize the risk and uncertainty brought about by changing market demographics, culture, and economy.

This strategy would also allow the group to review and reflect on the whole business model. Consumers these days do not just buy jewelry products. The purchase and possession of jewelry are a manifestation of their attitude towards life. The perspective and lifestyle of young people are very different from those of their previous generation, resulting in different needs. They form their own ecosystem.

Aside from multi-brands that offer highly differentiated products, Chow Tai Fook is also exploring multi-channel strategies to reach and engage new consumers effectively. Besides online shopping on Tmall and JD.com, mobile is a significant interface that facilitates one-on-one communication and interaction (Image 2.4).

IMAGE 2.4   Forgot to buy a birthday gift for someone important? No worries, this "private corner" offered by Chow Tai Fook can serve your needs 24/7. Credit: ctfjewellerygroup.com.

Technology and data have transformed the planning and doing of business beyond products and services. They open more doors for jewelry companies to expand their sphere of influence in areas such as financing by leveraging the tremendous insights generated by the data of each customer. This expansion can also lead to collaboration with other industries such as banks, thus fulfilling the customer's needs throughout the different stages of their lives.

Needless to say, multi-brands have to complement the core business. It is unnecessary to have too many brands or too much overlap between them. Their purpose is to fulfill different customers or the different needs of the same customer.

For instance, there are customers in their fifties who buy MONOLOGUE because they are young and vibrant at heart. Demographics is no longer the most useful dimension for matching customers to brands (Image 2.5).

To elaborate, the role of multi-brands is to acquire new customers and to retain existing ones by creating more reasons for them to remain interested in us. Although there is no mentioning upfront that these new brands are part of the Chow Tai Fook family, eventually revealing that they belong to the same group is an important factor for assuring consumers of the product's quality. After all, jewelry is a high-value item that must be authentic, so having a brand that is trustworthy and longstanding is affirming. In fact, aside from the team's hard work and out-of-the-box thinking, the substantial infrastructure of Chow

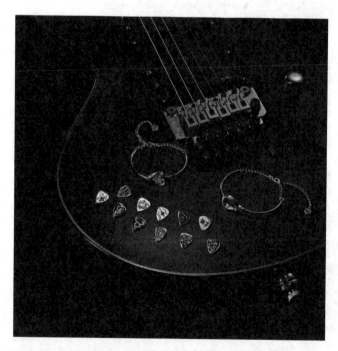

IMAGE 2.5 MONOLOGUE is another new brand that offers a new jewelry experience. Credit: ctfjewellerygroup.com.

Tai Fook (including its sourcing, logistics, IT, etc.) is another major factor that contributed to the success of its multi-brands within such a short time.

To summarize, Chow Tai Fook's multi-brand strategy is totally in line with the group's core value and philosophy that can be summarized by a famous Chinese saying, translated as *harmonious yet not homogeneous, decentralization yet not disconnected.* The strategy can be effectively enforced with data to reflect the real and measurable progress of any initiative.

Notes

1 "Flight Overbooks the Barbaric Norm." *The Standard*, April 12, 2017. https://www.thestandard.com.hk/section-news/section/17/181793/Flight-overbooks-the-barbaric-norm.
2 eMarketer. "Mobile Ad Spending to Surpass All Traditional Media Combined by 2020," October 16, 2018. https://www.emarketer.com/content/mobile-ad-spending-to-surpass-all-traditional-media-combined-by-2020.
3 Xi, Wei. "Chinese Audiences Unhappy with Clumsy Product Placement." *Global Times*, June 29, 2016. https://www.globaltimes.cn/content/991371.shtml.
4 Brooke, Eliza. "Abercrombie & Fitch Is Getting Rid of Its Shirtless Store Models." *Fashionista*, April 24, 2015. https://fashionista.com/2015/04/abercrombie-fitch-shirtless-models.
5 Smith, Kit. "126 Amazing Social Media Statistics and Facts." *Brandwatch*, December 30, 2019. https://www.brandwatch.com/blog/amazing-social-media-statistics-and-facts/.
6 Iqbal, Mansoor. "App Download and Usage Statistics (2019)." *Business of Apps*, July 30, 2019. https://www.businessofapps.com/data/app-statistics/.
7 Madsen, Nineveh. "Council Post: Six Steps to Create a Great Public Relations Story and Earn a Place in the Media Spotlight." *Forbes*, July 7, 2017. https://www.forbes.com/sites/forbescommunicationscouncil/2017/07/07/six-steps-to-create-a-great-public-relations-story-and-earn-a-place-in-the-media-spotlight/.
8 Encyclopedia.com. "The Ogilvy Group, Inc.," October 8, 2020. https://www.encyclopedia.com/books/politics-and-business-magazines/ogilvy-group-inc.
9 Schultz, Don E., and Heidi F. Schultz. "Transitioning Marketing Communication into the Twenty-First Century." *Journal of Marketing Communications* 4, no. 1 (January 1, 1998): 9–26. doi: 10.1080/135272698345852.
10 Stern, Stefan. "The Importance of Creating and Keeping a Customer." *Financial Times*, October 10, 2011. https://www.ft.com/content/88803a36-f108-11e0-b56f-00144feab49a.
11 Drucker, Peter F., and Joseph A. Maciariello. "The Purpose and Objectives of a Business." In *Management*, Rev. ed., 98. New York: Collins, 2008.
12 Chow Tai Fook Jewellery Group. "About Our Group," June 12, 2020. https://www.ctfjewellerygroup.com/en/group/about-us.html.

3

ESSENCE OF BRANDING

The concept of branding predates you and me. In fact, it existed before people had any idea about what branding was. Imagine someone from 100 years ago going to see a doctor or a tailor. I bet he wouldn't just randomly visit any doctor or tailor. Whether to seek medical advice or learn how to dress better, he would go to someone he trusted. "Trust" is the cornerstone of branding.

Branding has become an inseparable part of our lives. When we buy things, we think of brands. We think of buying a Colgate or Oral B, not just a toothpaste. Some people believe the act of marking livestock with a branding iron in ancient times was one of the first ways people practiced "branding." The goal of marking the livestock was to express ownership and separate your belongings from others. These days, a brand still functions as a badge, but it has also taken on more symbolic significance and become an important part of human interactions.

A brand stands for absolute quality and implies a more satisfying experience. A trusted brand gives people assurance and peace of mind. As such, people engage in brands they believe in. The brand becomes a promise, and it nurtures relationships based on this promise. This is why branding is so critical in business dealings; business is all about building long-term partnerships based on mutual trust and expectation.

This may all sound like common sense, except having common sense is not very common these days. Sometimes, people tend to over-complicate or over-analyze issues. This chapter intends to examine the construct of branding from various perspectives and provide some clarity on the subject. It will also serve as a good foundation for further discussions of branding in the age of disruption.

Defining "brand" today

I have met more than one business owner who believes that brand-building is very costly, and out of their budget. First, brand-building is an investment, not a cost. I hope that before you finish reading this book, you will realize and agree that brand-building is not only a worthwhile pursuit, but a must: *your brand exists before you start to promote or advertise it.* Your customers will form an impression of you after interacting with you, even before they do business with you. If you do not actively manage your brand and guide people on how to appreciate it, you are leaving it to the audience to define your brand. A 15-year-old can spend an entire day talking about a Ferrari with great enthusiasm and can probably accurately describe its functionality. However, it is highly unlikely that he has ever driven a Ferrari. He may not even have a driving license! The same goes for your customers. They may not have awarded you with a contract yet, but your reputation precedes you (hopefully in a positive way). Our job as marketers is to provide all the clues in a structured manner on an ongoing basis so that people can effortlessly put together a picture of what we do and who we are.

From here, we may realize that the term "loyal customer" may need a new definition. Traditionally, loyal customers are defined as individuals or corporations that do business with us frequently or have done so for a considerable period of time. This is the way many institutions classify their customers based on their sales record. If a customer increases their spending year after year with us, they surely must be a loyal and satisfied customer. And yet, this assumption may be invalid. An individual might have an account with a certain bank, but that does not necessarily mean he or she has a genuine relationship with it. Their employer may just prefer its staff to open an account with a particular bank for payroll processing (at the end of Chapter Eleven, there is a transcript of an interview with William Leung, who has managed both traditional and virtual banks. He will share insights on how banks can win the hearts of customers before winning their wallets). Even if someone spends more with us over the years, he may be spending even more with our competitors. We need to gauge our relationship with the customers through data, observations, and experience to arrive at a complete understanding of the situation.

In the digital world, consumers talk to and support each other by sharing information and experiences online. This communication reduces their risk of purchasing the wrong or less desirable product. They will also go to someone who is qualified to offer a credible opinion about the specific product category. In other words, corporations not only have to manage the people who buy or use their brand, but also influence the influencers whose opinions can help their business. Customers who frequently buy your products are important assets to the company. Yet *a loyal customer is not necessarily someone who buys your brand regularly but one who promotes your brand and defends your brand voluntarily.* We have to identify these warriors and empower them to protect our brand. We also need to educate and nurture more of our customers so that they will join this group and become our brand advocates. They are the most effective and powerful sales team that any corporation could ever imagine.

Some marketers will classify some of their marketing programs as brand-building efforts, while other programs are for promoting sales. Because of this mentality, some marketers tend to focus more on initiatives that they believe tie in more directly with sales. This is an outdated or even mistaken concept. There is no trade-off between building a brand and building sales. They complement each other due to the simple fact that a well-crafted brand will attract buyers, and the more that people use the product, the more they appreciate what the brand can do for them. Every marketing initiative, therefore, should contribute to building the brand and safeguarding its position in the market.

Arguably, building a brand should come before making sales. This is apparent in the business-to-business (B2B) sector, where a client has to meet a vendor for different rounds of discussions before concluding any business deals. A brand strategy can be defensive or offensive. A defensive move can fend off competitors who are trying to steal your customers. An offensive brand strategy can expand the customer base to tap a "blue ocean." Exercising both defensive and offensive strategies is paramount in the digital age, where social media is inundated by comments that are accurate, false, constructive, and destructive. The national team that wins the World Cup must be good at defensive and offensive playing in order to secure the championship, and the same goes for the business world. We need to stay alert and be ready to seize any opportunity or preempt any erosion of our customer base.

Every brand has a life cycle, from entering a market to becoming a mature player, with a group of steady followers. Yet the life cycle of the brand has been severely disrupted or even shortened in the digital world. The justification of where and how to spend money has evolved alongside the rapidly changing tastes and expectations of modern consumers. For example, a study by McKinsey found that consumers in China prefer to buy more understated jewelry pieces and watches.[1] They are more interested in the movement of a watch than a gold-plated case with diamonds. Similarly, the luxury phone manufacturer Vertu closed its UK manufacturing operations in 2017 because consumers decided that digital functionality outweighs appearance.[2] We will discuss later in this chapter on how a brand can stay young and rejuvenate itself.

Price has always been an instrumental component of a brand. It indicates how much the brand is worth and filters out customers who cannot afford the brand. Pricing is also a branding statement that connotes quality and exclusivity. Premium pricing has to be justified by superior quality and product performance, or else the brand will not last long in the market. As we discussed in Chapter Two, corporations these days are completely "naked" in front of consumers due to the information available on the Internet. Pricing, for instance, is entirely transparent. Some websites even compare the pricing and performance of different brands so that users have all the information they need to make a more informed decision.

Traditionally, a brand can choose to establish a premium or value position, or somewhere in between. A premium positioning commands premium pricing with superior product quality. A value positioning offers an affordable alternative with acceptable quality. In this day and age, due to improvements in production technology and supply chain management, some brands have rewritten the quality and pricing equation. A brand can be low-cost but not low-end. Consumers do not have to be apologetic anymore about wearing or using a relatively cheaper item. Uniqlo is enjoying global success for feeding the market with basic, functional, and quality clothing that is very accommodating as far as pricing is concerned. Zara and H&M are also allowing consumers to experience in-season, Fifth Avenue–style fashion that doesn't cost an arm and a leg. A Kia Stinger GT comes with a 3.3-liter twin-turbo V6 engine that generates 365 hp at 6,000 rpm and 510 N m of torque from 1,500 to 4,500 rpm. It can accelerate from 0 to 62 mph in just 4.9 seconds. If you are amazed by its look and performance, you will be even more surprised by its price – it costs less than a quarter of a BMW M5's price. All these brands have disrupted the market and educated consumers on how to perceive brands.

At the same time, the market is still willing to pay a premium for exclusive club memberships, high-end residential properties, or even prestigious schools. Harrow International School in Hong Kong charges an annual tuition of around $26,000 for senior students plus a capital levy charge of $7,700 per year for pupils without Capital Certificates and Debentures.[3] To many parents, the steep tuition fee is acceptable if it allows them to send their kids to a school associated with the Harrow brand, a school founded under the Royal Charter of Queen Elizabeth I with more than 440 years of establishment.

In this volatile market, traditional luxury brands such as Hermès and Louis Vuitton are able to defend their positions and stay in the game. They have demonstrated that there is no compromise between exclusivity and popularity. Their shops in Paris are always packed with tourists who have a massive appetite for shopping. In Hong Kong, it is very common to see a long queue outside the high-end stores on Tsim Sha Tsui's Canton Road, where eager customers wait with their shopping lists and credit cards at the ready. Knowing that a luxury brand may lose its cachet when so many customers carry the brand everywhere, even at the supermarket, Louis Vuitton rolled out their "Journeys" campaign in 2008. Featuring Mikhail S. Gorbachev, Sean Connery, Keith Richards of the Rolling Stones, and astronauts Buzz Aldrin, Sally Ride, and Jim Lovell, "Journeys" aimed to reinforce the core values of the brand.[4] These iconic figures have one thing in common – their journeys have touched the hearts of many people and created a significant impact on our world. For the past 160 years and more, Louis Vuitton has accompanied people with discerning tastes as they travel the world and gain different life experiences. The campaign has helped them reconnect with their loyal consumers by reinforcing that the core value of the brand has not faded.

Stunning campaigns have considerable stopping power and may invite people to reappraise a brand. Yet more than just attractive advertising is needed to ensure the long-term market viability of a brand. To merit the ongoing support of their users, brands must maintain the following qualities:

- Experience: to satisfy the users and enrich their lives in a tangible way;
- Entertainment: to engage the users with exceptional sensations;

- Collaboration: to involve the users in manifesting the values of the brand;
- Technology: to enhance the delivery system and infrastructure;
- Newsiness: to offer upgrades and surprises that are in line with the brand proposition.

The conventional 4Ps of marketing are no longer sufficient for ensuring business success. Reliable quality, reasonable price, easy access, regular advertising, and promotion are becoming hygiene factors. These are the necessary prerequisites a product must fulfill to even to be considered This can be understood as the "new OS" in brand-building, which will be explained further in the interview with Kent Wertime of Ogilvy at the end of the next chapter.

Value of brands

A brand represents tremendous value to an organization. There is a growing interest in ascertaining and quantifying the value of a brand. The two most widely cited studies on brand valuation are Kantar Millward Brown's annual BrandZ report[5] and Interbrand's Brand Valuation methodology.[6] Though they approach the subject with different methodologies, both studies gave the same four companies the highest rankings in 2019 – Apple, Google, Amazon, and Microsoft – though not necessarily in the same order.

To shed some light on this topic, I spoke with accounting veterans Philip Tsai and Richard Sun. Philip is the Chairman of Deloitte China. Richard is the Lead Director of PwC China, Hong Kong, Taiwan, and Singapore. Their inputs have been amazingly consistent. Overall, branding is about perception, and is rather generic by nature. While trademarks and patents can be registered, there is no standard practice in valuing a brand. And since the brand is an intangible asset generated internally, it cannot be recognized on the balance sheet.

The International Accounting Standards (IAS 38) specifically prohibits the recognition of brands, mastheads, publishing titles, customer lists, and similarly internally generated substances as intangible assets. The IAS 38 Committee believed that internally generated, intangible items of this kind would rarely, and perhaps never, meet its recognition criteria.

The value of a brand, however, can be recognized after its acquisition. When Prada S.p.A. was listed on the Hong Kong Exchange in 2011, there was no intangible asset recognized for the Prada brand itself, but there was a valuation for Miu Miu, a subsidiary of Prada. It is worth noting that the market appeal of the acquired brand may have increased over time, but its increase in value cannot be quantified in accounting terms.

In the merger and acquisition process, a significant portion of the investment may go towards the brand instead of the physical asset. For instance, when LVMH took an 80% stake of Rimowa in 2016, 475 million euros out of the 640 million euros investment went to the brand.[7] Similarly, when Reckitt Benckiser bought Mead Johnson in 2017, the total acquisition cost was 13 billion pounds, of which 9 billion was for the brand.[8]

Although your brand may not appear on your balance sheet, your brand is probably the biggest reason why talents come to work for you. It is also the reason why consumers are confident in buying your products. *Your brand, therefore, can be regarded as your most valuable asset.* It is the result of all the hard work you have put into your business and the market reputation that you have earned over the years.

From product to brand

The value of a brand can be further highlighted when we try to distinguish the difference between a product and a brand. Out of all the definitions that explain the difference between products and brands, the one from WPP plc is probably the easiest to comprehend and the most indisputable: *Products are what are made in factories. Brands are what consumers buy.*[9] This statement is very true, and we experience it all the time in our daily lives. We do not just buy a smartphone. We buy an iPhone, Samsung, Huawei, or Xiaomi. Since 2005, Toyota and Subaru have been leveraging each other's technical expertise to co-develop new cars. In 2011, both manufacturers unveiled two near-identical cars at the Tokyo Auto Show. In terms of design and performance, the Toyota 86 and the Subaru BRZ are virtually the same product; the most notable difference is the two separate logos located above the grilles.[10] Still, the fact that they are able to appeal to different buyers is an interesting proof that consumers are indeed still buying brands.

A brand can be further broken down into different tiers of sub-brands. The Mercedes E-Class is more luxurious and expensive than the Mercedes C-Class. A Mercedes E350 is 60% more expensive than a C200, yet the AMG C63 (which is also part of the C-Class family) is priced 70% higher than the E350. Mercedes Benz is the master brand or the corporate brand, while E-Class and C-Class can be regarded as the product brands. We will expand on this example to explain the concept of brand architecture when we discuss brand DNA in the next section.

Branding is not a sales tool, although hot brands sell well. This is logical because brands are what consumers go after. Products are generic, like commodities. When people buy commodities, they just compare prices and believe that their takeaway from the different products will be more or less the same. However, when consumers engage in a brand, their thought process is very different from when they consume a product. *A brand will draw the consumers to focus on the value they can get rather than the price they have to pay.* As such, a company is immune to a price war when it does not have to compete with price. Brands like Tiffany and Chanel will never have to discount their products. When there was a rumor that Chanel would soon increase its retail pricing, people rushed to Chanel stores to buy its handbags – even during COVID-19.[11]

Gift-giving is a common ritual in all cultures. People around the world celebrate birthdays, weddings, anniversaries, newborn babies, etc. A branded gift will mean much more than a generic present to both the giver and the receiver. When a gift is wrapped by Harrods or Galeries Lafayette, the quality of the content inside is almost guaranteed. This is the power of branding.

Given the value of brands, why are so many companies still engaged in selling products instead of creating brands? It is understandable for companies, especially small and mid-size enterprises (SMEs), to focus on their product and services when they first enter a market. After they have achieved a certain business momentum, they will then think about building brands. This logic is probably based on the belief that selling products makes money, and building brands spends money. Therefore, they expect to first make a profit, and then set aside a certain percentage of the profit for brand-building when funds are sufficient.

However, this approach is only half-correct. When a business is growing, more marketing efforts are needed to support its market expansion. Yet even in the early stages of a business, the company should have a clear vision about its brand positioning and how it differs from current market operators in answering customer needs. In other words, why should the prospects even consider your product? As mentioned in the previous chapter, there are different types of media that corporations can tap to communicate their messages. Having a presence on Facebook, Instagram, WeChat, YouTube, and a registered brand website is fundamental to starting a business. Actively updating these channels and posting relevant content is also vital.

A brand does not always happen when you advertise. Hiring a celebrity to endorse your product does not guarantee that you will have an awesome and adorable brand. *A product becomes a brand when it has a personality.* A product can be easily copied, especially with today's technology, but a brand is unique. *Building a brand is different from selling a product because it is not just about what you do as a corporation, but also how and why you do it.* A product is about providing a service. A brand is about delivering a service and provoking feelings. When the brand moves beyond functionality, it is less easily replaced or substituted. A brand allows an organization to have a dynamic rather than a linear relationship with the users. It is less likely to be severely affected by the disruptive forces in the market. *In the age of disruption, companies that continue to produce a standard product will fade away, but those who possess strong and enduring brands will persevere.*

Every brand has its DNA

A brand is unique because of its brand DNA. This DNA derives from the brand's country of origin, industry, culture, core competence, and any other factors that contribute to its originality. There is no right or wrong in brand DNA; it simply has to do with how the general public perceives or is taught to look at the world. A German car is technically more reliable. French wine is more palatable. These ideas may change over time, depending on how well the industries of the country perform. Thirty years ago, consumer electronics that were manufactured in Japan were favored over those made in South Korea. Yet Samsung is now a leading brand in many categories such as smartphones, quantum dot LED TVs, and kitchen appliances. As a result, "made in S. Korea" is now an endorsement of the design and quality of consumer products. In the old days, casinos mainly catered to gamblers. Yet by incorporating live spectacles and world-class entertainment into its casino resorts, Macau now boasts a total sales turnover that triples that of Las Vegas. Brands like The Venetian, MGM, City of Dreams, and Studio City are destinations for families because they provide not only gambling, but also fine dining and entertainment. To illustrate a final example – Ferrari, Maserati, and Alfa Romeo are reputable manufacturers of sports cars. They are all from Italy and are owned or partially owned by the same group, Fiat Chrysler Automobiles. Yet the three brands each have their own brand DNA because of their individual characteristics and distinct heritage. Different car enthusiasts are attracted to each of the three brands not because of the differences in pricing, but because of the variability in their personalities.

The good, the bad, and the ugly

A brand is gradually formed over time based on people's interactions with it. *A brand is therefore defined by the people who relate to it rather than the brand-owner itself.* A brand exists in the mind of people instead of in the market. The term "stakeholders" is used to collectively describe the different people who have a relationship with the brand, including customers, staff, collaborators, investors, media, influencers, regulators, etc.

These stakeholders are fully aware that the brand exists but may not like or respect it, for reasons that are not always fair. That is not the point. As Cesar Millan, the host of the famous TV series *Dog Whisperer*, always said, "I rehabilitate dogs. I train people."[12] The takeaway from this quote is that we should not blame people not liking us. Instead, we should find out why we are not likable. Some marketers fail to stick to a plan while others are stuck with the wrong plan. That is why only a few brands will make it to the final shortlist. The remaining brands will neither be noticeable nor memorable.

Generally speaking, we can classify brands into three groups – the good, the bad, and the ugly (Figure 3.1). The good brands are distinctive, consistent, and relevant. A unique image helps them stand out. The Internet has created a borderless market. We are facing all kinds of competition from around the world. Consumers are spoiled for choice and are not obliged to purchase any product. Presenting a clear and desirable image is the first step in sticking in the minds of consumers. Consumers may have to encounter a brand couple of times or more, depending on the category and circumstance, before they build up sufficient interest in the brand.

Thus, consistency is critical in customer retention. Being consistent is more than following a rigid design template in the communication materials. It is also

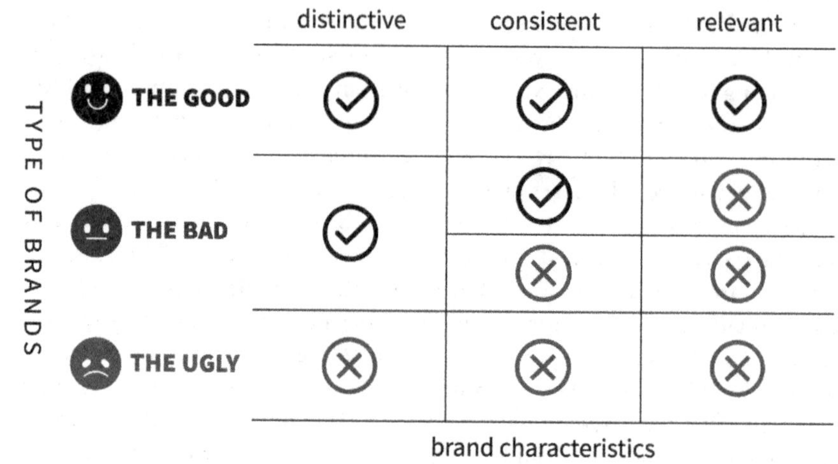

	distinctive	consistent	relevant
THE GOOD	✓	✓	✓
THE BAD	✓	✓	✗
		✗	✗
THE UGLY	✗	✗	✗

TYPE OF BRANDS

brand characteristics

FIGURE 3.1 The different types of brands based on their respective brand characteristics.

different from being repetitive. A consistent brand can be very dynamic and exciting. It does not have to say the same thing, in the same way, every time. We can never bore consumers into buying our products. The consumers will not buy our brand if they do not "click" with it. To be relevant is to translate our competitive advantage into consumer benefit so that people will understand and like what we do.

Bad brands may have a distinctive image and enjoy high visibility. Many people may have even heard of or tried their products. People may not like their image but remember it nonetheless due to the brand's massive advertising budget or extensive distribution network. They are usually quite consistent in a traditional sense, as they tend to repeat the same advertising over and over again. They believe in putting most of their budget in media buying rather than crafting the right creative executions. When their TV commercial pops up during the commercial break, viewers can't help but switch the channel because they have had enough with their boring and repetitive content. These brands may talk about how great they are and tend to highlight things that matter to them rather than the audience. As a result, there is no strong, compelling reason for consumers to actively engage with them. People may buy them occasionally out of convenience or lack of other options. Their positions will be immediately challenged when new brands that can identify and address unfulfilled needs enter the market.

Finally, ugly brands are the ones that are non-distinctive, inconsistent, and irrelevant. Some of them lack discipline in their marketing process while others are unconfident about their own strategy and switch from one positioning to another, resulting in a blurred or confusing image. As they are not customer-centric, there is a fundamental disconnect between the brand and the consumers. Failure is the only outcome. It is just a matter of time.

Every customer will go through a journey before making a purchase. The journey could be long or short, depending on the urgency of the occasion plus other push and pull factors. If there is a special promotion that temporarily changes the value equation, the customers may take prompt action to maximize their gain during the transaction. Brands have to be part of this customer journey and accompany the customer from beginning to end. To do so, they have to first enter the brand repertoire. For every category, we usually have three to five favorite brands. We rank these brands based on criteria such as price, overall quality, suitability for a particular occasion, etc. The criteria will differ for different categories. They will also change according to our experience, taste, budget, and lifestyle. After successfully joining the league, a brand will have to reach to the top so that it will be the first one the customer considers. "Good" brands are more likely to be shortlisted and ranked highly because they are distinctive, consistent, and relevant.

Major brand-building pitfalls

Major pitfall one

Ending the brand-building effort with sales, failing to educate consumers on appreciating the brand

It is ironic to see so many corporations spend considerable effort to win over customers, only to disappoint them once they are on board. There is nothing wrong with chasing the sales target. We all are salesmen in one way or another. But there is no excuse not to look after the people who have just supported your business. Many online platforms and mobile apps offer a basic membership for free and then upsell the user to a subscription service that includes more features and privileges. Some users are enticed by the sales pitch and agree to pay a monthly or annual fee. However, they are soon left entirely alone to navigate the digital jungle by themselves. They are unable to talk to any human representatives, and only have a list of FAQs for troubleshooting problems. After several attempts, the once-enthusiastic users become so frustrated and disillusioned that they eventually terminate their subscription for good. It is unforgivable to push away these wonderful supporters who will likely be gone forever.

Major pitfall two

A brand starts to fade when it starts taking customers for granted

Almost all corporations nowadays have their own loyalty programs, which were pioneered by the airline industry. Most of these programs simply ask customers to spend and then earn points for future gift-redemption. However, most of the gifts are not particularly appealing, making it hard for the customers to burn the points. Worst of all, these points expire after a certain period of time, such that diligently earned points are often gone when members finally remember to check their account. Redemption programs like these will not always advance the relationship between the brand and its users. In fact, all kinds of relationships will go through ups and downs, and face temptation along the way. A brand should continue to romance its users and create new excitements from time to time. In their book *Romancing the Customers*, Martin Trott and Paul Temporal explain that customer relationship management (CRM) is not about the software. It is about respecting and caring for the customers genuinely.[13] It is a matter of adopting the correct mindset. Technology is only a tool. Just like as Theodore Roosevelt, the 26th president of the United States, once said, "People do not care about how much you know until they care how much you care."

Major pitfall three

Making empty brand promises that don't realize at the end

I am a proud cardmember of American Express. "Don't leave home without it" and "Membership has its privilege" were my two most favorite campaigns during the early days of my advertising career. The Amex card was in a class above the Visa and Master Card, such that the other staff members in our agency envied the team that worked on the Amex account. I got my Amex Green Card in 1987, and to this day Amex is still the first card that I pull out of my wallet in front of the cashier. Before I proposed to my wife, I gave her a Supplementary Gold Card (luckily, she said yes). A few years went by, and I got my Amex Platinum Card. Finally, in 1999, I found a humongous black box sitting on my desk when I returned from a meeting one day. When I unwrapped it, I was stunned to find a Centurion Card – the mysterious, invitation-only black card made of titanium (Image 3.1). The Amex

IMAGE 3.1 Amex's member since – A good example of major pitfalls for brands.

Centurion became the only card that I would use for any kind of purchase, including one time when I was paying for a Steinway & Sons grand piano.

Yet as I mentioned before, there will always be ups and downs in the journey shared by the brand and its users, and my relationship with Amex was no exception. I was a somewhat satisfied customer until one day in 2012, when I called the Centurion hotline and asked the concierge whether Amex would do anything to celebrate our 25th anniversary. The concierge who answered the phone was quite puzzled, and after double-checking with his duty manager, he confirmed that there was no such policy within Amex.

I always believed that "Member since" was one of the most genius marketing inventions in history, since it doesn't cost anything to punch two more digits on the card. Still, it serves as a memento and sign of commitment between Amex and its cardmembers. It is a seal of trust and respect. I was quite shocked to discover that "Member since" was nothing more than a marketing gimmick. This type of shortfall is bad enough for any brand, but for Amex, which has founded its brand on these two words, it is quite unimaginable. It was a tough decision, but I eventually returned the Centurion card to Amex. *Branding is not about making but delivering the promise.*

Major pitfall four

Assuming celebrity is the magic potion for brand-building

I read somewhere that one out of three ads in the United States involves a celebrity. The ratio can be significantly higher for some industries. Even Clinique, which was once possibly the only skincare and cosmetic brand that didn't feature any celebrity, hired Emilia Clarke to be their first ambassador in January 2020.[14] The apparent advantages of using celebrities include the favorable click-through-rate on their ads and the potential transfer of their values onto the brand. After all, celebrities themselves are brands. The leading sports brand in China was named after its founder Li Ning, who won three Olympic gold medals (in floor exercise, pommel horse, and rings).

Hiring a celebrity can be a very costly proposition, and the more popular a celebrity is, the more likely that they are endorsing multiple brands at the same time. The consumers are fully aware that many of these celebrities, so-called spokespersons or brand-ambassadors, are only endorsing brands because they are paid to do so. Some of them do not even like or use the brand in their personal lives. The famous Brazilian footballer Ronaldinho was spotted drinking two cans of Pepsi at a press conference in 2012 when he was supposed to be endorsing Coke at the time.[15] Dropping his contract didn't cause the giant beverage brand any less embarrassment. Furthermore, the brands that continued to hire Ronaldinho would find that they had more PR crises to solve when he was arrested in Paraguay in March 2020 for using a fake passport. Another example of a celebrity endorsement backfiring is Sharon Stone's partnership with Christian Dior in China. The partnership lasted until Stone commented during an interview that the 2008 Sichuan earthquake, which had a death toll of almost 70,000, was "bad karma" because Tibetans were badly treated by China.[16] The cosmetics brand immediately announced their separation with her; had they failed to do so promptly, the brand might have been severely affected as a consequence.

Building a brand is like playing chess. You need to understand your opponents, then work out a viable strategy and plan a few steps ahead before you make any move. Once you realize you have fallen into a trap, it may already be too late, and you may have reached a point of no return. Many marketers are spending a disproportionate amount of their time putting out fires rather than seizing new business opportunities because they have allowed their brands to fall into a tricky position.

These are some of the common traps that may restrict the future growth of brands:

Parent's brand: *a brand that is seen as out of date and used by the older generations.* To appeal to a younger generation, Armani launched Armani Jeans, Armani Exchange, and EA7 for consumers who may find Armani Collezioni too formal and mature for their tastes.

Someone's brand: *a brand that belongs to someone else.* Tiffany tactfully engages first-time buyers by offering them jewelry items that are made of silver so that younger consumers won't be intimated by the brand's premium pricing.

Playboy's brand: *a brand that is too flashy and loud on the outside, usually without real substance on the inside.* There is a fine line between being bold and loud. Panerai Luminor watches are easily recognizable even from a distance but will never come across as being ostentatious.

Kid's brand: *a brand that is too childish or lacks sophistication and seriousness.* The color tone, material, and packaging of a product will anchor a brand to some extent. All expensive watches come with rather elaborate packaging. The wooden box, certificate, and wax seal hologram tag of a Rolex watch are more than sufficient evidence of its authenticity. The presentation and level of detail that goes into packaging are part of the brand experience, especially when it is purchased as a precious gift for someone important.

Beggar's brand: *a brand that is seen as too desperate and characterized by frequent discounting.* Offering a discount is not a crime. What is undesirable is sending out a wrong signal to the market that the product is unwanted and does not warrant its original price. Every consumer welcome freebies and discounts. The key is to avoid compromising the brand image during the process. Founded in 1850, Lane Crawford is an upscale department store in Mainland China and Hong Kong that targets the affluent segment. It runs two annual promotions that are highly anticipated events for many smart shoppers. These sales promotions are like carnivals where customers can enjoy the same level of professional customer service provided during the sales period. Lane Crawford also organizes a pre-sale such that their VIP customers can indulge themselves with the special discounts without having to compete with non-regular customers.

The above traps highlight the different threats posed to a brand, and we have seen how some brands tackle these challenges. They share one thing in common – people see the brand as being not right for them and do not bother to consider or pay attention to it.

This "not for me" syndrome can be a death penalty for brands because the consumer's mind will filter out anything to do with a brand that they regard as irrelevant. A consumer may see a brand as being not for them because they don't need it. Someone who doesn't drive may not show interest in a car brand. Or a consumer may need a car, but selectively seek out a brand that they deem suitable. A young driver is less likely to be interested in Volvo because of its mature and conservative image. The brand imagery is made up of two parts – the product imagery and user imagery. The product imagery refers to the perceived quality, performance, style, and characteristics of the product, while the user imagery is the perceived personality and character of the product's typical user. Product and user imageries are not two isolated constructs, but tightly interlocked concepts that connect both players: a particular type of user is more likely to look for a certain product quality and performance. A well-groomed brand image will effectively address both the "needs" and "desires" of the consumer.

Volvo is a well-regarded car brand worldwide. It is synonymous with "safety," and is one of the few brands that can project a consistent brand image across different markets. In recent years, Volvo has dedicated much effort to revitalizing its product imagery. The launch of the XC series with its slick and contemporary design was a great attempt to change how people appraise its products. The bigger challenge that Volvo has to tackle is probably its user imagery, which is more difficult to change once it is established in the mind of consumers.

Fanta is well-liked by kids because of its fruity flavor. Adults may feel weird ordering Fanta for themselves at a social gathering. To expand its customer base without deviating from its brand DNA, Fanta rolled out a new campaign advocating that "we do not have to be so grown-up all the time." The animation style of the execution appealed to kids, while the witty subtext of the ad resonated with adults. Fanta was able to retain its core users and give adults a reason to not feel apologetic for consuming Fanta. By widening its base while still presenting a fruity and pleasant drink, Fanta has stepped up its overall brand imagery.

Aging brands and brand rejuvenation

Will a brand get old? Yes, of course.
When will a brand start to age? It depends.

The aging of brands bears no correlation with their years of existence. Both BMW and Ford are more than 100 years old, but their cars are still driven around the world today (BMW and Ford were established in 1916 and 1903, respectively). Colgate was founded in 1806 and is still available in almost every supermarket. It is interesting to note that Colgate didn't start out by making toothpaste, however. If it had not made a conscious decision to switch from making soap and candles to toothpaste, it might not even be around today. JPMorgan Chase opened in New York City in 1799, it continues to be the largest bank in America, with a total asset of over $3.1 trillion[17]. In the technology world, Samsung has also come a long way. It was founded in 1938 and the corporation made a strategic move to dive into the digital world in the mid-1990s. Its total commitment to the digital revolution has completely transformed the company and the entire sector.

The above cases show that a brand can still be strong and vibrant regardless of how long it has been around. On the contrary, there are brands that were introduced only 10 or 20 years ago but have already ceased operating. Those that are still in the market may be struggling to make a profit. *Regardless of its age, a brand will start to age when it loses its relevance to the users.*

To stay relevant, brand-owners have to distinguish between trends and fads (Figure 3.2). Dieting may be a trend, but there are many different ways to achieve this goal. Some of the products that claim to be solutions are fads (e.g. low-carb "diet" products) and will be quickly replaced by another idea that appears to be more fashionable (e.g. long-term weight-loss programs). If a brand rides on

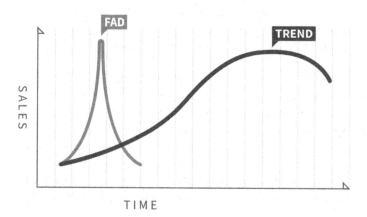

FIGURE 3.2 A comparison of the product life cycle of a trend vs. a fad.

fads to build its market presence, it puts itself in a dangerous position of losing relevance quickly.

On the other hand, there are brands that will never go out of fashion. A Chanel bag purchased 30 years ago is just as elegant and attractive as a new bag because it is regarded as a vintage. A Porsche made in the 1960s is a classic car that catches people's eyes on the road possibly more than any current sportscar would. These brands are not only trendsetters but also icons that represent certain generational breakthroughs in style, design, or technology. People respect them not only because of what they do but also what they symbolize.

As previously mentioned, every brand has a life cycle. In a digital age influenced by trends, technology has fast-tracked the research and development process, and corporations are racing to push new products into the market. The life cycle is more condensed than ever, and some brands may age more rapidly as a result. Pokémon Go is a good example of how quickly a hot idea can cool down in the Internet age. It was launched in July 2016 and instantly became a global hit. People were obsessed by the game and couldn't stop playing it. But in just a matter of months or even weeks, the intensity of downloading and playing the game dramatically diminished (Image 3.2). For traditional businesses like the automobile industry, manufacturers are also conscious to sustain market interest in their brands. Cars are given facelifts every two years before they are replaced by new models. These continuous upgrades have trained consumers to be more demanding and to look for new features and superior product performance in every purchase. Consumers themselves are also constantly exposed to new stimuli on the Internet. The convergence of industries has expanded their options, giving them no reason to settle for less.

IMAGE 3.2 Pokémon Go can be regarded as a fad as it came and went so quickly. Credit: am730.

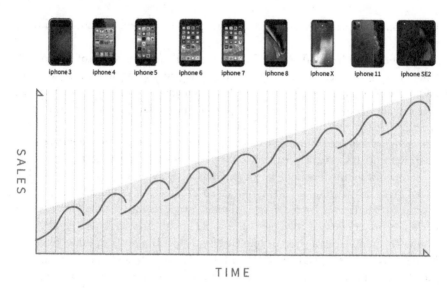

FIGURE 3.3 The rolling out of new iPhone models every year creates a lasting product life cycle.

Staying young requires more than rolling out a new ad campaign or hiring a new spokesperson. *To revitalize a brand is to make it relevant again by reconnecting with the consumers of today.* The best way to combat aging as a brand is to avoid even entering the stage of aging. *Brands can stretch their life cycle by keeping abreast of the latest market and consumer trends or introducing new variants guided by their brand DNA.* For example, iPhone has always led its users instead of being led by them. Apple is a master of creating needs by challenging its own inventions (Figure 3.3). Lego is a brand that needs no introduction. With all the computer and online games flooding the market, traditional toys like Lego can easily be pushed aside. Quite the contrary, the Denmark brand from 1932 is going from strength to strength because of its product innovations and brilliant marketing campaigns. Its "rebuild the world" campaign was a major undertaking that maintained its vibrancy and relevance. By connecting parents and children in a unique way, Lego is a priceless product that cannot be replaced by any video game.

Protecting your most valuable asset

Because the brand is such an important asset to any organization, protecting it and avoiding negative publicity should be a top priority. Still, numerous PR crises have struck brands of sizable corporations over the years. Most, if not all, of these crises were caused internally, due to product malfunctions or an insensitivity towards cultural issues. In other words, the crises that caused severe damage to the reputation and financial performance of the company could have been entirely avoided.

In 2003, Toyota had to openly apologize for publishing an ad in China that featured a Prado car crossing a bridge that highly resembled the Marco Polo Bridge – the entry point of Japan's invasion of China in 1937. The traditional Chinese guardian lion was shown saluting the Prado car beneath the headline, "you have to pay respect to it."[18] The setting of the ad, combined with its unfortunate headline and the stone sculpture, was a perfect recipe for disaster for promoting a Japanese brand in China. Similarly, in October 2019, the Japanese apparel brand Uniqlo launched a global ad campaign featuring the 98-year-old American fashion icon Iris Apfel to mark the 25th anniversary of fleece. The Korean subtitle of the commercial was, "How could I remember? It was eighty years ago." Korean consumers were extremely offended by the ad, which was perceived as a deliberate reference to the Japanese occupation of the Korean peninsula from 1910 to 1945, during which many Korean women were forced to serve as "comfort women."[19]

Another widely publicized incident occurred in January 2018, when H&M shared an image of a black child wearing a hoodie that bore the words "the coolest monkey in the jungle." The retail fashion brand was immediately accused of being racist and spreading stereotypes about black culture.[20]

David Ogilvy once said, "Never write an advertisement which you wouldn't want your family to read." His words offer great insight on how to filter out the inappropriate content that may hurt a brand but without compromising on creativity. In today's digital age, we may have to rephrase his quote to "Never do anything that you dare not post on social media." Your product or idea will be judged by anyone from anywhere in the world, including those who are not your target but may be able to influence the decision of your customers.

Although all the brands mentioned above swiftly expressed their apologies, that did not stop outraged citizens from marching to their stores to protest and in some cases even smash shop windows. Perhaps they should take notes from KFC, which mastered the art of apology. In early 2018, KFC was forced to close hundreds of its stores in the UK due to problems with its chicken supplier. It placed a full-page ad in the local newspapers showing an empty bucket of chicken with crumbs spilling out. The magic of the ad was that the KFC logo on the bucket was flipped to read "FCK" – humorously admitting that it was not ideal for a fried chicken store not to have chicken.[21] KFC also used the ad space as an opportunity to thank all the staff and customers for their patience and understanding. Not only did they enjoy much free media coverage, they also managed to redirect the focus from the "chicken run" to the wittiness of how they managed the crisis.

A confident brand can laugh at its own logo and even break its brand promise (in a positive way, of course). Nestlé in Australia gave away 250,000 packs of Kit Kat with a big "Thank You" graphic printed on it to thank healthcare workers for "not taking a break" during COVID-19.[22] Giving away free chocolates to frontline workers was already a "sweet" gesture; taking this exceptional

opportunity to subtly reinforce its brand promise that "Kit Kat is perfect for taking a break" was a genius move.

From the above case studies, we can see that consumers are very critical about
the behavior of corporations these days and will not hesitate to confront them
openly. That said, they are willing to give the brand a second chance when a
crisis happens, depending on how it responds to the situation. On October 4,
2013, I received an e-letter from Elon Musk with the title "About the Model S
Fire" (Image 3.3). The letter was quite thorough and was written because a Tesla
Model S caught fire in Seattle after it was hit by a huge metallic object. The letter detailed how the design of the car allowed it to contain the damage and keep
the driver safe.

I received the letter because I was put on Tesla's prospective customer database
after once attending a test drive. Apparently, they contacted every single owner

T≡5Lក

October 4, 2013
About the Model S fire
By Elon Musk, *Chairman, Product Architect & CEO*

Earlier this week, a Model S traveling at highway speed struck a large metal object,
causing significant damage to the vehicle. A curved section that fell off a semi-trailer was
recovered from the roadway near where the accident occurred and, according to the
road crew that was on the scene, appears to be the culprit. The geometry of the object
caused a powerful lever action as it went under the car, punching upward and impaling
the Model S with a peak force on the order of 25 tons. Only a force of this magnitude
would be strong enough to punch a 3 inch diameter hole through the quarter inch armor
plate protecting the base of the vehicle.

The Model S owner was nonetheless able to exit the highway as instructed by the
onboard alert system, bring the car to a stop and depart the vehicle without injury. A fire
caused by the impact began in the front battery module – the battery pack has a total of
16 modules – but was contained to the front section of the car by internal firewalls within
the pack. Vents built into the battery pack directed the flames down towards the road
and away from the vehicle.

Tesla Motors | 3500 Deer Creek Road | Palo Alto, CA 94304
Privacy Policy | Unsubscribe

IMAGE 3.3   An e-letter from Elon Musk explaining why the Model S caught fire in
Seattle (only a portion of the letter is shown here).

and potential owner of Tesla around the world shortly after the car accident because they knew the news would go viral on the Internet. Instead of allowing people to watch the viral video and worry about the car's safety features, Tesla proactively reached out to the people that matter most to them but might know very little about the details of the accident. They continued to send me updates about the case from time to time for three months. Then they wrapped it up with an email on December 27, 2013, stating that the National Highway Traffic Safety Administration (NHTSA) had reaffirmed the 5-Star safety ranking for the Tesla Model S and all its sub-categories for 2014 (Image 3.4). Tesla's prompt and thorough follow-up actions regained the confidence of its users and helped its stock bounce back from the huge dip it suffered at the beginning of the crisis.

A crisis may befall any organization, but the more famous the brand is, the more it will be reported in the press and on social media. Every brand–owner and marketer should be mentally and logistically prepared for the unlikely event that a crisis of any nature might happen at any moment. The following disciplines are some of the key takeaways from studying how different corporations in various markets respond to brand-threatening crises:

T≡5LΠ

NHTSA REAFFIRMS MODEL S 5-STAR SAFETY RATING IN ALL CATEGORIES FOR MODEL YEAR 2014

PALO ALTO, Calif. – The National Highway Traffic Safety Administration (NHTSA) has reaffirmed the 5-star safety rating of the Tesla Model S and in all subcategories for Model Year 2014, confirming the highest safety rating in America. While Tesla is awaiting feedback from NHTSA regarding their investigation of recent fire incidents, the German Federal Motor Transport Authority, Kraftfahrt-Bundesamt (KBA), recently concluded its review of the incidents, finding no manufacturer-related defects or need for further action.

It is worth noting that a Tesla vehicle is over five times less likely to experience a fire than the average gasoline car and that there have been zero serious injuries or deaths for any reason ever, fire or otherwise, in a Model S. Over the course of more than 100 million miles driven in almost every possible terrain, weather and crash conditions, the Tesla Model S has consistently protected its driver and passengers, achieving the best safety track record of any car on the road.

Tesla Motors | 3500 Deer Creek Road | Palo Alto, CA 94304
Privacy Policy | Unsubscribe

IMAGE 3.4 Email from Tesla to state that NHTSA reaffirmed the Model S with 5-Star safety.

1. **Crisis management starts before the crisis**

   If you come up with an action plan after something bad happens, it is already too late. When you are hit by a serious crisis, you are likely to be caught by surprise, and you simply do not have the time to think. You will be forced to respond instantly, and your whole team will be in reactive mode, making it easier to make mistakes, which is the last thing you want in the middle of a crisis.

   Chances are your PR team and your PR partner will have already prepared a crisis manual. It makes sense not only to update its contents from time to time but to ensure all team members concerned will be fully briefed on their roles and be given proper guidance on how to deal with different types of tricky situations. Anticipation is the best strategy for crisis management. Various industries are, by default, facing different kinds of potential dangers. If you are Disneyland, you want to make sure your rides are totally bullet-proof before putting any visitor on them. If you are Häagen-Dazs, you want to make sure all your products will be kept under the stringent and required temperature conditions throughout the entire transportation process.

   When I was the Executive Director of Hong Kong Futures Exchange in 1999, we underwent numerous rounds of drill-and-practice in dealing with an exhaustive list of possible scenarios regarding the Y2K/Millennium bug problem. We involved not only the internal staff, but also related parties such as the financial secretary at that time.

2. **Build your network of allies**

   The media has no obligation to protect your reputation. If you have an ongoing professional rapport with them, however, they will know who to contact when something unusual happens and may even report your side of the story as well. Media relationships are especially important in the digital age, where articles are published online on a real-time basis.

3. **Speed matters**

   Yes, the speed of putting out the fire is crucial, but the effort of dealing with the situation should be well planned, orchestrated, or even rehearsed. Keeping all team members on the same page will reduce the possibility of sending out conflicting messages.

4. **People expect transparency**

   Consumers understand that mistakes may happen and may even accommodate them. But they will not forgive dishonesty or shady cover-ups. Being open and transparent does not mean exposing your brand to unnecessary misinterpretation. By contrast, it helps people better understand the context of the problem or technical subtleties that are best communicated by the brand itself.

5. **Focus on the solution rather than the blame**

   The method for handling the crisis will differ depending on its type and seriousness. Human errors, intentional misreporting, or even unlawful practice may give rise to the problem, as was the case with the 2001 Enron scandal, where internal corruption led to the downfall of a once-major corporation.

Tackling the problem at its root is imperative. Regaining public confidence and safeguarding the brand reputation should be of the utmost priority.

6. **Manage the different stakeholders**

   Obviously, all stakeholders will be concerned about the issue. Some of them may not be directly involved in handling the case, but it does not mean they should not be promptly informed about its progress. In October 2004, DBS Bank accidentally disposed of the safety boxes (including the possessions stored inside) of its customers when renovating its Mei Foo branch in Hong Kong. My team was involved in a major town hall meeting to re-boost the morale of their frontline staff and discuss how to face the harsh comments and inquiries from retail customers.

7. **Prioritize forward-looking actions and commitment**

   Dealing with the problem is only half the job. Regaining momentum and taking the brand to a brighter future should always be part of crisis management. Hong Kong McDonald's was put under the scrutiny of local health authorities in July 2014 when one of its suppliers was found to be processing expired meat for the leading burger chain and other restaurant operators. What could have been a major showstopper was quickly resolved within just 12 weeks, as McDonald's conducted a complete review of its entire supply chain and rolled out a robust, step-by-step campaign to reconnect with its customers. By setting up a social listening team to monitor the market pulse, McDonald's was able to address any issue strategically in real-time.

8. **It's more than just legal liability**

   The biggest mistake many corporations make is to only focus on sorting out potential legal disputes. To them, if they have published a disclaimer or legitimately shifted the blame to a third party, they have nothing to worry about. Yet crisis management is about preempting any adverse public perception of the brand by taking all the necessary marketing and operational actions. That is why corporations should still take proactive measures to manage the situation even when they are free from any legal liability.

9. **Build up your credibility and trustworthiness**

   Investing in your brand is like building a massive reservoir before there is a drought. The volume of the water stored in the reservoir represents the level of credibility and trustworthiness you can command in the market. Even if there is a crack in the dam caused by erosion or some other reason, you should have sufficient buffer space to fix the problem before all the water has been drained. A brand with strong equity and a proven track record is more prepared to combat challenges without causing significant damage to its course in the long run.

Corporate branding and CEO branding

In the old days, a corporation could be big and successful without publicizing its business owner or the chief representative. If it were not a listed company, the owner could stay behind the curtain and remain completely anonymous. This will never be the case in the digital age. Knowing that the media, bloggers, and consumers are able to dig up the background of the founder or chief executive of any enterprise, companies understand that their leaders cannot hide away. They are prepared to put a face to the corporation, not just to fulfill the curiosity of people, but also to satisfy the rules of the new marketplace. If they can play this card well, it will add significant value to corporations because consumers tend to buy the messenger before they buy the message. The charisma of leaders has become an essential part of corporate branding. It helps "humanize" the organization. Humans are attracted by other humans, not machines. In fact, there is considerable overlap between corporate branding and CEO branding. Consumers will use the same words to describe Apple and Steve Jobs, or Virgin and Richard Branson. In fact, the founder of a corporation is its soul. Their values and qualities will be transferred to the corporation, and vice versa. Today's CEOs do not only appear in the business or finance sections of the paper. They are a new type of celebrity, and sometimes generate even more buzz than a Hollywood star.

Back in 2012, Richard Branson posted his first "a day in the life" YouTube video to document his everyday life as the founder of Virgin. The video is a well-orchestrated effort that subtly conveys important aspects of Virgin group's corporate culture. The video shows Richard commuting to different places in a convertible Audi RS4 and a Mercedes E-class, which may very well reflect his personal taste, but also project a young and dynamic image on his behalf. Sometimes, Richard will sit in the backseat while working and tweeting. Otherwise, he will sit in the passenger seat, giving off a friendly and easy-going impression. Instead of showing him dining in Michelin 3-star restaurants, the video shows him meeting a "Star of the Year" staff member in a cafeteria. Throughout the video, various heads of the different Virgin companies talk about the group's corporate culture in a very consistent way, giving people the impression that Virgin does not only rely on one person; rather, there is a strong leadership team in place connected by a very cohesive mission. In the video, Richard also attends the premiere of a documentary filmed by his son, showing that he can strike a balance between his personal and professional life. Most importantly, Richard announces at the very beginning of the video that he will be attending a mix of business and social events, which gel together to articulate the corporate values of Virgin.[23]

Some people may not be familiar with Salesforce, aside from knowing that it occupies the tallest building in San Francisco. Based on its name and its business model of selling cloud-based computer software, Salesforce may be perceived as a cold and rigid organization. Yet when people read about how Marc Benioff is fostering gender equality in the workplace by closing the gender pay gap and ensuring that at least 30% of meeting participants are women, they will have quite a different impression of the organization.[24]

As the figurehead of a company, the CEO has to be held accountable for corporate performance. In April 2010, BP experienced possibly the largest marine oil spill in history when its Deepwater Horizon oil rig exploded in the Gulf of Mexico. The disaster caused significant environmental damage and led to the sharp criticism and subsequent resignation of Tony Hayward, who was the CEO of BP at that time.[25]

It is a known fact that a brand will outlive its creator. Steve Jobs passed away on October 5, 2011, at the age of 56. Tim Cook succeeded him as the CEO, and Apple remains one of the most admirable brands in the world today. The globally renowned martial artist and philosopher Bruce Lee died suddenly at the age of 33 at the peak of his career. Yet it is incredible to see how many young people around the world today are still aware of Bruce and his accomplishments in life. Bruce invented Jeet Kune Do, a revolutionary way of interpreting martial arts without the restrictions of form or shape. His "like water" philosophy has inspired many followers to experience the limitless in different facets of life by being direct, efficient, and straightforward.

Destination branding, NGO branding, and personal branding

The concept of branding applies not only to commercial products but also to cities, countries, NGOs, and people. " **I ♡ NY**" is probably one of the most recognizable icons in destination branding. It was created by Milton Glaser in 1977, and just like the city itself, it will never go out of style. It is bold, passionate, and expressive. It is a statement, as well as an invitation. It has the magnetic power that mere words cannot explain and encapsulates the spirit of the city that never sleeps. "What happens in Vegas, stays in Vegas" is another brilliant expression that matches the personality of a city. It is up to the individual to interpret the meaning of this slogan, but no matter what their takeaway is, it will probably evoke Las Vegas' glittering and enigmatic lifestyle. Although not expressed explicitly, the unstoppable and larger-than-life Vegas experience can be felt instantaneously.

Just as the heart symbol represents the word "love" in " **I ♡ NY**," India uses the exclamation mark to replace the letter "I" in its "Incredible !ndia" campaign. Launched in 2002, the campaign is still used today to capture the rich heritage and myriad attractions of India. Aside from aptly describing the food, culture, and people of India, "Incredible" also alliterates with "India," thus creating a memorable and catchy slogan.

Sometimes, a clever tactical campaign can make a destination famous overnight. "The Best Job in the World" was one of the most successful promotions in marketing history both in terms of its substantial global coverage and the tangible, enduring brand image it created for Queensland. Launched in January 2009, the campaign advertised a six-month, highly compensated opportunity to be an island caretaker for the Great Barrier Reef. Candidates from all over the world applied for the dream position, sustaining the campaign through enormous user-generated content. The blogs written by the candidates and the winner before, during, and after the competition were more compelling than any professional travel magazine due to their authenticity and first-hand experience.[26]

In the same way that it helps commercial enterprises, branding can anchor non-profit organizations by connecting them with their supporters through a carefully crafted, shared mission statement. A common challenge faced by NGOs is sustaining the enthusiasm of their supporters. Many of these supporters drop out not because they are less willing to give aid, but because they feel excluded or uncertain about whether their contributions can make a positive difference. As a father of two, I can easily identify with organizations that focus on helping children. In 2006, I received an exceptional postcard from Oxfam. The letter never once mentioned the keyword that usually appears in all correspondences between an NGO and its supporters – "donor." Instead, Oxfam purposely replaced the word "donor" with "education partner," repositioning my role from a passive supporter to an active collaborator (Image 3.5). What's more, the letter came with a certificate of appreciation that included my name and the length of our partnership (Image 3.6). Oxfam's branding strategy goes to show how an NGO can motivate its supporters to stay on course and reinforce their contributions.

Established in 1937, Plan International is another leading development and humanitarian organization that specifically focuses on children. Headquartered

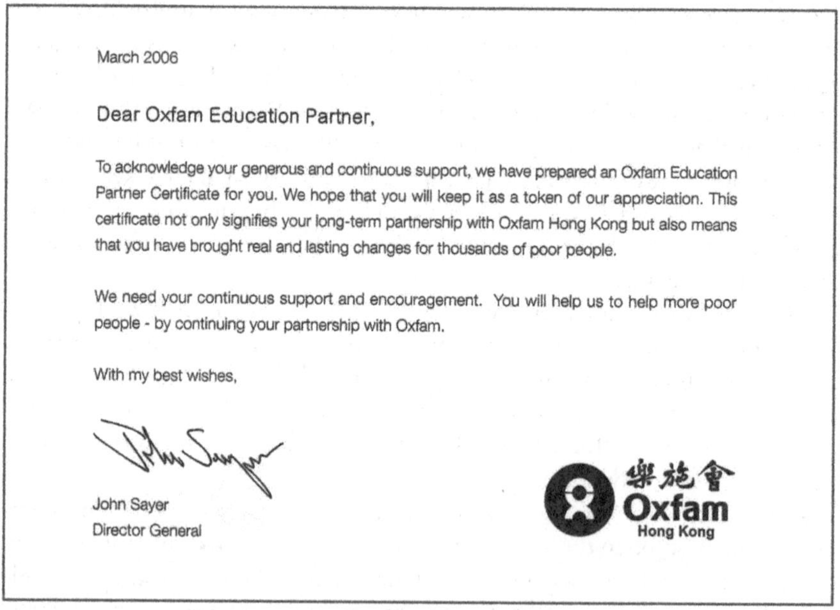

March 2006

Dear Oxfam Education Partner,

To acknowledge your generous and continuous support, we have prepared an Oxfam Education Partner Certificate for you. We hope that you will keep it as a token of our appreciation. This certificate not only signifies your long-term partnership with Oxfam Hong Kong but also means that you have brought real and lasting changes for thousands of poor people.

We need your continuous support and encouragement. You will help us to help more poor people - by continuing your partnership with Oxfam.

With my best wishes,

John Sayer
Director General

Oxfam
Hong Kong

IMAGE 3.5 The word "donor" was replaced by "education partner" to successfully reframe the relationship between Oxfam and its supporters.

IMAGE 3.6 The Oxfam Education Partner Certificate is a clever way to recognize its supporters.

in the UK, it operates in 71 countries to improve the quality of life for children in the areas of education, early childhood development, and more. To set itself apart from peer organizations that also serve children, Plan International initiated a global movement titled "Because I am a Girl (BIAAG)" to raise awareness about the double standards, academic obstacles, and safety threats that young girls face in developing countries. The movement has evolved into the "Girls Get Equal" global campaign for gender equality, which aims to empower every girl and young woman to take control over her own life and shape the world around her. By focusing on an issue that resonates deeply with people, Plan International has gained substantial recognition and won the support of many like-minded supporters. At the end of this chapter is an interview with the CEO of Plan HK, who will further discuss how NGOs leverage branding for worthwhile causes.

By now, you have read three chapters of this book and I hope you find it interesting and useful. I would like to wrap up this section by talking about how this book is relevant to you – not only your work and business, but also literally you, as a person. You are, in fact, a brand.

When people mention your name in a conversation, certain images will pop up in their minds, representing a collection of what they have heard about you and their personal experience with you as a family, friend, colleague, or client. People remember you because of your abilities and more importantly your character. You occupy a certain place in their mind the same way a commercial brand does. They will think of you and approach you when they believe that you can play a role in a project they have in mind. If you want to get the level of recognition you deserve, you have to actively manage your brand to make sure it is distinctive, consistent, and relevant.

We have talked about some great corporate leaders in this chapter and I am sure you have no trouble choosing words to describe them. I would encourage you to do the same with yourself, by picking the three words that you want people to use when they describe you. These are your desired brand attributes. You can then ask some of your trusted friends or colleagues to candidly share with you the three words they would use to describe you. You may be amazed how similar or different the two sets of words are. If people use words that are similar to the ones you chose, you enjoy a clear image. However, if what people use to describe you differs or even contradicts what you have picked for yourself, you may want to assess why this is the case. Do not worry. This is quite common. What we need to be mindful of is that our brand is not defined by ourselves, but by the people who have a relationship with us. In other words, we are what and how people see us. The logical next step is for us to think hard about what we should do to narrow the gap in perception. This is a great way to self-reflect and rethink how we may want to engage people from now onwards, including the language we use, the tone we adopt, and the actions we take, so that we can live up to the roles we are supposed to play and enjoy more fruitful relationships with the people around us.

Insights on branding from Global Leaders

Branding is a topic that does not only interest marketers. Over the years, many iconic figures have talked about "branding" in different ways, simply because it matters to them. Through their work or life experience, they have seen branding in action and understand the positive difference it can bring to any organization.

In this section, I have compiled a range of quotes from leaders of different disciplines and different eras. Their words stimulate and expand our thoughts about brands. It is amazing how fluid the concept of branding is and how it can stand the test of time.

Meg Whitman, CEO of Quibi and formerly CEO of Hewlett Packard, believes that it is quite powerful for us to use a brand as a verb in our daily lives. We all say things like, "Google it," "I'll WhatsApp or WeChat you later," "Please FedEx it to the New York office," "I'll Skype you tonight," or "See you on ZOOM." Why is this so remarkable? Because it means that the brand has become synonymous with its function. It is the leader and role model for other players in the same market. It sets the standard for the industry. Using the name of a brand in everyday conversation is a great testimony to the brand's enormous popularity. Needless to say, it is likely to be the consumer's preferred choice as it has occupied the top-of-mind position in their head already.

Warren Buffet certainly understands the implications of making a wrong move or decision. He has remarked that it takes a long time to establish a market reputation, but just one incident to destroy it. Indeed, it takes time to build a brand, even in the digital age when things are traveling at the speed of light, because awareness doesn't mean recognition. A brand has to go through constant validations in the market until it has earned its reputation. Even after it has established its position in the market, it will have to undergo continuous appraisals by its users.

A person or an organization ruins their reputation usually not because of others, but by themselves, by saying or doing something inappropriate or unacceptable. *Brand-building is not only about what we do, but also what we don't do.* The more popular the brand is, the more it will be put under the spotlight and monitored. Once the brand has crossed a line, the news will spread around the world through social media. Thus, actively managing brand reputation is absolutely essential.

Our history is what makes us who we are today. Not only should we stay true to it, we should also take full advantage of it. This is the reason why most luxury brands are from Europe, where craftmanship is a cornerstone of their heritage. This is something money can't buy. English designer Alice Temperley equates a brand with its heritage, which is what makes a brand truly unique. Of course, it is not about the good old days, but a solid foundation and culture that has enriched the story of the brand. A brand with a long history can also be modern and cutting-edge. There is no tradeoff between heritage and innovation. Sometimes, brand-owners are too greedy and try to step into a new territory that has a conflict with their brand DNA. This may tarnish its current brand proposition yet without making any headway in the new arena. We should never pretend to be who we are not.

Mark Zuckerberg sees Facebook as a platform where people can keep up with friends and family while at the same consciously or sub-consciously building their own brands. What people post on Facebook or in fact any social network sends out signals to project a certain image and will attract people with similar interests. As such, branding is about making connections. It can be considered the bridge between a corporation and its stakeholders. Branding is also about community. People who follow the same brand belong to a community. They share some common interests, and their lives are enriched because of the same brand. That's why there is a Porsche Club or Ferrari Club in almost every country. And it's not just physical or pricy products that create community, either. Rotary is a brand with more than 1.2 million members worldwide who connect over a shared mission—to create lasting change around the globe, in our communities, and in ourselves. A strong brand is the center of gravity that draws all like-minded people together, and what they do in unison can be quite phenomenal.

Elon Musk is a visionary and risk-taker. He believes in and is totally committed to what he does, which is why people follow him, even with blind faith.

People buy his dreams before they buy his products. Be it PayPal, Tesla, or SpaceX, Musk promises something different each time, something that people have never seen or experienced before. As he said, he uses results and evidence to tangibilize the intangible. A brand can be an ideology or abstract concept, but it cannot solely consist of empty promises or bluffing. It has to be substantiated by a product or service that people can hold, use, and feel. He believes that the perception and reality of a brand will eventually converge, and that we have to work hard on our offerings because they are how we will be judged.

Sending someone into space may seem like an unimaginable feat, but on May 30, 2020, SpaceX became the first private company to put a human into orbit.[27] This is a fantastic example of a brand delivering its promise, even when the promise may appear to be larger than life.

> You now have to decide what "image" you want for your brand.
> Image means personality. Products, like people, have personalities, and they can make or break them in the marketplace.
>
> – David Ogilvy

According to the American Psychological Association, "personality" refers to individual differences in characteristic patterns of thinking, feeling, and behaving. The study of personality focuses on two broad areas: understanding individual differences in particular personality characteristics and understanding how the various parts of a person come together as a whole.

David Ogilvy emphasized that a brand is not a brand without a personality (Image 3.7). It is conventional, unremarkable, and dull. It will hardly stand out from the crowd, let alone attract consumers. In the past, when advertising was the primary vehicle to brand creation, a personality was something crafted and projected to the market. Today, public perception still forms an essential piece of the puzzle. Consumers still cross-check the product design, quality, and performance to see if the projected image is genuine. The same goes for the corporate reputation on how it conducts business and treats its staff. It is based on a combination of impression, observation, and experience that constitute a brand personality.

As mentioned earlier, the brand holds everything and everyone together within an organization. Frontline staff have a direct impact on how consumers feel about the brand since they represent the brand in front of consumers. As basic as it may sound, still not every company gets it. Imagine if the first line of defense is not familiar with or even doubts the brand. Consumers can sense this, and the mistrust will spread to other consumers. Simon Mainwaring believes that the employees of an organization are the most effective form of advertising if they fully understand the brand. They constantly interact with other people, and nothing is more powerful than direct contact and exchange.

Even staff members who work in the backend will voluntarily put in the effort to make sure the product is assembled precisely the way it should be if they truly understand the brand's mission. The most successful brands in the world

IMAGE 3.7   David Ogilvy was an innovator in defining brands and advertising. Credit: ogilvy.com.

are those where all members involved with the brand share the same belief and deliver the promise together seamlessly.

Being first is not unimportant. In *Positioning*, a 1980 marketing classic by Al Ries and Jack Trout that still refreshes the way people look at brands today, many practical examples illustrate the different principles of branding and marketing. One compelling case asks, "who was the first astronaut to walk on the moon?"[28] Readers will have no problem naming Neil Armstrong, who was indeed the first man to step on the moon on July 20, 1969. But when asked about the second astronaut to walk the moon, people answer in a different way: who cares, and who knows? Speed is sometimes as critical as quality. This is particularly true in the digital age, where users look for instant gratification. Being the first also implies occupying the most apparent position in the consumer's mind. It has tremendous trade leverage because the trade has no choice but to carry the products that consumers want. Stefan Persson of H&M considers quality a primary factor for ensuring customer loyalty. Closing the deal is only the beginning, not the end. The customer's usage and involvement with the brand's products and services will determine whether or not they return.

When it comes to building brand loyalty, being first also has its advantages. The brand is likely to engage innovators and early adopters who are at the forefront of the "adoption curve." They are less price-sensitive and can accept flaws in a product as long as its novelty element can outweigh minor glitches. They are usually opinion leaders who will publicize their experience of experimenting with a new product on social media. They can have a tremendous influence on mainstream users who form the bulk of the market. Originality is highly valued by users. By contrast, a better but me-too product may not make the cut. Of course, if the quality does not meet users' expectations, then both repurchase and referral rates will be low. In this disruptive marketing era, speed and quality are major factors contributing to brand loyalty. To cope with changing market dynamics, a brand should continue to reinvent itself so it will be seen as the "best" no matter how the market evolves.

There is a reason why Under Armour emerged as a new force in the footwear and casual apparel market. Its founder, Kevin Plank, is committed to building a brand with an exceptional story, not just good merchandise. A great story invites its readers to enter a world in another dimension with unlimited possibilities. A great brand story has incredible drawing power and will allow users to immerse themselves in the brand world. Yet the story should not be just about the past. It should be an ongoing story with current and relevant content. Moreover, the story cannot be fabricated. Inauthenticity is what consumers hate most these days. People demand transparency and honesty. More will be said about the importance of "authenticity" in brand communication in the later part of this book.

Tommy Hilfiger is not simply interested in designing clothes. He devoted his energy to designing a lifestyle brand. People pay more for branded apparel, but not only because of the logo printed on the front. The design, quality, and style are also sensationally satisfying. Branded clothes express people's personality and help them blend in with others who share the same attire. It can make someone feel more confident and authoritative, either subtly or explicitly. A fashion brand is about putting something special on people's minds, not their bodies.

A brand journey is not linear. In fact, a great brand has never existed linearly, according to Angela Ahrendts. It is an evolving construct that touches people's hearts at different moments throughout their life. The first Patek Philippe you got for yourself is a great reward, and one of those highlights in life that you will always remember. When you pass the same watch to your child, it adds another dimension, and stands for something so special that words alone cannot explain. This timepiece will always be one of the most precious belongings to your child. After all, *you never actually own a Patek Philippe. You merely look after it for the next generation.*

To maintain an ongoing relationship with users, brands must reach out to users and try to connect with them. At the same time, it is equally essential that the brand should represent something so crucial to the users that they will continue to want more from the brand.

A brand-builder's perspective

Interview with Dr. Kanie Siu, CEO of Plan International (Hong Kong)

Dr. Kanie Siu is Plan International's Chief Executive Officer for the Hong Kong office. She joined Plan International in January 2015. Dr. Siu is an expert fundraiser, marketer, and administrator. She spent ten years working in marketing and public relations across several commercial industries before joining Oxfam Hong Kong (OHK) in 1998, where she helped pioneer the application of those skills to the non-governmental organization (NGO) sector. In 2013, Dr. Siu was named OHK's Director of Fundraising and Communications, a role in which she became responsible for fundraising, communications, and branding strategies in Hong Kong, Macau, Taiwan, and Mainland China. Over the years, she also played a significant role in marketing and product development for the agency, which operates international development programs in China, Asia, and Africa. In 2015, she was appointed CEO of Plan International Hong Kong, one of the leading international development organizations with 80 years of history that is committed to fulfilling children's rights and ending poverty worldwide. With her contributions to philanthropy in both Hong Kong and Mainland China, Dr. Siu has been named one of the awardees in the Second Global Outstanding Young Leader Award, organized by YaZhou Zhoukan in 2017.

Royce Yuen: How important is "branding" to NGOs and why?

Dr. Kanie Siu: Branding is essential to NGOs as people offer their support to an NGO mostly because of its image, credibility, and reputation. Branding can help an NGO build a positive and credible image that gradually contributes to the building up of a positive reputation.

RY: How do you build the brand for Plan using presumably less resources than a commercial organization can?

KS: Due to fewer resources and budget constraints, we rely on free publicity and pro-bono support from different partners, namely the media, celebrities, advertising agencies, and ex-beneficiaries (Image 3.8).

We make use of the stories we gather from Plan's project site to appeal for media interviews or generate media content. The stories show what hardships disadvantaged children, especially girls, face in their lives. They also show how Plan has been helping them combat these situations. Harmful practices, such as early marriage and female genital mutilations, are seldom talked about in Asia. The media helps raise awareness about these problems and the role that Plan is playing.

In addition, we use the stories of our former beneficiaries to show how Plan had been helping children since the 1950s and 1960s. Hopefully, these stories can boost Plan's positive image and increase its local relevance, encouraging the public to support Plan HK when they see our appeals in online and offline channels.

RY: Is brand-building today different from what it used to be say, ten or even five years ago? And why?

KS: Before 2008, there was less competition in the market; the donor's demand for NGO accountability was not as high.

IMAGE 3.8 "Run for Girls" is a signature annual event organized by Plan International HK to raise funds for marginalized young women around the world. Credit: plan.org.hk.

After 2008, the market grew more competitive as new international NGOs (INGOs) entered the market (such as UNHCR, Save the Children, Fred Hollows, etc.). With more players operating in the market and competing in the same media space, the cost of media has gone up as well.

Previously, only a few large NGOs built their brands through fundraising activities, such as Tung Wah, Po Leung Kuk, Community Chest, World Vision, Oxfam, Orbis, Unicef, and Doctors Without Borders. But in recent years, more and more large and small NGOs and INGOs have raised their profile through different media, leading to more fundraising events and a very crowded market.

RY: Do you feel the impact of the digital revolution? Is the effect on Plan positive or negative?

KS: I indeed feel the impact of the digital revolution. It can be both positive and negative to Plan.

As Plan is only a medium-size INGO, and we rely on public donations mainly through individuals, mass appeals through media are vital for us in brand-building. As such, social media is a comparatively cheaper means for publicity and promotion when compared with traditional media such as TV and radio.

However, it also means that we have to be more creative to grab the attention of the general public as there is so much information on social media. We cannot afford to have a dedicated social media coordinator or team at the moment.

RY: How does the brand of Plan differ from that of other NGOs that also focus on serving underprivileged children?

KS: While Plan also serves underprivileged children, we focus more on girls in developing countries.

In my 16 years of working in the NGO sector, I have observed that all major INGOs working for children focus more on issues of general poverty and often show photos of disadvantaged children in developing countries.

As Plan is a small organization locally without a renowned brand name, we have to focus on something that differentiates ourselves so that we can stand out from the crowd. Girls' issues in developing countries are seldom publicized. Women's rights will generate interest from the media, which can then convey our stories to a wider audience.

RY: How do you engage donors so that they can truly and fully appreciate the brand of Plan?

KS: We make use of our events to engage donors and supporters. For example, we sell pencils at our "Donate a Pencil" charity sale and inform donors that the funds raised will be used to support girls' projects, protect them from early marriage, and allow them to stay in school. We recruit sponsors on the spot, and we mainly highlight girls as the sponsored children to reinforce our message.

Only women can join "Run for Girls," another one of our annual events. We display information about girls' issues at the venue and emphasize girls in our promotional materials so that the participants are well aware that they are supporting girls in developing countries.

In addition, our "Youth Conference" is a platform where students from grades 9 to 11 (this year we also welcomed university students) can learn about and discuss the issues that affect girls in developing countries. Some students will also join our "Be a Change-Maker" program, during which they will learn about the topics in-depth by visiting our project sites and conducting projects on child protection, particularly as it relates to young women.

A brand-builder's perspective

Interview with Chong Got, former Senior Corporate Director of Dah Chong Hong Holdings

Mr. Chong Got was the Senior Corporate Director of Dah Chong Hong Holdings responsible for overseeing the automotive (Audi, Bentley, Honda, Nissan, INFINITI, MAN, DAF, and Sinotruk) and luxury yacht businesses. Prior to that, he was the Managing Director of Wallace Harper as well as the Vice-Chairman of the Dealers' Advisory Board for Ford Motors. In 2013, he led the Bentley business in China to achieve worldwide number two in sales. He was named CEO of the year by Capital Magazine in the same year. Mr. Got was also the Chairman of the Hong Kong Motor Traders' Association for three consecutive years. Mr. Got is currently a life coach and executive consultant. He is also a Managing Partner of MaLogic.

Royce Yuen: What are consumers actually looking for or trying to fulfill when they purchase a luxury car or a yacht?

Chong Got: The stereotypical reason for people buying supercars and yachts is to show off personal wealth. This may well be the case for some people, but most of the customers that I know are not spending tens of millions of dollars or more just to show off. They are much wiser than that. They belong to high society, and they already own many luxury or even collector's items. They may have a practical reason for purchasing high-end items for business entertainment, or it can be for purely personal enjoyment. The biggest motivation is still to own and experience something that makes life more exciting or fulfilling. The old rich are interested in making money, but the new rich are interested in both making and spending money. Sometimes, it is a reward for their hard work. In other cases, they need the right items to match or fulfill their extravagant lifestyle. Consumers are becoming more informed these days, and they receive a lot of information from various sources. Especially if you are of ultra-high net worth, many brands will approach you to invite you to join their exclusive circles. Many high-end customers prefer to be in the "driver's seat" rather than sitting in the back all the time. This is how they can genuinely gain first-hand experience of these meticulously crafted luxury items.

RY: How important is the "brand" and what role does it play throughout the consumer purchase journey?

CG: The brand plays a vital role in the purchase journey for luxury goods. First of all, if you are not a well-known brand, you will not be able to make the short-list or even get consumers' attention. In the premium segment, all products will command a certain quality as their price point will allow them to use the finest materials and also the best craftsmanship. The brand, therefore, can be a determining factor in the customer's choice. Genuinely prestigious brands do not bluff about how great they are. This is particularly true for automobiles and yachts, as there are objective measurements of the performance of different models. It is not just about counting how many diamonds are mounted on the case. An enduring brand in the luxury sector has heritage and reputation, which cannot be fabricated. Luxury is all about "substance with style." Furthermore, the most distinctive and successful luxury brands are not designed for everyone. They possess a special character that may appeal to a certain type of customer. Some people may be wealthy enough to buy certain brands, but they do not identify with them. Most of these brands are not built overnight. They earn their status and recognition over years. They are endorsed by many people around the world who can tell the great from the good. Their histories are filled with amazing stories, and their customers are legends themselves.

RY: *Is the role of "branding" becoming less or more important in this digital era?*

CG: Branding is becoming even more critical in the digital age because technology has equalized the functional performance of products. The only element that cannot be copied is probably the brand. Also, things are very transparent on the Internet; you can never fool a customer into buying a product. Whether they are looking for an everyday necessity or an exclusive high-ticket item, the customer will make sure what they are getting is worth every dollar they spend. A remarkable brand can achieve cut-through and be noticed by real connoisseurs.

RY: *How is brand-building different these days as compared to, say, ten or even five years ago?*

CG: The way of building brands today is indeed very different from how it was done before. In the past, you could build a brand through advertising with a big production budget and big media spending. Looking for the most prominent outdoor billboard and putting up a giant poster is already something that an average brand cannot afford to do. Organizing an exclusive "by invitation only" event, placing an ad on the centerspread of some glossy lifestyle magazines, or featuring a top celebrity wearing your brand on the front cover were the usual tactics. But consumers are now more than a passive audience. Brands are built by experience and commentaries on the web.

Since word of mouth is so important throughout the customer journey for luxury items, brand-owners are paying more attention and investing the time and resources to provide the proper orientation or even coaching to customers. Nothing is more detrimental than a current customer who does not understand your brand passing on unfair comments to their peers. So, "don't let your VIP customer kill your brand," because their words carry weight. People will trust the comments of a user more than what they see and hear in advertising. Selling is just the beginning; luxury brands have to follow through and turn their customers into ambassadors who possesses the knowledge and depth that allow them to genuinely fall in love with your brand.

Case study – Memorigin tourbillon watch

Taking a local brand to a global stage

A Hong Kong–made brand that now sells tourbillon watches in 18 countries worldwide, Memorigin has demonstrated that competing in a high-end luxury market is not mission impossible (Image 3.9). Memorigin is the first Hong Kong watch brand that specializes in tourbillon watches. Its watches blend oriental and Western elements by integrating pristine oriental sculpture with Western watchmaking traditions.

Memorigin tourbillon watches are manufactured by innovative designers who assemble high-quality materials from different countries with Memorigin's in-house

IMAGE 3.9 Diamond Legend from the JONQUET series is a Tourbillon watch valued at $289,465. Credit: memorigin.com.

movement. Customers can even engrave special words on the movement, making every watch a truly unique timepiece. Memorigin has had its tourbillon watch reviewed by Ogawa Satoshi Yukari from Osaka's renowned Watch Repair Master testing center, and both time accuracy and waterproof tests show that Memorigin meets the highest international standard for watch craftmanship (Image 3.10).[29]

Interview with William Shum, Founder and CEO of Memorigin

The founder and CEO of Memorigin Watch Company, Mr. William Shum graduated from Cornell University with master's degrees in applied economics and management. After working as an investment banker for a year, Mr. Shum quit his job to embark on his entrepreneurial journey. In 2015, Memorigin partnered with Disney to produce Avengers-themed watches that were sold worldwide. Partnering with blockbuster movies seems to be a winning formula, adding another entertaining and unique dimension to the timepiece (Image 3.11–3.12). Mr. Shum was awarded one of the Young Industrialist Awards of Hong Kong in 2015 and the Global Chinese Outstanding Youth Award in 2016. He also won the Executive of the Year for Luxury Retail at the Business Management Excellence Awards in 2018.

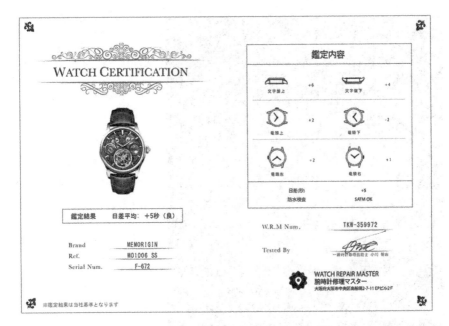

IMAGE 3.10 A Memorigin watch is certified to have reached the highest international standard. Credit: mermorigin.com.

IMAGE 3.11 A giant outdoor poster to promote both the movie as well as the special collection of Memorigin during the screening period of *Transformers*. Credit: memorigin.com.

IMAGE 3.12 The crossover with *The Dark Knight Rises* is just one of the many collaborations between Memorigin and popular Hollywood movies. Credit: memorigin.com.

Royce Yuen: What are the biggest challenges of building a brand from ground zero?

William Shum: The biggest challenge is to overcome the pressure that comes from Everywhere – including from people who are close to you and do not want to see you fail. It can be a very lonely journey, and there are hundreds of reasons not to pursue it further. Many people will ruthlessly crush your dream and destroy your self-esteem. I was rejected by uncountable watch retailers. Sometimes, their facial expression and body gestures can be ten times harsher than words.

RY: What are the critical success factors for brand-building?

WS: To be persistent and uphold your beliefs even when everyone is giving up on you. Try to be thankful for those who rejected you as they are pushing you to work even harder. Do what the competition can't – for instance, I try to leverage my nimble workshop to produce limited quantities for each design, making every piece a collector's item. Never compromise on product quality and try to give as much as possible to your customers. Eventually, they will recognize how much you have put in, and they will come back to ask for more.

Crossover with other corporations to present different themes such as local heritage, superhero, Hong Kong spirit, etc. Collaborate with different celebrities if possible. Be socially responsible, and then the money will come.

RY: *What is the difference, if any, between a local brand and an international brand?*

WS: Obviously, internationally acclaimed brands enjoy the halo effect that commands recognition, respect, and trustworthiness. It is tough for a local and relatively unknown brand to ask for a premium price, even when their quality is just as good. This is, in fact, the magic of branding.

RY: *How and when can a local brand become an international brand?*

WS: It is a long and tough journey … and can be very costly, too. It demands the highest level of commitment and self-belief. Our brand strategy is very clear – to reach the top level of awareness, be noticeable, and find a way for people to remember you. Remember that every effort counts, and nothing is wasted even if there may not be visible positive results initially.

Try to understand what consumers around the world want in common and try to offer something that is tangibly better than what they have now. Nothing can beat authenticity and originality – a brand can gain the "international" label as long as it reaches the global design and quality standards, even if it is not internationally made.

RY: *Do e-commerce and online shopping trends have any impact on your brand-building effort or business?*

WS: They have a very substantial impact indeed. Social media can make or break a brand anytime. If you have a good story, it can possibly go viral globally and allow you to connect with any potential customer around the world. Yet the Internet is full of fake news, and there is an ocean of information that may bury the truth. You must attack with purpose and turn the disadvantage into your advantage to achieve a phenomenal effect.

Dan Gable once said, "Gold medals aren't really made of gold. They're made of sweat, determination, and a hard-to-find alloy called guts."

Notes

1 "China Luxury Report 2019: How Young Chinese Consumers are Reshaping Global Luxury." McKinsey & Company, April 2019.
2 Vincent, James. "Luxury Phone Maker Vertu is Shutting Down its UK Manufacturing Operation." *The Verge*, July 13, 2017. https://www.theverge.com/2017/7/13/15963 656/vertu-luxury-phone-manufacturing-bankrupt.
3 "Harrow International School Hong Kong Fees." Accessed September 30, 2020. https://www.harrowschool.hk/admissions/fees.

4 Binkley, Christina. "Behind the Choice of a Luxury-Bag Pitchman." *Wall Street Journal*, June 7, 2012, sec. Life and Style. https://online.wsj.com/article/SB1000142 405270230366590457745071183033032.html.

5 "BrandZ Global Top 100 Most Valuable Brands 2019." KANTAR, 2019. http://online.pubhtml5.com/bydd/ksdy/#p=8.

6 Interbrand. "Best Brands." *Interbrand* (blog). Accessed September 30, 2020. https://www.interbrand.com/best-brands/best-global-brands/2019/ranking/.

7 Green, Dennis. "Celebrities Love this Aluminum Suitcase Maker that Luxury Goods Giant LVMH Just Bought for $717 Million." *Business Insider*. Accessed September 30, 2020. https://www.businessinsider.com/lvmh-buys-rimowa-for-717-million-2016-10.

8 Geller, Martinne. "Reckitt Finalises Deal to Buy Mead Johnson for $16.6 Billion." *Reuters*, February 10, 2017. https://br.reuters.com/article/uk-mead-johnson-m-a-reckitt-benc-grp-idUKKBN15P0MX.

9 Tybout, Alice M., and Gregory S. Carpenter. "Creating and Managing Brands." In *Kellogg on Marketing*, edited by Alice M. Tybout and Bobby J. Calder, 2nd ed., 78. Hoboken, New Jersey: John Wiley & Sons, 2001.

10 Squatriglia, Chuck. "Toyota, Subaru Sports Coupes Set Our Hearts Aflutter." *Wired*, November 30, 2011. https://www.wired.com/2011/11/toyota-gt-86-subaru-brz/.

11 Yu, Silvia Aloisi, Sophie. "Luxury Handbags Jump in Price as Brands Make Up for Coronavirus Hit." *Reuters*, May 14, 2020. https://www.reuters.com/article/us-health-coronavirus-luxury-prices-idUSKBN22Q2UW.

12 Millan, Cesar, and Melissa Jo Peltier. "Introduction." In *Cesar's Rules: Your Way to Train a Well-Behaved Dog*, 1. New York: Three Rivers Press, 2011.

13 Temporal, Paul, and Martin Trott. *Romancing the Customer: Maximizing Brand Value through Powerful Relationship Management*. 1st edition. New York: Wiley, 2001.

14 Murray, Becki. "Emilia Clarke is Clinique's First Global Brand Ambassador." *Harper's BAZAAR*, January 16, 2020. https://www.harpersbazaar.com/uk/beauty/skincare/a30532453/emilia-clarke-clinique-first-ever-ambassador/.

15 Weinreich, Marc. "Ronaldinho Loses $750,000 Coke Sponsorship for Drinking Pepsi at Press Conference." *Sports Illustrated*. Accessed September 30, 2020. https://www.si.com/si-wire/2012/07/11/ronaldinho-coke-sponsorship-pepsi-soccer.

16 Henry, Barnes. "Stone: China Earthquake 'Was Karma for Tibet.'" *The Guardian*, May 28, 2008, sec. Film. http://www.theguardian.com/film/2008/may/28/news.chinaearthquake.

17 Coyne, Marley. "America's Largest Public Companies in 2020: JPMorgan Chase Leads for the Second Year in a Row." *Forbes*, May 13, 2020. https://www.forbes.com/sites/marleycoyne/2020/05/13/americas-largest-public-companies-in-2020-jpmorgan-chase-leads-for-the-second-year-in-a-row/#4b6328b66593.

18 "Toyota Apologizes for 'Humiliating' Ads." *China Daily HK*, December 5, 2003. https://www.chinadaily.com.cn/en/doc/2003-12/05/content_287571.htm.

19 Cha, Sangmi. "Uniqlo Ad Sparks Protest, Parody as South Korea–Japan Dispute Flares." *Reuters*, October 22, 2019. https://www.reuters.com/article/us-southkorea-japan-uniqlo-idUSKBN1X106Q.

20 Patton, Stacey. "Turning H&M's Racist Image around on White Kids Won't Fix Anything." *The Washington Post*, January 12, 2008. https://www.washingtonpost.com/news/posteverything/wp/2018/01/12/turning-hms-racist-image-around-on-white-kids-wont-fix-anything/.

21 Petroff, Alanna. "KFC Apologizes for Chicken Shortage with a Hilarious Hidden Message." *CNNMoney*, February 23, 2018. https://money.cnn.com/2018/02/23/news/kfc-apology-ad-shortage-chicken/index.html.

22 Bensen, Jenna. "KitKat Gives 250,000 'Thank You' Labelled Bars to Thousands of Healthcare Workers." *WSFM 101.7 Sydney* (blog), May 20, 2020. https://www.wsfm

.com.au/lifestyle/health-beauty/kitkat-gives-250000-thank-you-labelled-bars-to-thousands-of-healthcare-workers/.

23 *A Day in the Life*, 2012. https://www.youtube.com/watch?v=oRqhoy4AVIM&ab_channel=RichardBranson.

24 Langley, Monica, and Marc Benioff. "How Salesforce Closed the Pay Gap between Men and Women." *Wired*, October 15, 2019. https://www.wired.com/story/how-salesforce-closed-pay-gap-between-men-women/.

25 Walsh, Bryan. "Oil Spill: Goodbye, Mr. Hayward." *Time*, July 25, 2010. https://science.time.com/2010/07/25/oil-spill-goodbye-mr-hayward/.

26 Goldsmith, Belinda. "Briton Wins 'Best Job in the World' on Australia Island." *Reuters*, May 6, 2009. https://www.reuters.com/article/us-job-australia-idUSTRE54514U20090506.

27 Sheetz, Michael. "SpaceX Launches Two NASA Astronauts to Space for the First Time in Historic US Mission." *CNBC*, May 30, 2020, sec. Investing in Space. https://www.cnbc.com/2020/05/30/spacex-launches-two-nasa-astronauts-to-space-for-the-first-time.html.

28 Ries, Al, Jack Trout, and Philip Kotler. "Getting into the Mind." In *Positioning: The Battle for Your Mind*, 1st edition., 20. New York: McGraw-Hill Education, 2001.

29 Memorigin. "About Us." Accessed September 30, 2020. https://memorigin.com/mobile/about_us.php?lang=eng.

4

THE RISE OF DISRUPTIVE BRANDS

The market would not have been severely disrupted if it weren't for the emergence of "disruptive brands." These brands redefine categories, challenge established players, and offer a new or different kind of experience to consumers. In this chapter, we will examine some of the most profound disruptive brands in the world and see what we can learn from their shared strengths.

Of the four cases that we are going to study, two are tech-based companies that operate completely in the digital space; one runs its business entirely in the physical world; and one is close to half a century old. In other words, brands of any business nature can disrupt an industry and cause a paradigm shift as long as they have the vision and capability to change the game for good. In the later part of this chapter, we will propose a new way to look at the competition by expanding the "Five Competitive Forces" advocated by Prof. Michael Porter to consider the impact of many more stakeholders in the market we operate.

Airbnb – The best hotel may not have a bellboy

The first case we are going to study is a role model for new startups. From a humble idea to a now-iconic brand, Airbnb is further proof that it pays to "dare to dream big."

What began as a way for three college kids to earn some extra cash by letting strangers crash on their floor is now a massive enterprise that offers over 7 million accommodations and 50,000 experiences in more than 220 countries. Airbnb is powered by a global community of hosts who list places to stay – from treehouses to castles – that anyone can book as an alternative to making a typical hotel reservation. Hosts can also offer experiences, from cooking classes to hiking adventures, to enrich the travel experiences of guests. Airbnb is a way for people to make a living, as well as an opportunity for travelers to experience more personalizable, unique forms of living.[1]

Since its founding in August 2008, the San Francisco–based company has never stopped refining its brand proposition, not only to gain more market share but also more mindshare. In 2014, Airbnb debuted a new logo, the "Bélo," which was designed to represent four elements: people, places, love, and the "A" of Airbnb.[2] Although the logo quickly became an internet meme, as people compared it to the shape of a pretzel, squid, and most controversially, certain body parts, Airbnb took the online attention in its stride by responding (humorously) that the logo's widespread interpretation only reinforces it as a true symbol of "belonging."[3] By welcoming the different reactions to its logo, even the backlash, Airbnb not only generated more brand awareness, but also showed that the brand has something for everyone.

I belong to the class of travelers that has traveled the world but never actually seen the world. My usual route is "airport – hotel – office – back to hotel – airport." My assistant will book me a room at the same hotel (she has no reason to pick a different one unless I request it) according to my itinerary. I have no reason to complain because the hotel serves my accommodation needs just fine during my business trip. Yet I have no reason to rejoice either, as it is just part of the usual routine. One may argue that staying in a hotel is a solid choice for business travelers because people may not want too many "surprises" during their business trips. The counter-argument is that Airbnb may then be a better option for tourists who want to diverge from their daily routine and explore a different world. If we follow this logic, Airbnb and its counterparts may someday own the leisure traveling segment, while traditional hotels with marble staircases and enormous crystal chandeliers will be confined to accommodating business travelers.

The difference between hotels and Airbnbs should remind business operators of a golden marketing rule that often slips their minds: "one size doesn't fit all." Even Airbnb has expanded its portfolio to include both affordable and high-end alternatives so that it can meet the tastes, expectations, and budgets of different travelers. Disruptive brands do not necessarily fragment the market; they simply respond to what consumers have always desired.

Most leisure travelers face an interesting dilemma each time they travel. On the one hand, they want to discover something different from what they experience at home. On the other hand, they may feel nervous or intimidated to navigate a totally foreign environment. Airbnb presents an ideal compromise: guests can stay in a place that is totally new, and also feel the warmth of a home. What's more, it is the authenticity and human touch that makes every Airbnb stay special.

So far, our discussion has centered on the Airbnb's "cozy" and "personal" aspects instead of its more practical and serviceable features. This is not surprising if we trace the root of the word "hotel," which derives from the Latin *hospes*, a word that refers to both the host and the visitor. *Hospes* is also the root for the English word "hospitable," which describes someone who is kind and caring to guests.[4]

The essence of a hotel is its hospitality, not its building or rooms. By understanding this concept, Airbnb can focus its attention on what matters most to travelers. After all, consumers are not marketers. They never analyze, but they can sense what "clicks" with them and what does not. All five-star hotels try to provide meticulous customer service, but they have to handle hundreds of customers at the same time, while Airbnb makes "you" the VIP in a particular property without other customers competing for the same services. This partly explains the growing popularity of Airbnb.

The other dimension that sets Airbnb apart from traditional hotels is that its listings are rated by the users, not the industry. Review Trackers estimates that 94% of consumers choose whether to support a business based on online reviews, while 80% of consumers put the most faith in businesses with 4–5-star ratings.[5] Airbnb's rating system is an integral part of its business model, as both hosts and guests evaluate each other after a stay or experience is completed. On Airbnb, guests may leave starred ratings, public reviews, or private messages to the host regarding the ease and convenience of their stay. Hosts are expected to be responsive, available, and honest. But it takes two to tango; in turn, the host will rank the guest based on how they treat the property and whether they honor the original terms of their stay. In particular – and this is worth noting – guests should not treat their Airbnb like a hotel where room service or housekeeping is guaranteed. In an arrangement where the host may not be trained in the hospitality business and the guest is looking for a homier experience, both sides need to adopt a new mindset.

Airbnb is smart enough to understand that any poor ratings on their site will tarnish their reputation. That's why corporations should not just focus on their work, but also keep an eye on the service delivery of their partners. That is, if the package fails to deliver on time or in good condition, both the logistics company and the brand that owns the e-commerce site will take the heat. Ensuring that guests and hosts enjoy a positive experience is therefore key to Airbnb's business sustainability.[6]

The digital economy has removed many traditional "middle-men" who no longer have a role to play in the eco-system. Why go to a travel agent when you can book your hotel directly online based on transparent reviews and deals? One of the unique features of the digital economy is that customers are a key driving force that improves the entire delivery system. Perhaps they usher in the emergence of a "new" middle-man who is neither an agent nor a broker, but someone who enriches the whole process while participating in it themselves. As a disruptive brand, Airbnb does not merely offer a novel platform for booking accommodations; it nurtures a new culture that facilitates the collaboration between the seller and the buyer.

Uber – You don't need a taxi, you need a lift

An unpleasant taxi ride can ruin your entire journey. Common complaints about terrible taxi experiences typically have to do with unreasonable or even unlawful charges, miscommunications with the driver, failure to reach the correct destination (sometimes intentionally), rude drivers, and safety-related issues (some taxis do not even have seatbelts!). Imagine having more control over the kind of car you step into and the accountability of your driver. Here is where Uber enters the picture – the multinational ride-hailing company has disrupted the market by making transportation services much more transparent and reliable.

In an era where consumers want to access everything from their phones, Uber began as a simple concept – "tap a button, get a ride." Since the first Uber trip on July 5, 2010, the app has evolved to change the way we think about getting from place to place. Everything, except for the ride itself, happens on the phone. Uber replaces the hassle of hailing a cab, worrying about change, and having to explain your destination address. Users can customize the kind of vehicle that picks them up, ranging from the standard UberX to the Premium Black SUV that specializes in offering luxury rides. Your driver arrives knowing the fastest way to reach your destination, and you can step out of the vehicle after the ride is completed knowing that the payment has already been settled through the app. To save money, riders can also opt for an Uber Pool and split the cost of the ride with a stranger heading in a similar direction. Uber accommodates different styles of travel, too; users can rent a Lime Scooter or request a wheelchair-accessible ride. Since 2015, Uber Eats has also transformed the app into a go-to option for food delivery.

As of 2018, Uber has an estimated 91 million monthly active users and 3.9 million drivers, and completes 14 million trips each day. Uber has become so representative of today's sharing economy that the process of transitioning to a service-based industry has been named "uberization."[7]

In most of the markets where it operates, Uber is a popular alternative to a traditional taxi, especially for the younger generation. Yet in other markets, the platform can be quite controversial in terms of its legitimacy and safety issues. In Hong Kong, for instance, Uber is not legalized. It faces stiff resistance from the local taxi industry, where there are 18,163 licensed taxis serving a population of only seven million.[8] In July 2018, 28 Hong Kong Uber drivers were fined between HK$3,800 (US$487) and HK$4,500 (US$576) after being found guilty of driving passengers without a hire car permit. On September 1, 2020, 24 Uber drivers found guilty of carrying passengers for hire or reward in Hong Kong lost their final court of appeal. Even so, Uber is not giving up and will continue to lobby local authorities (Image 4.1).[9]

The tenacity of Uber as a brand is also reflected in the way it has handled internal branding issues over the years. Although Uber's former CEO, Travis Kalanick, helped the company take off as a successful business, his reputation as a toxic leader severely tarnished the brand's image. Following increasing

IMAGE 4.1 Entering certain markets proves harder than expected, but this disruptive brand shows no sign of giving up. Credit: am730.

complaints about workplace discrimination and sexual harassment, Kalanick was replaced in 2017 by Dara Khosrowshahi, whose first task was cut out for him: to rebrand Uber and regain customer support.[10]

A picture is worth a thousand words, so Uber's rebranding strategy began with its logo. If one traces the evolution of Uber's logos over the years, one can see the evolution of its brand identity. The company's first logo was created when the app was still called "ubercab," and the company was still a startup. The pragmatic design showed that the company was more focused on logistics than branding. Then in 2013, the logo changed into a bold and glossy graphic, highlighting its position as a market disruptor. In 2016, the logo morphed once more into a sleek, futuristic design that emphasized Uber's technological edge. Both the 2013 and 2016 logos give off a sharp and even elitist impression, which one could associate with its former CEO's macho and hostile style of leadership. To truly rebrand Uber, its new logo would have to look completely different – which brings us to the 2018 and current iteration, a simple typographic logo. Designed with Wolff-Olins studio, the logo was designed to emphasize simplicity and universal recognizability.[11] Moreover, it signals a complete aesthetic shift from its predecessors and, along with it, a cultural reset for the brand. Memorable and unpretentious, the new "Uber" logo summed up the core goals of its rebranding strategy.

The major takeaway from the Uber case is not about redesigning one's logo every two to three years. As a disruptive brand, Uber chose to take proactive measures to reinvent itself, following Peter Drucker's advice that "the most effective way to manage change successfully is to create it." As other ride-hailing companies such as Lyft and Grab populate the market, Uber must stay on its toes to enjoy its top-of-mind awareness, and to prove why it is the eponymous trailblazer of "uberization."

Operating in Southeast Asia, Grab realizes that transportation does not always equate to cars in some markets. And hence Grab offers GrabTaxi, GrabBike, GrabWheel, and GrabTuktuk. In fact, Grab has quickly evolved to become a super app that provides everyday services such as ride-hailing; food, package, and grocery delivery; mobile payments; and financial services to millions of Southeast Asians. Its mission is to use technology to empower its communities and elevate the quality of life for everyone. Grab sets an excellent example that explains the positive implications of the concept of "disruption."

WeWork – Sharing a dream is more appealing than sharing an office

When someone mentions the word "coworking" these days, there is a high chance that they are talking about WeWork. Founded in 2010, the workspace provider supplies office suites, dedicated desk spaces, meeting rooms, and more workspace amenities to almost 700,000 members in 149 cities around the world.[12] As a place for companies and freelancers to mingle, WeWork offers all the office amenities you can imagine, from reliable Internet connection to strong coffee. And yet, WeWork spaces are not just about the "work," but also the "we" – you won't find lonely cubicles in a WeWork building, but communal spaces that are perfect for hosting events and networking opportunities. By reimagining the workspace, WeWork ultimately aims to create community out of colleagues.

WeWork is not the oldest or largest coworking space around, but it is the most rapidly expanding and perhaps most trendy company in the sector. The company has ample cash reserves and the support of blue-chip investors who make it possible for it to rent prime real estate in major cities such as San Francisco and New York.[13] Each WeWork location is also stylishly designed and furnished, projecting the image of a contemporary, enviable workspace. As such, WeWork has been able to build a strong brand presence in locations that are already known for attracting entrepreneurs and young professionals.

The 2019 Global Startup Ecosystem Report estimates that the global startup economy in 2019 was worth nearly $3 trillion, which is larger than the GDP of countries such as the UK or France, and represents a 20% increase from 2017. Technology-driven startups do not simply drive economic growth; they *are* economic growth.[14] Young and energetic entrepreneurs will no longer find traditional office environment or "business centers" (readers may no longer recognize this outdated term) a good fit for them. Instead, they will gravitate towards WeWork's "work and play" environment.

It is worth noting that even some blue-chip companies and the Big Four house their staff at WeWork. For example, KPMG has already moved several of their teams to WeWork locations around the world. In an interview with the *Financial Times*, KPMG explained that their collaboration with WeWork is in part a "branding exercise" to see whether working alongside startups may change its corporate image for the better. In an open office where big businesses and new startups work side by side, different company cultures can become mutually advantageous; businesses may learn more about the emerging trends that new startups identify easily, and young entrepreneurs can receive mentorship from established companies. In particular, big businesses can build relationships with up-and-coming entrepreneurs and rely on their fresh expertise to stay in touch with current consumer trends.[15]

Another prominent player that has decided to invest in WeWork is HSBC, which became one of the company's largest tenants after leasing more than 1,000 desks in London's Waterloo district.[16] HSBC's partnership with WeWork is taking place in Asia, too; the banking titan moved 300 staff members into WeWork's office in Causeway Bay, one of the busiest districts in Hong Kong. HSBC emphasized that migrating some employees to WeWork, which costs less than a traditional office space in Hong Kong, was not motivated by economic considerations. Rather, they believe that an open office plan could cultivate partnerships between HSBC staff and the technology-based startups at WeWork, benefiting HSBC as it builds its digital presence.[17]

Yet as larger companies move into WeWork, the company faces the challenge of holding on to its younger, less-established members. Corporations can afford the best co-working spaces, while freelancers may find that the expense of renting out a desk in a building largely occupied by big businesses is no longer worthwhile, despite WeWork's flexible leasing policies.[18] For WeWork to survive, it will have to refine its brand values to stay abreast of changes in the market.

I visited three WeWork locations in Hong Kong and randomly spoke with two tenants in each place, hoping to find out why they chose WeWork over a business center or another co-working space. During our conversations, the same words kept popping up – "global," "buzz," "community," "superior," "ambition," etc. It is apparent that people feel proud to be associated with the WeWork brand, especially those who are just starting out and lack recognition in the market. By associating themselves with WeWork, they feel more confident about connecting with potential investors or partners. Moreover, the sense of belonging to a community that is at the forefront of new trends is a great source of motivation for aspiring entrepreneurs. Like Airbnb, WeWork taps into the human desire to belong, and its capacity to continue disrupting the market lies in its ability to fulfill this brand promise.

iPhone – Taking gorgeous pictures without a traditional camera

While Apple is known for a line of impressive products, including MacBooks, iPads, Apple Watches, and more, this section will focus on one particular product that has prominently shaped Apple's role as a disruptor: the iPhone. Apple stopped reporting its iPhone sales figures in 2018. In the 12 years following its initial release, around 2.2 billion iPhones have been sold worldwide. Ranked by Forbes as the number one most valuable brand in the world, Apple was valued at $205.5 billion in 2019.[19] As the final disruptive brand that we are going to study in this chapter, let's first reveal some of the astonishing statistics associated with Apple and iPhone:[20]

- Since 2001, Apple stocks have risen by 15,000%, reaching USD 1 trillion.
- Apple generated a whopping USD 260 billion in revenue during 2019.
- iPhone sales are responsible for more than half of the total revenue generated by Apple.
- Apple made over USD 142 billion from iPhone sales alone in 2019.

I had the pleasure of being involved with Apple back in 1988 when I worked at BBDO, the agency serving Apple at that time. I was the proud owner of a Mac SE and later a PowerBook (which cost approximately $4,000 back in 1995). Apple has always played the role of a "disrupter" with its "what you see is what you get" graphic interface and its superior desktop publishing capabilities. Its marketing is equally impressive, especially in the way it defines a powerful computer. Apple has found a way to communicate the power of computers that is understandable even to a five-year-old. According to Apple, the power of computers has nothing to do with BITS or MIPS. The most powerful computer is the computer that people use.

A user-friendly, simple, and avant-garde yet not flashy design has always been part of Apple's brand DNA. The iPhone has been an excellent manifestation of these values since its launch in 2007. Some people even draw a comparison between the iPhone and Newton, which was the first Personal Digital Assistant (PDA) launched by Apple in 1992. The device could take notes, store contacts, and manage calendars. It could send a fax and even translate handwriting into text. Now, these are features that any basic smartphone can do today, but they were revolutionary in the early 1990s. Unfortunately, Newton was not regarded as a successful product, mainly because of its steep price (USD 5,000) and the fact that the technology at the time and maybe even users were not yet ready for such a device.

Steve Jobs, who had been ousted from the company in 1985, returned to Apple in 1996 after his company NeXT was acquired by Apple. The following year, he became the company's interim CEO and eventually stayed in the position. On June 29, 2007, Jobs launched the world's highly anticipated iPhone.

Because of its name, some manufacturers may have mistaken the iPhone for merely a "phone." By the time they came to their senses, it was already too late; the iPhone eroded other categories, rendering many brands or even entire industries obsolete (see Image 1.2 in Chapter One for a list of products that have been made redundant by smartphones). The iPhone's photo-taking capabilities have drastically improved throughout its different generations, and Apple ads tend to highlight the high-definition photos that can be captured with an iPhone. But the real reason it shakes up the market is that it influences changing consumer behaviors and lifestyles. These days, pictures and videos taken by consumers are meant to be shared on social media. The fact that people can upload files onto iCloud has also resolved the problem of storage. Moreover, every user can customize their smartphone by downloading a range of mobile apps for both business and leisure purposes. Not to mention that many die-hard Apple fans have multiple Apple products that can be connected to the iPhone to make life more convenient and pleasurable. In the case study presented in the next chapter, we will examine how the sales of once-popular compact digital cameras have been severely affected by smartphones, and how the global camera giant Canon is reshaping its entire corporate strategy to cope with the changing marketplace.

10 common characteristics of disruptive brands

The four brands that we have studied operate their businesses in totally different contexts, yet we see the emergence of a few common themes that can be summarized by the following points:

Mission-driven
> All four disruptive brands have clearly demonstrated why they exist, and their reasons extend beyond a neatly crafted mission statement. Their sense of purpose and direction guides the entire corporation to advance, or should I say leap, and conquer a promised land. It is because of their absolute clarity and consistency that they can act in unison among all their stakeholders (staff, partners, users, investors, etc.). Even brands that may have kickstarted their businesses without a long-range strategic plan can redefine their mission with sufficient momentum and self-awareness, allowing their business to reach new heights.

Continuous reinvention
> Standing still is never an option for a disruptive brand. From the way they revamp their brand identities to the way they stretch their total business offerings, they constantly pre-empt threats from competitors to stay in the forefront. Apple releases a new iPhone every year, a typical example of creating not just to meet consumers' needs, but to create those needs in the first place. One of the biggest hurdles in business advancement is complacency, where the corporation is either too content with their achievement or too scared to change. Disruptive brands are characterized by their eagerness to create new waves in the market and challenge the status quo.

Built by experience, not ads
> These brands are not heavy advertising spenders. Some of them do not even advertise regularly. That does not mean they are not investing in their brands. Rather, they have shifted their focus from window dressing to literally making things work better, both functionally and emotionally, and creating an exceptional customer experience. Positive word of mouth is the

driving force that makes these brands a part of daily conversations. As such, they occupy the top-of-mind of both users and prospects, maintaining a high conversion rate throughout.

Bigger than the category

Disruptive brands do not simply focus on coming up with more or better product features. Furthermore, their products are more than just a better alternative. They provide a new way to fulfill customers' needs and disrupt the industry by adding value to customers' lives. Naturally, customers will support them and reward them with their loyalty. As a result, disruptive brands become game-changers that profoundly redefine how business should be conducted.

Unrivaled speed and scale

These disruptive brands are usually empowered by technology to create a tremendous impact. But it is not the technology that makes them so influential. It is the speed of expansion and coverage that make them so formidable, with technology serving as a catalyst. They reach a mega scale so rapidly that they become a dominating power in the market and can re-write the rules of the game.

Simplify our complicated lives

Now that information is abundant and everyone owns a number of smart devices, we are somehow obliged to be more accessible by family, friends, colleagues, and clients. We realize we have an ever-expanding "to-do list." Anxiety is on the rise, especially among young people in the social media age. The number of UK youth who say that they do not believe life is worth living has doubled in the last decade, and the overwhelming pressure of social media contributes to internalized feelings of self-doubt.[21] Although they may have disrupted the industry, leading brands play a role in breaking down the complexity of daily life by allowing people to do everyday tasks with fewer burdens. Disruptive brands can counter some of the anxieties felt in life by allowing people to attain their goals more effortlessly.

Doesn't have to be perfect to be likable

Disruptive brands have taught us that we do not need to be perfect to earn the support of users. It is more important to be genuine than flawless. However, this does not mean that consumers are expecting less from brands. Rather, they would prefer be involved as co-creators of a better product or experience. They have a new mentality for engaging brands, and expect continuous improvement based on the user's feedback – hence the importance of "speed" and "self-reinvention" mentioned above.

Appeal to our curiosity

A common attribute that we all share is curiosity. This instinct helps us acquire knowledge and understand the world. This vital quality is often downplayed and suppressed as we grow older. We tend to behave habitually rather than explore new things because we fear making mistakes. The older we become, the more baggage we have, and the more risk-averse we become. Disruptive brands give us opportunities to release our inner child and gain new exposure. The pleasant experience of trying these brands will become a kind of positive reinforcement that drives us to follow them.

Big personality

All these brands have a distinctive character and bold personality, and attract people with their charisma and beliefs. In other words, *people follow brands because of who they represent, and not just what they can offer.* This also explains why brands do not have to be "flawless," as they need to resonate with the general public. This is not so different from a nation following a new leader who starts a revolution for the betterment of their people. Their conviction is contagious, which is why some people even describe highly influential brands as their "religion."

High touch, not just high tech

As mentioned above, technology is the means, not the end. Consumers never buy technology. They buy what technology can do for them. In all the cases we have studied, technology can help us tackle some of the problems we face in life. Many of these obstacles exist because companies do not always have consumers' best interests at heart. Instead, the industry has created a set of regulations that cater to the smooth running of their operation for the sake of higher productivity and profitability. Disruptive brands can shift the focus back to the consumer and remove these barriers for good.

From five to nine competitive forces

In 1979, Michael E. Porter developed the *Five Forces of Competitive Position Analysis,* a framework for evaluating the competitive strength and position of a business organization.

His theory posits that the success of an organization in a certain market depends on the balance of five different forces that impact the competitive intensity of that industry. By considering all five factors in tandem instead of fixating on a specific threat, organizations can be better positioned to decide whether or not entering a particular market will be profitable for them in the long run. Porter's five forces are:

1. **Supplier power**
   The ease with which suppliers can inflate prices is determined by how many suppliers are producing a particular input, their relative size and strength, and the cost of switching between suppliers. The uniqueness of the product or service will also have an impact on supplier power.

2. **Buyer power**
   The intensity of competition is driven by the number of buyers in the market, their individual importance to the organization, and the cost to the buyer of switching between brands. A business with just a few powerful buyers will operate under a more vulnerable position.

3. **Existing rivalry**

   The quantity and strength of competitors in the market will impact a business's staying power in the market. The market becomes less attractive if it is already populated by organizations offering similar products and services.

4. **Threat of substitution**

   In a market where consumers can easily choose alternative, cheaper products in response to price hikes, the organization hoping to enter the market has lower chances of making a profit. This reduces the supplier power and the market's overall attractiveness.

5. **Threat of new entrants**

   Finally, profitable markets with low barriers to entry will attract new entrants, which decreases profitability for individual organizations. The market will be more competitive unless there are strong barriers to entry in place such as patents, economies of scale, capital requirements, or government policies. As a result, the government can also be considered a sixth force in industries whose strength depends on government regulation.[22]

When Porter developed this framework in the late 1970s, he obviously could not take the impact of the digital era into account. Since then, the market has changed quite dramatically, posing the question of whether this framework is still valid for analyzing the operating environment of today. To better understand the challenges we currently face, we will have to consider four more forces that will affect the way we conduct business.

The *Nine Competitive Forces Framework* shown below builds on the Five Forces model by adding four new dimensions that are essential to current market dynamics (Figure 4.1):

1. **Other users and UGC.** In today's eco-system, consumers are not dealing with the service-providers alone. An unspoken alliance exists among users around the world, who exchange their views and product feedback on social media. It is a known fact that users trust "user-generated content" more than the information listed on a corporation's official website. People are not only interested in product performance, but also the integrity and trustworthiness of corporations. As such, operators have to constantly stay alert to the overall market sentiments about their entire industry (e.g. environmental or health-related issues) as well as specific views about them and their competitors.

2. **Key opinion leaders (KOLs).** Aside from other users, KOLs are another reliable source that users go to for obtaining information and advice. Some of these KOLs act as the bridge between brands and users. They are sometimes in a delicate position, for when reviewing a product they want to both earn commercial interest from sponsors and maintain the trust of their "fans." If they play it well, KOL can add value to both the service providers and the users. Some KOLs are so influential on social media that their

FIGURE 4.1 The Nine Competitive Forces Framework provides an updated and more complete view of the competitive landscape.

comments can promote or demote a brand instantly. Although brand-owners can work with KOL, their impartial position has made them another competitive force that does not fall under any organization's total control.

3. **E-commerce platforms and fulfillment partners**. Online shopping for any product category will only gain more popularity over time, especially in a post-COVID-19 era. E-commerce platforms or online marketplaces such as Amazon, Tmall, JD.com, and Shopify will play a critical role in the buying and selling of any product. They are the major gateways through which brands can reach out to prospects anytime, anywhere. The policies set by these platforms will directly affect the operating environment and, therefore, the competitive pressure within the market. Whether operators sell through these e-tailers or their own e-commerce sites, fulfillment is always an essential part of the purchase journey. The logistics support provided by third-party vendors, who may decide the speed, quality, and return process of product deliveries, can also impact the overall viability of the business.

4. **Review and comparison websites.** There is nothing more reliable than seeking the advice of someone who has just used a particular product or service. Their word of mouth or word of "mouse" has a direct and significant effect on other buyers' decisions. In other words, operators not only have to

manage consumer perceptions, but also their actual experiences. Users are quite accustomed to visiting websites such as Tripadvisor or DianPing to consider all reviews and ratings before they make a decision. There are also sites that are dedicated to pricing comparison, such as trivago. Operators cannot choose to opt-out of reviews, which have become an integral part of the business equation and will determine an organization's overall appeal and competitiveness in a market.

Many disruptive brands were born in the new economy era, so possess an inherited advantage in understanding and dealing with the four new forces. Their familiarity with the digital marketplace is also the reason why they can disrupt or even take the reins of an entire industry.

A brand-builder's perspective

Interview with Kent Wertime, co-CEO of Ogilvy & Mather Asia Pacific

Mr. Kent Wertime has lived and worked in Asia for the past 30 years. During this time, he has held various senior advertising and marketing positions based in Hong Kong, Bangkok, Tokyo, and Singapore.

Mr. Wertime's tenure with Ogilvy began in 1999 when he joined Ogilvy to head its Interactive division. He helped Ogilvy establish the largest Interactive agency operation in Asia, with offices in 12 markets. In January 2004, Mr. Wertime was promoted to President, OgilvyOne Asia. In March 2009, he moved to Japan and took on the added responsibility of the presidency of Ogilvy & Mather Japan. In 2010, he was promoted to Chief Operating Officer, and in 2016 he was named co-CEO of Ogilvy & Mather Asia-Pacific.

Mr. Wertime is an experienced writer and speaker. His first book, *Building Brands and Believers*, was published in 2002. In late 2007, Mr. Wertime co-authored a second book, *DigiMarketing: The Essential Guide to New Media & Digital Marketing*. His writing has also appeared over the years in *The Asian Wall Street Journal*, *Media*, *Asiaweek*, *China Daily*, and *Brand News*. Mr. Wertime is a frequent speaker at industry conferences in Asia and around the world.

Same logic. New physics

Royce Yuen: What impact has digitalization had on both marketers and consumers?

Kent Wertime: While most people agree that digitalization has rapidly changed the world, the digitalization process of most brands over the past 30 years *has been far too slow*. There has arguably been an underspend of 100 billion US dollars, if marketing resources were to truly match the human shift of their time to digital channels. So, many marketers still need to do more and better digital marketing.

Consumers have dramatically shifted their time – faster than the majority of brands have. They have been doing this for a basic reason. From the consumers' perspective, digitalization has given them a variety of benefits: new entertainment, more choices, more power to contribute, and a raft of new options and services. Marketers should see this as a boon for the way they reach and interact with prospects and loyal consumers.

However, many brand-owners have been – and some still are – hesitant to make the dramatic changes required to make their marketing and business models fully future-ready in a digital world. It's not that they don't want to change. Some of them just don't know how and also don't know what things will become beyond their comfort zone. Marketers need to embrace a new way of marketing built around addressable, digital channels that offer them so much more power of personalization, location, mobility, and other aspects that are core benefits of digital marketing.

RY: How do some brands embrace this disruption and turn it into an opportunity?

KW: "Disruption" is a concern for a raft of businesses, but particularly for entrenched businesses that have been built on old business models without the benefits of digital technology. Therefore, many corporations these days are obsessed with young and nimble brands that have consumer cachet and have been built "digital first."

There are some key options for companies that want to avoid falling behind and being disrupted. The first route is to acquire new, digitally built brands. Companies sometimes see this as the fastest way to transform, given the pain of change, the time it takes to create a truly digital-first brand, and the reality that even new brands can't be built overnight.

Aside from acquiring brands, brand-owners are asking themselves how to create a seamless connection to consumers that will be intuitive, easy, and fluid. "Digital transformation" pops up in every meeting, with discussions on how to be digitally enabled, be socially enabled, be connected to eCommerce and e-payment, and distribute content effectively. Most companies are aware of the new and increasingly competitive landscape; the question is not *whether* to transform, but *how* to transform.

Lastly, a lot of existing brands pour tons of money into digital experience. Yet a further challenge is their legacy assets, agreement, and relationships that cannot be ignored. These includes things like long-term commitments to retail space, distributor agreements, franchise agreements, and the partnerships they have built over the years with substantial financial investment and ties.

However, the current marketplace is the reality. Young people may not ever visit a physical store to buy or look for what they want, and more consumers everywhere are shifting to online commerce. So, many brand-owners are in transition, many of them are going through the pains of change, but some of them are successfully adapting to new norms. It is fair to say that almost every brand needs to focus on transformation, or they will be dead.

RY: How should brands step up and manifest themselves differently?

KW: The market is a continuum and its physics has changed. Marketing is becoming automated, and there is a seamless connection to purchase and fulfillment.

When you get into a Tesla, you can upload a whole new operating system – something that many other automakers simply can't match. It is not just about reframing the brand. The "new physics" of how things work is profoundly different. People sometimes buy a whole new experience or a re-imagined experience of a traditional service or goods. It calls for a more radical change; not just a new channel, new campaign, or new connection, but all of the above and much more.

RY: Is the role of the agency changing, and how does it add value to its clients' businesses these days?

KW: Consumers are leading the way, marketers are behind, and some agencies are behind the marketers. Clients cannot wait to find more digital solutions. It is not just about the idea but also the execution of a marketing cloud with the right "technology" that is stable and secure across all the platforms. Agencies can learn from their CRM journey 20 years ago, but of course, this time it will be much more complicated and demanding.

Agencies still need the talent and people who can create something that end-consumers choose to watch, interact with, and increasingly respond to. The challenge is how to scale new business areas when other legacy areas of the business are shrinking. Instead of producing one multi-million-dollar film shoot, clients now want dozens of bite-sized videos that can cover a variety of content in a more timely manner. Consumers are impatient and they won't wait. They will move on to look for other solutions if the service-provider cannot fulfill their changing needs. Brands have to stay relevant every day. This is the new physics, which will have a direct impact on the brand experience. Today, the ultimate goal of clients is to build and grow their brands over the years, and successfully every day too, as they interact more with consumers. So part of their decision-making process is to ask, "who is going to help me to make sure my brand is alive every day?"

RY: How is brand-building different from before?

KW: We help brands explore their higher purpose to set their long-term direction both internally and externally. Having the brand ideal to tackle fundamental problems is essential, but that alone is not enough. We need a new "OS" that builds brands over various time horizons to build the brand overnight, and over time. The new operating system puts ideas to work and aligns everyone around a core set of objectives. It helps us focus on the right 10 degrees that matter most to the brand from the 360 degrees that are available.

Case study – Hotel Madera

Why check into a hotel room when you can check out the local community?

Located at the heart of Kowloon, Hotel Madera Hong Kong is a hidden gem in the city's urban bustle. In Spanish, "Madera" means "wood." Riding on such a concept, the hotel employs a balancing and synergistic architectural design with a natural harmony concept. Natural inspirations, calming rooms, and a moody sky lounge help you not only unwind and relax but also enjoy urban living in a hideaway. Featuring 88 luxurious hotel rooms, each with a spectacular view of the city, guests at Hotel Madera Hong Kong can luxuriate in its comfortable guest rooms while taking in the exhilarating vista of Kowloon (Image 4.2).

Interview with David Fong, Managing Director of Hip Shing Hong

Mr. David Fong is the Managing Director of Hip Shing Hong (Holdings) Co. Ltd., a leading property group with a portfolio of hotels, office buildings, high-end homes, and over 200 retail properties. Mr. Fong obtained a master's degree in Business Administration from the University of Hong Kong and an Honorary Fellow of the City University of Hong Kong. Mr. Fong is currently a National

IMAGE 4.2 Why choose a big hotel chain when you can have a big experience of the city? Credit: Madera Hospitality Group.

Committee Member of CPPCC, an Honorary Trustee of Peking University, and a member of the Board of Trustee of Jinan University.

Mr. Fong is also the Chairman of Hong Kong Strategy, Chairman of Betting and Lotteries Commission, Life Honorary Chairman of the Chinese General Chamber of Commerce, a Member of the Hospital Authority Board, a Council Member of the Hong Kong University of Science and Technology, Vice-Chairman of Hong Kong Committee for UNICEF and an Executive Council Member, and a trustee of WWF Hong Kong.

Royce Yuen: How do you make your brand stand out in a crowded hotel market that is already occupied by big global chains?

David Fong: The two boutique hotels under the brand Madera ranked in the top 40 among more than 600 hotel/guest houses in Hong Kong. The first hotel, Madera Hotel, Hong Kong (HK), opened in November 2011. We adopted a design by a Barcelona designer, which is uncommon in Hong Kong. This helps differentiate us from most local developers who use US, UK, or Hong Kong designers.

Besides, I have personally provided a lot of input on how to deliver great customer experience, including an old gallery of Hong Kong and a local smartphone that people can use anywhere in the city (Image 4.3). We never intend to compete on the hardware or even the location. We strive to offer a unique experience and touch so memorable that customers want to return. In a sense, we are not building hotels. We are building "friendships."

RY: What is it exactly that you want to offer to your hotel guests?

DF: We want to offer our guests a local neighborhood experience (like Temple Street, local eateries, etc.) where you see the real Hong Kong instead of the concrete in the central business district (Image 4.4). We help our guests maximize their experience in Hong Kong, no matter how little time they have in between meetings or appointments. The location of our hotel is not a stereotypical, posh area. It is not like Fifth Avenue in New York or Avenue des Champs-Elysées in Paris. Yet we are able to turn this seeming disadvantage into an advantage by tapping the local surrounding environment, allowing people to experience the authenticity and local flavor of the Pearl of the Orient (Image 4.5). We provide all the essential luxuries at an affordable tariff. We also have some high-end luxury suites and double-story penthouses for the most discerning guests.

RY: Do you think consumers these days do not necessarily go after the "big" brands? Why?

DF: Traveling is routine for many business executives or business owners. They are seasoned travelers and experience nothing new going to big hotels, which may appear cookie-cutter to them. They are bored with the expected and standard level of services. They may find boutique hotels that provide more personal and customized services a refreshing experience. In some cases, small is beautiful, and you will not get lost the way you might in a hotel with a thousand rooms.

IMAGE 4.3 Take the handy smartphone to explore the city with unlimited local and international calls (to seven countries) and unlimited data usage. Credit: Madera Hospitality Group.

RY: What are the other market changes that will impact or even "disrupt" the market?

DF: Airbnb is emerging as an interesting player and getting a lot of attention, even market share, from the traditional tourist market. It may be appealing to young travelers and families, who are more willing to try out a home–living style of accommodation. There may be more privacy as well with fewer facilities. Due to the wide range of properties, Airbnb offers many choices, including some that are more affordable. But it is a particular market that will not affect the business traveler segment whose traveling expenses are covered by their company. The other factors that reshape the traveling market are new intermediaries, like online booking platforms. They are more transparent, and they display many customer ratings – an increasingly important criterion for choosing a hotel.

RY: How would you describe the latest market development and market structure for the hospitality sector?

IMAGE 4.4 Navigating local street stores is a different experience from shopping in a high-end mall. Credit: Madera Hospitality Group.

IMAGE 4.5 Madera is conveniently located for visitors who are interested in trying out the local flavor. Credit: Madera Hospitality Group.

DF: There will be more consolidation, like mergers and acquisitions of big hotel chains. There will also be more online booking platforms hitting different market segments. Big chains will create more sub-brands (like boutique hotels) to compete with smaller, agile players and to regain the market share. High labor cost is a big issue, and people cannot be easily replaced by robots even if they provide all the services in a technical sense.

RY: How do you manage the market and geographical expansion of Madera?

DF: At the moment, we are very cautious about expanding geographically due to tough geopolitics. In terms of profitability, expanding is much less profitable than doing real estate development. It is a very long-term investment. Nevertheless, it allows our group to enrich our portfolio by entering a new category. It can bring new ideas into the organization and urge the team to think out-of-the-box. We will be very selective when opening new hotels and prefer to get it right each time. We are aiming at customer share instead of the market share at this stage.

RY: What are the biggest challenges and difficulties in building a brand from scratch?

DF: You need to put a lot of planning and thinking into what the brand represents, and to be crystal clear about its core values. There has to be substances instead of empty talk. Consumers won't analyze what you say, but they can feel whether it has substance. You also need to have patience; burning money does not guarantee a successful brand. It may only increase brand awareness.

RY: How will you manage the brand if Madera becomes a big chain one day?

DF: We would need to hire more professionals to guide us to the next stage. By then, it may be a different ball game, and we need to make sure our team is growing into a new position where they can comfortably perform without losing their original passion or the "heart" to bring exceptional experiences and unforgettable memories to our guests.

Notes

1 Airbnb Newsroom. "About Us." Accessed September 9, 2020. https://news.airbnb.com/about-us/.
2 Marion. "Airbnb's Consistent Rebrand Focuses on the Sense of Belonging to a Community." *The Branding Journal* (blog), July 23, 2014. https://www.thebrandingjournal.com/2014/07/airbnbs-consistent-rebrand-focuses-sense-belonging-community/.
3 The Airbnb Blog. "The Bélo Report: An Infographic on the New Airbnb Symbol," July 23, 2014. https://blog.atairbnb.com/belo-report-new-airbnb-symbol-infographic/.
4 Merriam-Webster. "Had a Long Day of Travel? Check into a Hospital." Accessed September 30, 2020. https://www.merriam-webster.com/words-at-play/word-history-hospital-hostel-hotel-hospice.

5 ReviewTrackers. "2018 ReviewTrackers Online Reviews Stats and Survey." Accessed September 30, 2020. https://www.reviewtrackers.com/reports/online-reviews-s urvey/.

6 Airbnb. "Hosting on Airbnb." Accessed September 30, 2020. https://www.airbnb .com/hospitality.

7 Pavie, Xavier. "'Uberization' and the Rise of the Service Economy." Essec Business School, May 17, 2017. http://knowledge.essec.edu/en/innovation/video-uberizat ion-and-rise-service-economy.html.

8 Yau, Cannix. "Uber Partnership with Taxi Firm Could Stall as Owner Faces Backlash." *South China Morning Post*, March 4, 2019. https://www.scmp.com/news /hong-kong/transport/article/2188596/uber-partnership-hong-kong-taxi-firm-tin -shing-motors-could.

9 Siu, Jasmine. "Uber Drivers Lose Final Appeal against Hong Kong Convictions." *South China Morning Post*, September 1, 2020. https://www.scmp.com/news/hong -kong/transport/article/3099732/uber-drivers-hong-kong-lose-final-court-appeal -against.

10 Kleinman, Zoe. "Uber: The Scandals that Drove Travis Kalanick Out." *BBC News*, June 21, 2017, sec. Technology. https://www.bbc.com/news/technology-4035 2868.

11 Bowman, Amanda. "Uber's Powerful Rebrand and What Your Business Can Learn from It." *Crowdspring* (blog), October 1, 2018. https://www.crowdspring.com/blog/ uber-rebrand/.

12 WeWork. "Newsroom." Accessed September 11, 2020. https://www.wework.com/ newsroom.

13 Sawerschel, Youri. "WeWork – The Brand that Redefined an Industry." *Hospitality Net*, July 9, 2018. https://www.hospitalitynet.org/opinion/4089189.html.

14 Sherrington, Ailsa. "The 2019 Global Startup Ecosystem Report Launches at TNW2019." *The Next Web*, May 9, 2019. https://thenextweb.com/tnw2019/2019 /05/09/the-2019-global-startup-ecosystem-report-launches-at-tnw2019/.

15 Jacobs, Emma. "Big Business Moves into Co-Working Spaces." *Financial Times*, April 28, 2016. https://www.ft.com/content/c8255158-fffe-11e5-ac98-3c15a1aa2e62.

16 Evans, Judith. "HSBC becomes One of WeWork's Biggest Tenants." *Financial Times*, June 19, 2019. https://www.ft.com/content/3d4c1690-92a2-11e9-b7ea-60 e35ef678d2.

17 Li, Sandy. "HSBC Moves 300 Staff into WeWork Hot-Desking Site in Causeway Bay." *South China Morning Post*, September 22, 2016. https://www.scmp.com/prop erty/hong-kong-china/article/2021679/hsbc-moves-300-staff-wework-hot-deskin g-site-causeway-bay.

18 Sawerschel, "WeWork."

19 Swant, Marty. "The 2020 World's Most Valuable Brands." *Forbes*. Accessed September 30, 2020. https://www.forbes.com/the-worlds-most-valuable-brands/.

20 Milenkovic, Jovan. "How Many iPhones Have Been Sold Worldwide? – iPhone Sales Analyzed." *KommandoTech* (blog), February 11, 2020. https://kommandotech.com/ statistics/how-many-iphones-have-been-sold-worldwide/.

21 Booth, Robert. "Anxiety on Rise among the Young in Social Media Age." *The Guardian*, February 4, 2019. https://www.theguardian.com/society/2019/feb/05/yo uth-unhappiness-uk-doubles-in-past-10-years.

22 CGMA. "Porter's Five Forces of Competitive Position Analysis," June 11, 2013. https ://www.cgma.org/resources/tools/essential-tools/porters-five-forces.html.

5

BRANDING REDEFINED

By now, you have finished one-third of the book. I hope you have found your time well spent and that you are still interested in reading onwards. The first part of the book aimed to review the most profound principles of branding that have contributed to many successful brands and businesses around the world. It also examined the evolution and progression of the concept of branding from various perspectives.

The market has never been so disruptive than it is now due to the convergence of exceptional forces that have inspired an explosive transformation – the advancement of technology, the emergence of borderless markets, the shift of power from manufacturers to consumers, the digitization of market practice, increasingly pressing global environmental issues, and an unprecedented pandemic. All of this has urged business-owners and marketers to rethink and redeploy their overall branding strategies to avoid joining the growing league of extinct enterprises or industries.

The remainder of the book will lay out a framework on how to help brands make the leap from good to great. Before we get to that, however, this chapter serves as a sectional conclusion to decode the meaning of branding. The most apparent impact of brands on consumers can be summarized in one line:

Branding provides rational reasons for consumers to behave irrationally.

Disagree?

Then why do we have so many shoes, to the extent that we have lost count of how many we own?

Why do we want to buy another car when we already have a car?

Why do we still buy watches when we no longer need watches to tell the time?

Why do we spend on a leather handbag the amount of money that could pay for our family's luxury vacation?

There is a common belief that marketers never persuade consumers. It is the consumers who convince themselves. We can never force a consumer to respond or comply. But we can provide all the hints that trigger an internal debate in their minds and hearts: to buy or not to buy? One major role of agencies in the past was to help client organizations find consumers' "soft spot" and use the most effective and relevant way to communicate with them. This approach is possible through understanding what matters most to the consumers based on experiences, observations, or research studies. Now that an increasing number of tools for analyzing and visualizing data is available to brand-owners, the need to conduct ad hoc research has significantly diminished. Corporations today have access to real-time data and insights that were not available to them in the past. Some corporations are even obsessed with data. But can data solve all marketing problems? How will brand-building change with the support of data? Is branding becoming more of a science? Do brand-builders have to adopt a new skill set and mindset in the future (a new O/S, as mentioned by Kent)? These questions will be explored in the subsequent sections, which also include excerpts from interviews with the CEO and data scientist of MaLogic on how data is transforming the way we do business and build brands.

Big data and big branding

Agencies have had to live with a curse for more than a century. It is a curse that they detest but cannot deny – "half of the advertising budget is wasted; we just don't know which half." Now with big data, we may finally be able to find the cure.

The reason why big data can potentially challenge this curse is that it empowers more effective marketing and business operations. It allows us to have a more thorough understanding of where we stand in the market and the extent to which we are fulfilling the "real" needs of customers. With this information, we can better strategize how to not necessarily sell more, but to better answer the unfulfilled needs of the people we have promised to serve.

Data allows us to be more certain of what we should be doing, such that we can roll out our plans with a higher level of confidence. Most importantly, data provides a scientific approach for us to measure results so that we can continue to refine our marketing campaigns.

It is a common industry practice to use the Four Vs to describe the characteristics of big data:

- Volume – the massive amount of data involved, with datasets as large as terabytes and zettabytes;
- Velocity – the rapid streaming of real-time data;
- Variety – the different types and formats of data from different sources;
- Veracity – the uncertainty resulting from biases, noises, and abnormalities in data.

Obviously, the most critical yet unspoken "V" that concerns business operators is the commercial "Value" that can be generated from data.

The 4 Vs of big data have empowered branding and communications with dynamic and real-time insights, which are critical in a data-driven operating environment. To complete the strategic framework, it is essential to add another "V" to the equation – Verdict (Figure 5.1). Sales history and patterns do not fully explain customers' involvement with the brand or the corporation. In fact, some customers who shop online are merely bargain-hunters. It is risky if a customer relationship is mainly built on discounts or incentives, since a genuine relationship can only be earned, not bribed. "Verdict" refers to the interrogation of the relationship between a brand and its advocates, attempting to understand the core reasons for people loving the brand. Based on data analysis, the corporation can form a judgment on each customer's comprehension and appreciation of the brand value. Hence, customer education can be devised to build active loyalty. By giving people "reasons" to love a brand, they will voluntarily buy its products.

Smart brands create market need and shape the behavior of users to drive brand preference and brand switching. They have a grand brand vision and big brand ambition while remaining meticulous in their execution details. They understand the psychology of different users by tracking their past and real-time behavior and dismissing all the obstacles that may possibly distract the customers from checking out their online shopping cart. For instance, guaranteeing a free refund is an important aspect of the fulfillment process, which contributes to the customer's sense of assurance throughout the purchase journey. Of course, the brand has to be confident enough that the rate of returning the goods will be manageable and that the profit margin will not be adversely affected.

In sum, the benefits of big data for building big brands can be summarized by the four main areas below – Assessing, Planning, Implementing, and Monitoring.

1. Assessing
   Sentiment audit: From sensing the market pulse to quantifying its relative strength, social data can provide a snapshot as well as a precise

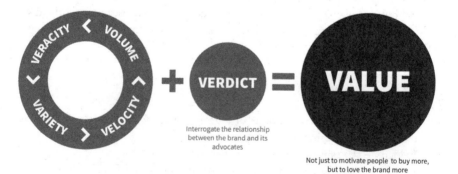

FIGURE 5.1   The 6 Vs of big data.

measurement of the brand's current performance. This data is useful for encouraging ongoing brand development.

Problem detection: Retention is critical to sustaining business success. Internal sales and customer data can detect the intensity of customer involvement and possibly identify the reasons for changes in attitude and behavior. Locating pressure points can prevent problems from escalating, especially among customers who may share the same experiences.

2. Planning

Prediction and segmentation: The insights derived from data can predict the behavior of consumers based on an analysis of their needs and wants. Consumers can be segmented into common clusters such that the brand may offer a customized solution to each and every customer. Prediction can also determine the inventory management strategy so as to cut operating costs and reduce time to market.

Profit maximization: Data can empower corporations to shift from "transaction" mode to "relationship" mode by aiming at customer lifetime value (LTV). By drawing conclusions from aggregated data, corporations can predict the individual's propensity to spend by better understanding the earning power, priorities, and profit potential of every customer throughout the customer life cycle. The 20/80 rule can then be applied to encourage more strategic marketing investment and classify customers into various tiers for deeper engagement and recognition.

3. Implementing

Recommender system: While problem detection can defend a corporation, the recommender system drives offensive marketing and significantly affects businesses when appropriately implemented. Many leading e-tailers rely on the recommender system to generate additional sales by suggestive selling and bundling based on data analysis. In some cases, the recommender system can generate up to as much as one-third of the sales turnover of an e-commerce site.

Aside from increasing the online shopper's basket, the system can also push relevant information to the users to cultivate stronger emotional attachments, encourage habitual visits to corporate sites, and even draw traffic to physical stores.

Targeted marketing: Measuring campaign performance can enhance a marketer's understanding of what does and does not work to identify what truly resonates with their customers. Tracking consumer interest in certain product lines or the competitor's products can lead to a higher conversion rate by providing the right offer at the right time. Corporations can construct profiles of converted customers to pick their "look-alikes," the next batch of target customers, within data pools.

Operational excellence: Devising a viable strategy cannot guarantee success; it has to be executed flawlessly. Algorithm-based data can generate automatic and timely decisions based on preset rules under different scenarios. This data is particularly valuable for the service industry due to its "perishable" business nature. Deep machine learning encourages constant refinement of marketing models to maximize efficiency and deliver total customer satisfaction while optimizing profit potential.

4. Monitoring

I use the word "monitoring" and not "measuring" here because the semantic meaning of "measure" often refers to post-mortem actions after a campaign, whereas "monitoring" is an ongoing process of constant tracking and refinement.

Benchmarking report: Industry sales data and social listening can provide insights on relative performance in terms of both the "share of market" and the "share of heart."

In fact, the share of the market can be understood as the outcome of the share of the heart.

Brands plot and predict market and consumer trends in order to stay at the forefront of the market instead of just adapting to change.

Branding: Science or art?

If science is defined as a structural and systematic way to enrich our knowledge of a subject based on experiences, observations, experiments, and evidence, then branding can be regarded as a science. This chapter explains how data and analytics empower marketers to make more timely and accurate decisions. This scientific approach will become more advanced and sophisticated as newer applications are developed in the future.

Brands only exist when humans appreciate them; they do not exist by themselves. Since the human element has such a significant bearing on the formation and manifestation of brands, we should approach branding as a unique science. To begin with, humans are not a bunch of numbers. Their attitudes and behaviors are highly dependent on many emotional and situational variables. For instance, a user can have a direct or indirect influence on another user that affects the second user's experience and interaction with a brand. In the past, the relationship between a brand and its user existed in a linear dimension. But *in the digital and interactive world, branding is a collective experience, and everyone can play a part that will either reinforce or diminish the brand experience and its reputation.* The concept of a collective experience is not new in our society. A private club will require its members to behave in certain ways by adhering to a particular etiquette and dress code. A school will demand students to follow the rules and behave properly since others judge the school based on the manner and behavior of its students. The difference today is that the user's experience will not be dictated by the operators. The collaborative nature of social media has nurtured a dynamic and continually evolving environment for brands, urging us to not overlook the artistic side of branding even while exploring its scientific aspect.

Through physical and virtual contacts, a brand can send out numerous sensory stimuli to enhance a user's experience. For instance, companies collaborate with key opinion leaders (KOL) and key opinion consumers (KOC) to distribute short videos that cover a broad spectrum of content and real-time broadcasting. Technology has also expanded the range of creative and innovative ways for users to interact with brands. The cosmetics and fashion industries are the forerunners in merging creative expressions and technology applications. As such, when branding becomes more of a science, it does not become less of an art.

Brand virtue

The digital revolution has opened up the market, but has it opened our minds?

Instead of seeing a bigger universe that is full of opportunities, some corporations are only concerned about the potential erosion of their existing businesses by new market forces. This response may be a knee-jerk reaction under the conditioned thinking of "survival of the fittest." This philosophy has led to the belief of a zero-sum game – one in which one's gain must derive from another's loss. Arguably, the notion of "survival of the fittest" is only applicable in a situation where the supplies of essentials are fixed, and the focus is primarily on short-term return.

Indeed, in this new horizon, growth does not have to come from dismissing other industry players. This new mindset is about co-survival and co-advancement, such that growth can occur by value creation through innovation. Peter Drucker has long reminded us that marketing and innovation are the only two bloodstreams of a corporation.[1] Innovation is not necessarily about challenging or eliminating competition. As the Olympics has shown us, we should promote healthy, not hostile, competition. Although there may be only a few medalists at the end of the day, all the contenders become stronger and better because of the game. According to the International Olympics Committee, the goal of the Olympic Movement is to build a better world through an inclusive, discrimination-free sports education. The Olympic spirit requires "mutual understanding with a spirit of friendship, solidarity, and fair play."[2]

Innovation and advancement aim to dismiss complacency (the old way of working) and selfishness (the old way of thinking). They push for more accountability to create a new equilibrium that can benefit all parties concerned. Here is where the *5-C Market Equilibrium* comes in; it describes a state of being where all parties get what they need while the market operates harmoniously and sustainably. The rewards are distributed according to the merits of each contributor in an efficient and self-regulated manner, so that brands are motivated to constantly improve how products are made and delivered.

The first C in the 5-C Market Equilibrium stands for *corporations*. They are the brand-owners and the providers of goods and services. They produce products that meet the demands of the market, and during the production process, they create job opportunities and promote economic activities. Under the new equilibrium, brand-owners are not solely profit-driven; as this chapter will explain, they are willing to take on a more prominent role to tackle social issues by leveraging what they do best.

The second C is the *consumers*. They consume the product and service and thus enable corporations to be commercially viable in operating their businesses. Consumers today are different from those in the past because they are not just passive buyers or users. They are *prosumers* who provide real-time feedback to corporations on what works and what does not so that brand-owners can always have a clear idea of where to focus and what to fine-tune. The consumers in this model play another crucial role, which is to monitor the overall performance of the corporations and drive them to actively engage in both commercial and social causes. With the consumers acting as watchdogs prepared to exercise their collective influential power, corporations are more inclined to do good. Consumers can also instinctively spot who is doing good out of their own free will and who is doing it as a matter of obligation and compliance.

The third C is the *collaborators*. Let's not call them "competitors," since these operators have a much bigger undertaking than only competing in the market. They can complement fellow players by fulfilling what others cannot or do not want to do. They can also choose to go head-to-head with each other and keep everyone on their toes as a result. Rigorous collaboration drives the industry forward by setting new standards and expanding both the breadth and depth of the market.

The fourth C is the *community*. While the first three Cs busily engage in their business activities, they do not ignore the individuals or social issues that require active intervention, or should I say active involvement, from time to time. No man is an island. The business sector cannot be cut off completely from the community. Its success and stability have to be built on the solid foundation of a stable and healthy society.

The last C is the shared goal of the new equilibrium, *civilization*. The overriding objective of all business activities is to enrich the physical, emotional, and spiritual well-being of people. Human civilization depends on nurturing a healthier and more technologically advanced society. It grows by being smarter about how to "utilize," not simply "use," resources. In the past, human beings focused on "using" and exploiting natural resources, which resulted in the many global issues that we face today. In a way, the biggest demons we have to confront and overcome are created by ourselves. We must learn to become more intelligent by knowing how to utilize and not just use natural resources.

As such, the sharing economy has a new dimension. It is no longer just about sharing resources (like Airbnb), but also about sharing accountability (like the

UN and WHO). Unlike the industry collusion that may lead to oligopoly, the new equilibrium does not seek to only benefit a few big players, but instead aims to create a win-win situation for all parties concerned. Our enemies are not our industry rivals. "Competition" should be defined as anything (either in physical or ideological form) that hinders the advancement of society as a whole. Our common enemies are the pressing global and environmental issues such as global warming, climate change, and unknown diseases like COVID-19. Our common goal is to re-build social harmony. This is a new market view and worldview. As such, leadership has also taken on a new definition – it is not about "bigness" but "greatness," and not only about "productivity" but also "accountability." It is about mutual respect, mutual support, and mutual prosperity. The advancements of different brands in a market do not have to be mutually exclusive. The art and science of a brand are only the manifestations of the nature and process of branding. The most important aspect of branding is the *virtue of the brand*.

Brand virtue consists of:

- Brand values: *the "heart" and original mission of the brand, defining the role it plays in people's lives and in the community.*
- Brand personality: *the combination of the characteristics, qualities, and style that form the unique character of the brand.*
- Brand behavior: *the actions and activities the brand undertakes in the marketplace, including its products and services, its marketing and promotions, and its online and social media content.*

People can see your behavior, feel your personality, and sense your values. Together, they represent the totality of who you are and what you stand for in the eyes of those interacting with your brand.

Therefore, in today's context, the complete definition of branding should be:

> *A brand is the set of values that it represents and the actual values that it can add to those who are involved with the brand.*

A great brand does not only add value to its users; it radiates positive energy that brings opportunities and possibilities to anyone who is involved with the brand, including but not limited to its staff members. *People are connected to the values of the brand, attracted by its personality, and impacted by its behavior.* Nowadays, adding value takes place through empowerment, which turns different stakeholders into co-creators of the brand. Because they are responsible for the co-creation of the brand, they will naturally do what they can to ensure its long-term success. Ultimately, the brands that add tangible value to people's lives are the ones that will survive and prosper.

A brand-builder's perspective

Interview with Eliza Wong, CEO of MaLogic, and David Qing, Data Scientist of MaLogic

Trained as a professional accountant, Ms. Eliza Wong decided to embark on a career in the field of market research. With her talent in managing numbers, Ms. Wong has quickly risen to the leadership positions for prominent research institutions, including Synovate (Greater China) and GfK (Hong Kong and Taiwan). Before taking on the position of co-CEO at MaLogic, Ms. Wong founded GMD (Go Much Deeper) with the goal of redefining the strategic role of research with the deployment of technology and big data. Ms. Wong has been actively involved in The Samaritans and puts her persuasion to use for worthy causes.

With his extensive experience in the market research industry, Mr. David Qing is involved in data analysis and market analysis for a variety of projects, including car clinics, brand analysis, product tests, loyalty indexes, pricing stress tests, segmentation validation, and media research. Mr. Qing worked at Synovate & Ipsos for more than 15 years. Apart from conducting technical work in the data analysis field, Mr. Qing was also responsible for department building and management at both local and national levels and was involved in strategic planning for Greater China. He moved to the Decision system in 2011, which enabled him to become well equipped with statistics and modeling analysis skills. From 2012 to 2015, Mr. Qing was the Digital Information & Data Integration Director at GfK. He was also the market science head for GfK Great China, in charge of data analysis and providing solutions for market research. Mr. Qing is currently a data scientist at MaLogic.

Royce Yuen: How would you define "big data"?

Eliza Wong: Big data is commonly referred to as the 4 Vs – Volume, Velocity, Variety, and Veracity. We try to deploy Deep Learning to work out the complex relationship of data. This will allow the machine to gradually pick up new dimensions of data variables and let the machine trigger decisions automatically. *David Qing:* As the name implies, big data is a term that describes a substantial amount of data flowing in and out of the system/platform at high speed and usually in real-time. The data can be quite complex, including many data types and formats, plus thousands or more features per data item. The data, in most cases, come from different sources.

RY: How is big data different from a traditional database?

EW: Firstly, the relationship: big data is typically stored in a DMP (data management platform) that allows the data to talk to each other and translate into meaningful values for the corporation. In a traditional database, the data usually sits in silos, not having any connection. Secondly, interpretation: big data provides a complete elaboration of a situation, while the database provides a linear or one-dimensional meaning of the fact. Thirdly, users: big data can be used and accessed by a big group of audience members at the same time. A traditional database may only be accessed by one or two individuals in the corporation at any one time. Finally, report frequency: big data can perform this at a much higher frequency than traditional data-mining analysis.

DQ: Traditional data types are structured and fit neatly in a relational database. Structured Data is easier to analyze and organize into the database. Big data includes unstructured and semi-structured data types, such as text, audio, and video signals that require additional preprocessing. Unstructured data is much harder to analyze, and it needs a more significant infrastructure and technical skills to derive meaning and support the operation of metadata.

RY: *How can corporations benefit from big data in general?*

EW: *Speed to market* is a critical success factor these days. Big data can empower corporations to seize leadership positions by taking prompt marketing actions. *Marginal savings in operating costs* will also cumulate to a significant profit and lead to higher operational efficiency. Furthermore, when more team members access the same database, it helps eliminate misunderstandings across various departments. When team members are more aligned, there will be greater teamwork geared towards achieving common goals. Big data also enables more *accurate predictions and forecasts*, eliminating mistakes and allowing corporations to get things right the first time.

DQ: As mentioned earlier, big data often comes from different data sources in real-time. It can help organizations increase their work efficiency, make better decisions, monitor the health of brands, and gain more relevant information to better support or serve their customers.

RY: *Specifically, how can big data help to build* brands?

EW: In the traditional sense, data is used as a tool to support the different stages of building a brand. Big data can reduce these steps and make quick and meaningful connections so that we can forecast and predict consumer behavior more accurately. Big data allows marketing and brand-building to be done more transparently and effectively, including but not limited to precision and targeted marketing,

DQ: Big data can derive critical information based on users' behaviors, spending patterns, and tendencies. It can help organizations identify the most appropriate and profitable target groups as well as optimize product or services to generate new growth opportunities and enhance brand loyalty.

RY: *Big data as a concept or topic is not new; to what extent is the market implementing big data to its full strength and advantage?*

EW: There are many successful deployments of big data in the US and Europe, including credit checks by banks leading to more robust risk management, and more effective management of retail business, from reducing the level of inventories to upholding the freshness of products (e.g. Walmart and Tesco). The other obvious example is social media, which captures users' substantial and continuous real-time data, allowing companies (e.g. Google and Facebook) to push the most appropriate content to them. In China, JD.com and Alibaba let consumers order groceries or clothes, and 80% of these products can be delivered to the customer within an hour. Big data has elevated consumer experiences tremendously by increasing convenience and fulfilling "unmet needs."

DQ: Data has a lot of intrinsic value, but it is useless until that true value is discovered. The data has to be merged and integrated alongside meaningful dimensions. The true value comes from data analytics, which consists of learning, measuring, and controlling the data that can eventually empower data-driven decision-making.

RY: *What are the prerequisites or requirements for a corporation to be able to deploy big data successfully?*

EW: The corporation needs to have the right leadership that embraces "big data" and is fully committed to driving the initiative and culture organically throughout the entire organization.

DQ: Big data technology and applications are cross-disciplinary. Successful big data deployment may require a significant cultural transformation that must be driven by teamwork, involving IT specialists, data scientists, and statisticians. Users also play an essential role in providing a focus and priority so that the resources can be utilized in the most sensible way.

RY: *What are the major misunderstandings or challenges faced by corporations when practicing big data?*

EW: The major misunderstanding and challenges these days are the assumptions that big data is a very costly proposition and that only sizable corporations are in the position to deploy such a system. Any corporation can pick and choose the data set that they need from big data providers, and pay a reasonable price to access a large pool of data for analysis.

DQ: Nowadays, data velocity is increasing, and data volume is enlarging. The uploading and transmitting of video files demand a more powerful hardware and robust algorithm to process the reservoir of data. People often think that the larger the dataset is, the better. Yet they should focus more on discovering its true value, not only its size, bearing in mind that there will be more noise in a large dataset.

RY: *What is the future of the development of big data?*

EW: Sooner rather than later, big data will be so readily available that it may become a commodity. When that happens, everybody will access information from different sources, and the price will continue to drop. Having massive data is no longer a differentiation. The key will be to come up with innovative and creative solutions or ideas that can outshine the competition.

DQ: The greatest value of data comes from the integration of data of different dimensions and industries. The concept of big data may disappear or continue to evolve, but the analysis and discovery of value will persist, leading to a smarter living environment and marketplace.

Case study – Canon

Experience or quality – What matters more?

> *Change is progress. Transformation is advancement.*
> *– Fujio Mitarai, Chairman & CEO, Canon Inc.*

Behind Canon's 80-year history and development as a business lies its corporate DNA: a respect for humanity, an emphasis on technology, and an enterprising spirit that the company has consistently championed since its foundation.

The "Three Selfs," the foundation of the company's guiding principles that has been passed down since Canon was founded, are *self-motivation* (take the initiative and be proactive in all things), *self-management* (conduct oneself with responsibility and accountability), and *self-awareness* (understand one's situation and role in all situations). For Canon, which strives to be a truly excellent global corporation while maintaining the legacy of its corporate DNA, the Three Selfs continue to serve as the company's most important guiding principles.

IMAGE 5.1 Canon is advancing imaging technology to help preserve experiences and emotions. Credit: Shutterstock.

To most retail customers, Canon is probably synonymous with "camera." It is a well-known and respected brand. You likely own a Canon or are aware of the brand and what it produces. However, as a company, Canon is much more than "camera." In Phase V of its medium-to-long-term Excellent Global Corporation Plan, beginning in 2016 and designed to achieve new growth by 2020, Canon has undertaken a grand strategic transformation to shift its core businesses from business-to-consumer (B2C) to business-to-business (B2B).

In 2018, Canon successfully completed the transformation of its business portfolio by employing such methods as Merger and acquisition (M&A) in its four new businesses—commercial printing, network cameras, medical and industrial equipment.

To drive future growth in these new businesses, Canon will focus on expanding its scale and enhancing productivity. Meanwhile, it will strengthen its existing businesses by incorporating current technologies such as cloud computing, artificial intelligence, and the Internet of Things to further increase market shares.

Interview with Vincent Cheung, Vice President of Business Process Re-engineering Group of Canon Singapore

Mr. Vincent Cheung has had more than 28 years of sales and marketing experience in consumer and business imaging products. After working for a few years in different consumer product companies, Mr. Cheung joined Canon Hong Kong in 1998 as Marketing Manager of the Camera and Video Division. As an amateur photographer, he helped promote photography culture in Hong Kong by setting up Club Canon in 2006, an online platform designed for photo, video, and Canon lovers. In 2017, Mr. Cheung was appointed Vice President of Office Imaging Product Group at Canon Singapore regional headquarters, overseeing 23 regions in the Asia market. Currently, Mr. Cheung is the Vice President of Business Process Re-engineering Group at Canon Singapore.

Royce Yuen: To what extent is your camera business being "disrupted" by smartphones, including but not limited to sales turnover?

Vincent Cheung: In the Imaging System sector, we saw a rapid decline in the demand for our cameras. For compact cameras, the market shrank by 19% to 8.5 million units in 2019. We also posted a decline in unit sales that was in line with the market. In 2019, the interchangeable-lens camera market shrank by 15% to 8.8 million units, but to a much lesser extent as users of more sophisticated cameras have different expectations and also command a different level of appreciation of imaging technology.

The market has evolved so much that the applications of some products may be severely diminished. For instance, e-boarding passes are widely acceptable by airlines these days, so there is no more reason for people to print out boarding passes at home. Also, some people prefer to receive a soft copy of documents due to environmental reasons or accessibility. As a result, consumers are showing less interest in products with restricted functionality that can be easily replaced or substituted.

RY: Could you predict that change was coming and foresee the impact it would have on your business?

VC: The erosion happens gradually. It's difficult to predict how and when consumers are going to change. Also, when a new smartphone launches, the market dynamics may change again depending on the new features and functions of the phone – or I should say "device," as it is no longer just a phone anymore. Even adding the word "smart" in front of "phone" cannot fully explain the impact it can have on users as well as the market.

RY: Has the market structure been redefined? How?

VC: In the past, the camera market structure was like a pyramid, with professional cameras on the top, prosumers in the middle, and entry-level or simple models that are small and convenient to carry at the bottom. Almost 80% of this bottom segment has been replaced by smartphones; this is the biggest change in the market.

A smartphone offers more than a reasonably good picture. It includes other features, especially "connectivity," which is difficult for compact digital cameras to provide.

The role of the "camera" has changed, and the concept of the camera has been redefined.

The need for professional images is not going to be diminished. The wireless connection capability of cameras makes them an irreplaceable product that captures great images. Photos and videos can be transferred through dedicated mobile apps or directly uploaded to cloud platforms, such that user can edit and share photos online instantly. This wireless workflow builds a mutually beneficial relationship for camera and smartphone markets (Image 5.2).

RY: Are you now dealing with consumers with different mindsets and expectations?

VC: Yes indeed. We are adapting ourselves and refining our strategies given the integrated user experience offered by smartphones. Consumers enjoy the thrill of using an evolving product with new technology being introduced constantly. They experience a lot of positive changes on top of "convenience." They also put more emphasis on "experience" than on "quality" when taking pictures.

We encounter too much information every day. If different mobile apps help us structure and access relevant information, having these apps is as important as having the information itself.

RY: How did you overcome this disruption?

IMAGE 5.2 Wireless workflow is becoming a trend for some industry professionals. Credit: https://asia.canon.

VC: Canon is in the midst of a grand strategic transformation designed to accelerate growth in our four new businesses: commercial printing, network cameras, medical equipment, and industrial equipment. From development to manufacturing and procurement, and all the way to the cultivation of human resources, we strive for complete success as a group. At the same time, in such mature businesses as cameras and printers, we are pursuing next-stage growth through the development of high-value-added products and cost reduction.

Canon is a global image technology company. It provides more services than consumer imaging, such as production printing, professional imaging, and medical imaging. By adjusting the business and managing the portfolio wisely, there will still be growth opportunities.

On a product level, we have to be the "friend" and not the "enemy" of smartphones, even though they have replaced some of our convenient models.

Sometimes consumers need a quality picture; we can offer software that will make a proper camera more compatible with smartphones, instead of trying to compete head-on with it.

For example, the new inkjet printer has no scanning function and therefore is cheaper, but it can easily connect with smartphones. The user can take a picture of the object, then our app will align the positioning and lighting of the photo taken when it is being printed. All in all, our product can be positioned as a more sensible solution that takes up less space, if printing and scanning are not frequently required.

IMAGE 5.3   Complementing smartphones makes Canon products even more appealing to users. Credit: https://asia.canon.

The Canon PRINT Inkjet/SELPHY app is a free software application that allows customers using the iPad, iPhone, or iPod Touch and Android-based smartphones or tablets to enjoy a variety of PIXMA printing capabilities such as wireless printing and scanning. The customer can also use this app with cloud-ready printers to enjoy remote access to the printer over the internet and direct printing from cloud services (Image 5.3).

RY: What role does the Canon brand play during this critical period?

VC: In any declining market, the number of players will be greatly reduced. Typically, only a handful of companies will stay in business and most of the profit in the market will go to one or two of its top leaders. During the market transformation, Canon has been evolving by expanding into new business segments such as medical imaging equipment and network cameras, while staying in the leading position of our traditional domains such as the digital camera and printer market. The Canon brand plays a crucial role in our success by developing new business and winning the survival game in declining domains.

RY: Now that you have seen how the brand is performing in both HK and Singapore markets, can you offer your comments on how to manage a global brand across different markets?

VC: There are always two options at least: globalization (standardized) and localization (customized). There is no right or wrong answer, but according to the nature of the business, the range of products the brand offers, the proposition of each product, the maturity of each segment in each market, the culture in each market, the history of the brand in each market, and many more factors, a company needs to set up its brand strategy across different markets by mixing and matching globalization and localization.

In the case of Canon, we are very well known globally for our advanced imaging technology. At the same time, we offer a very wide range of products that cover the various consumer segments. Thus, we have more room to adjust our brand strategy by focusing on specific market segments, which could differ by region. I imagine if I were managing a luxury watch brand, the flexibility to localize the brand strategy would be relatively more limited.

Notes

1 Trout, Jack. "Peter Drucker on Marketing." *Forbes*, July 3, 2006. https://www.forbes .com/2006/06/30/jack-trout-on-marketing-cx_jt_0703drucker.html.
2 "Fundamental Principles of Olympism." In *Olympic Charter*, 11. International Olympics Committee, 2020. https://www.olympic.org/the-ioc/promote-olympism.

6

THE 10 Cs OF SUSTAINABLE BRANDING

The pandemic has put many brands to the test and revealed the vulnerability of some businesses. Marketers begin to realize that their judgment day could come at any time, without warning. For business operators who want to endure, keeping brands resilient in the era of disruption has become a top priority.

To keep brands sustainable, simply pouring money into marketing and promotion efforts will not suffice. Hiring trendy celebrities to appear in ad campaigns is not a bulletproof solution either. As mentioned previously, brands must justify their existence by providing tangible added value to their users. They must also stay abreast of the constantly evolving market environment. Users will regularly appraise their relationships with different brands, and there is no obligation for them to stick to the same brand for any category. It is indeed becoming tougher to achieve brand loyalty these days. Users are smart enough to understand that for the same kind of products or services, prices are likely to fall while quality is expected to improve over time.

This chapter intends to introduce a strategic framework for obtaining a holistic view of the relative strength of a brand – *The 10 Cs of Sustainable Branding* (Figure 6.1). It will examine a brand from various dimensions to identify the specific areas that require immediate attention. The 10 Cs may be understood as a "health check" for a brand. Once a brand identifies an underperforming area, they can take the right actions to prevent the problem from escalating and spend their marketing investment sensibly and effectively. More importantly, the 10 Cs bolster the sustainability and endurance of the brand, preparing it to face any challenge. This strategic framework is constructed based on the fundamental principle that "a brand is the set of values that it represents and the actual values that it can add to those who are involved with the brand." The framework consists of four main clusters. We will begin by reviewing the overall logic and

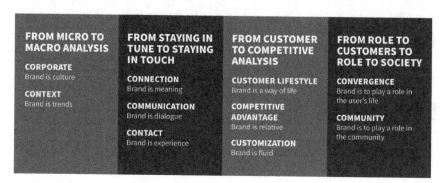

FIGURE 6.1 The 10 Cs of Sustainable Branding.

structure of the framework before subsequent chapters further elaborate each cluster in greater detail alongside real-life scenarios.

From micro to macro analysis

When a brand undergoes a "health checkup," the logical starting point for reviewing the brand is its origins – the *corporate*. It is critical to ensure that the brand is properly understood and embraced by the team whose task it is to promote the brand to the outside world. If they are not convinced about the values of the brand themselves, there is no way that they can convince others.

Furthermore, a brand must operate in a *context*. This is how it fits into the market environment and appeals to different stakeholders. Every market has its unique set of rules, and understanding the rules is a prerequisite to joining a game. It is worth noting that brands with disruptive power can redefine the game and how it is played. Hence, brands must review their market position from time to time, or they may be outcast.

From staying in tune to staying in touch

There can be no relationship without ongoing *communication*. Brand-owners cannot expect consumers to go to them all the time. They should take the lead in communicating with customers to nurture a deeper sense of mutual understanding. Communication can inform, educate, intrigue, and steer. It also triggers feedback and promotes a loop of constant exchange.

The whole point of communication is to drive *contact*. Contact can take many forms, such as the consumer visiting the brand's physical stores, checking out its website, or simply picking up the phone to call customer service. Making contact is extremely important because it is the "moment of truth" and a major step forward in the customer journey.

Ultimately, our goal is to *connect* with the customers after they have initiated contact. Connecting signals the existence of shared values, and this emotional alignment is what contributes to the most unbreakable bond between the brand

and its advocates. After all, the endgame of all marketing activities is to achieve customer loyalty.

From customer to competitive analysis

Marketing starts and ends with the *customers*. A brand is worthless if it is not appreciated by the people it serves. Yet understanding and pleasing customers is easier said than done. A brand must not take anything for granted and should try to offer more than what is expected of them. After all, customers will only value the brands that genuinely add value to their lives.

A customer may voluntarily seek other alternatives if he is unsatisfied or simply bored with the brand he currently uses. It is also natural that brand *competitors* will flirt with customers by offering enticing incentives that may outweigh the trouble of brand-switching. At the end of the day, a brand can only blame itself for any customer defection, for being good is no longer good enough.

As mentioned in Chapter Two, the days of mass marketing are long gone. "One-size-fits-all" is not only wishful thinking; it is an outdated mindset. If a manufacturer only sees things through its own perspective, it is deemed to fail. Customers now expect some degree of *customization* so that the brand can more precisely answer their specific needs.

From role to customers to role to society

A brand exists because it has a role to play in people's lives. This *convergence* between the brand and the customer's life defines the mission of the brand. The more significant the role, the more attached the customer. This is precisely the "actual added value" that we refer to in our definition of branding.

A truly respected and admired brand extends its positive influence from the industry to the *community*. The brand does not simply orchestrate a strategy to generate more publicity or brand exposure; its positive contributions derive from a sense of responsibility and commitment. By giving back to a receptive community, the brand can naturally emerge as a leader because leaders attract followers. This final "C" explains why the framework is called the "10 Cs of Sustainable Branding"—it helps brands become more sustainable while also fostering sustainability in the community.

Implementing the 10 Cs

Step one

To conduct a brand assessment based on the 10 Cs, the company should assemble a project team led by the head of marketing or branding, someone who understands the brand inside-out. To eliminate blind spots, as much as possible, other team members can be recruited from disciplines outside of the marketing team.

Step two

It will be prudent to gather views from regular users of the brand since their feelings towards the brand are the most critical and representative. After consolidating both internal and external inputs, the project team can objectively plot the assessment of the brand on *The 10 Cs Sustainable Branding Checklist* (Figure 6.2). The ten-point scale from "vulnerable" to "irreplaceable" is easy to compare and understand. It will provide a snapshot of what the brand is doing well and what needs to improve.

Unless the assessment is carried out with a sufficiently large sample size, this framework is meant for indicative purposes only. A qualitative approach is recommended when engaging with users since the key is not to obtain a score from them but to understand more precisely the reasons behind the score.

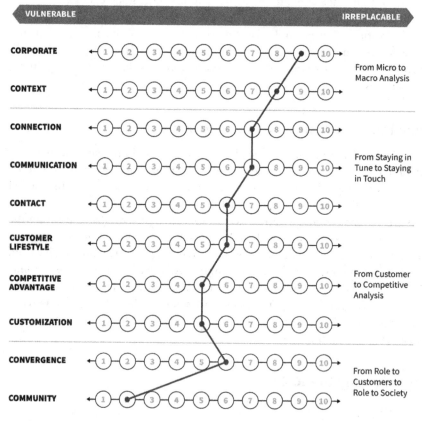

FIGURE 6.2 The 10 Cs Sustainable Branding Checklist provides a multi-dimensional snapshot of brand performance.

Step three

To complete the picture, it will be useful to plot the performance of the brand's closest competitor on the same chart by following the same procedures. This will allow the project team to compare and contrast the relative performance of their brand (Brand X) against its direct competitor (Brand Y) in a comprehensive manner. The example below shows how the performance of Brand X and Brand Y can be easily compared on a single chart (Figure 6.3). It appears that Brand Y ranks higher than Brand X in terms of customization, likely due to its extensive product range that suits the tastes and preferences of different market segments. Better customization may lead to more effective communication since messaging

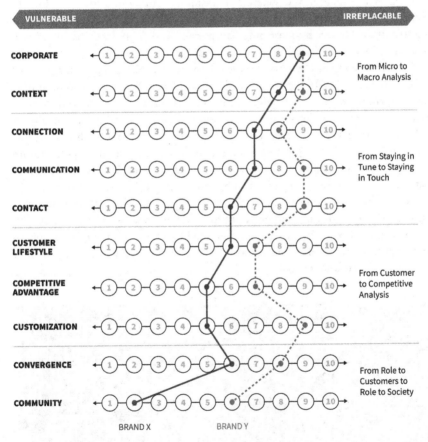

FIGURE 6.3 The comparison between Brand X and Brand Y on the 10 Cs Sustainable Branding Checklist.

can be tailor-made for each segment. Brand Y is also much more advanced in terms of its involvement in the community, which indicates another area where Brand X needs to step up to close the gap.

In Chapter Two, we examined how a brand can manifest itself and serve its users holistically. The 10 Cs framework outlined the different aspects of a brand, with each of the four clusters corresponding to different elements (Figure 6.4).

When internal staff members and key stakeholders align on brand value, vision, and direction, the product and other operational matters will naturally fall into place. The ideal way to nurture a brand is for the team to implement ideas freely while adhering to a shared vision, mission, and accountability. They will know precisely what to do and what to avoid, what will fit well with the brand and what will not.

Of course, strategic plans must be based on a thorough and realistic understanding of the market and where it is heading. This will allow the team to effectively identify and come up with viable ways to seize or even create business opportunities. Hence, by mastering "corporate" and "context," the brand will likely fulfill its "functional" role for its users.

The Maslow Hierarchy states that it is human nature to pursue a higher level of fulfillment in life after our basic needs are met.[1] A well-executed communication campaign can project an alluring image that provokes attraction. Physical contact with a brand can reinforce the notion that it is a must-have in life. A truly "aspirational" brand can command exceptional pricing, such that its followers are always able to justify purchasing its products. In some ways, premium pricing is an essential factor that contributes to the prestigious status of brands that cater to an exclusive group of individuals who appreciate the finer things in life. Yet glamour alone cannot guarantee sustainability, and even the most status-conscious consumers do not want to own these brands simply to show off. All the leading luxury brands are substantiated by their unique heritage, superb craftsmanship, and tireless innovation. They impart special meaning to their customers and customers-to-be.

FROM MICRO TO MACRO ANALYSIS	**FROM STAYING IN TUNE TO STAYING IN TOUCH**	**FROM CUSTOMER TO COMPETITIVE ANALYSIS**	**FROM ROLE TO CUSTOMERS TO ROLE TO SOCIETY**
CORPORATE Brand is culture	**CONNECTION** Brand is meaning	**CUSTOMER LIFESTYLE** Brand is a way of life	**CONVERGENCE** Brand is to play a role in the user's life
CONTEXT Brand is trends	**COMMUNICATION** Brand is dialogue	**COMPETITIVE ADVANTAGE** Brand is relative	**COMMUNITY** Brand is to play a role in the community
	CONTACT Brand is experience	**CUSTOMIZATION** Brand is fluid	
FUNCTIONAL	**ASPIRATIONAL**	**LIFESTYLE**	**RESPONSIBLE**

FIGURE 6.4 The 10 Cs branding framework maps out the four key aspects of branding.

As the market develops, consumers will become increasingly demanding. In a typical adoption curve, the opinion leaders will make the first move, followed by mainstream customers. A sustainable brand is one that understands and can meet changing expectations by offering the most appealing and up-to-date merchandise according to "customer lifestyle."

What's more, brands should be fully aware of their competitor's offerings in order to find a clever angle that highlights its "competitive advantage." At the same time, it should cater to the needs of different segments by offering "customized" solutions attract different types of buyers. With these tactics in place, the brand will be able to help users fully embrace the "lifestyle" they desire.

When the brand has established its role in a user's life as an enriching and essential force, the user will take all the necessary steps to protect their relationship with the brand. This explains why some brands can be resilient despite changes in the market paradigm. These days, consumers no longer care solely about their own well-being. Instead, they believe that their present-day privileges should not undermine the opportunities of future generations. The more educated and affluent consumers are, the more they understand the importance of fostering a sustainable society. Therefore, a brand that plays a role in the community will naturally appeal to modern consumers looking for brands that are capable (offering tangible values) and responsible (maintaining important values). This pattern fits perfectly in line with the notion of building a "new market equilibrium" to promote the pursuit of "brand virtues."

A brand-builder's perspective

Interview with Wilson Chan, Director of MaadTech Consortium

Mr. Wilson Chan is the Director of MaadTech Consortium. He is also a Partner of Gravitas. Prior to that, he was the CEO of Ammirati Puris Lintas in Hong Kong. Mr. Chan has held senior positions at several international advertising agencies, including Saatchi & Saatchi, FCB, and BBDO. He also founded his own agency, Storm Communications.

Royce Yuen: To what extent have marketing practices or overall business operations been disrupted?

Wilson Chan: The purpose and functionality of modern marketing remain consistent: to "create and manage customers, brands/products, and channels via market–customer insights and effective strategy implementation." The essence of marketing has not changed from the analog age to the digital era, but new skillsets and application tools have emerged from the digital transformation.

There are two main disruptors to the previous practices. Firstly, the emergence of technology (Internet, World Wide Web, social media, Internet of Things, etc.) impacts the lifestyle and behavior of consumers, notably due to millennials overtaking boomers. Secondly, the abundance of data allows marketers to improve accountability and efficiency, despite data usually being a completely alien (and intimidating) subject among marketers.

As a result, the practice of marketing (but not its essence) has become more of a science than an art compared to how it was perceived in the past.

RY: Has the concept of branding evolved or changed over the years?

WC: Very much so, from a manufacturer-driven mindset to a customer-centric approach and now to brand experience management.

RY: How is brand-building today different from what it used to be in the past?

WC: Traditional brand-building concepts emphasized creating brand identity and differentiation, usually through one-way traffic from marketer to consumer. The current best practices call for building image and value affinity with consumers via multi-channel dynamic interactions and customer journey management.

RY: Has the role of branding diminished in the digital age, or is it becoming even more critical?

WC: The role of branding will be even more critical in the digital age as "trust" is now the ultimate reason for consumers to follow any corporation. More advanced skillsets and resources are required to deliver a fully "dimensionalized" brand experience. In other words, the value of brands will remain a certainty. What is uncertain is how the true and gratifying brand experience will be performed constantly throughout the entire customer journey.

Case study – Carlsberg

Probably the best case of beer marketing in the world

At Carlsberg, the pursuit of better beer is in its DNA. More than 100 years after its founder J.C. Jacobsen mastered the art of brewing great pilsner, Carlsberg is still looking for ways to improve its beer. Its perfectly balanced Danish pilsner is wonderfully crisp and refreshing, with a full flavor and a distinctive hoppy aroma. It is "probably" the best beer in the world.

According to Carlsberg, the group increased its international focus by opening up breweries in various parts of the world between 1968 and 1981. The first overseas brewery opened in 1968. In 1972, 1974, and 1981, Carlsberg opened up breweries in Malaysia, the UK, and Hong Kong, respectively.

In the period after 1976, sales of Carlsberg and Tuborg outside Denmark exceed domestic sales by far. The success of Carlsberg and Tuborg's products in all parts of the world is attributed to its quality consciousness, know-how, and technological proficiency.

Carlsberg's international presence continued to grow in the 1990s as the company increased its degree of ownership or acquired new shareholdings in breweries in Portugal, Sweden, Italy, Vietnam, China, Poland, Latvia, and Croatia.[2]

Interview with Sunny Wong, former Chairman of Carlsberg Greater China

Mr. Sunny Wong was Chairman of Carlsberg Greater China and then senior advisor to Carlsberg Asia from September 2011 to November 2014. He is now Chief Advisor at the publicly listed Tibet Water Resources Ltd.

Apart from his roles as Chairman and CEO of Carlsberg from 2006 to 2014, Mr. Wong was also the chief of its M&A team. He set the strategic M&A plan for Carlsberg's long-term development in China and led a team in identifying potential targets, negotiating, closing deals, and conducting post-acquisition activities. Since 2002, the team has successfully acquired 59 breweries in 12 provinces in China and increased the number of production plants from 1 to 60, with a total workforce of up to 15,000.

Mr. Wong has a strong and successful background with more than 30 years' experience in the China fast-moving consumer goods (FMCG) industry, of which more than 25 years were spent in the Chinese beer market for top international companies like Carlsberg and Bass Brewers. Mr. Wong is an Adjunct Professor who teaches strategic marketing for the Hong Kong Baptist University's BBA program.

Royce Yuen: What is the role of branding for an industry like beer?

Sunny Wong: Beer is a very subjective category … Some like a strong bitter taste, and others prefer light, easy-drinking beer. However, in blind taste tests, people often confuse their favorite brand with others. It is ultimately the brand and its full marketing effort that we buy. Branding is also vital for beer because up to half of the total beer volume consumption occurs in socially visible outlets like bars and restaurants. You want to drink a brand that fits your social image. I think most beer drinkers care about the brand when consuming it in public, but they care less about it when drinking at home.

RY: With your wealth of experience in business management, how would you define "brand" in one line?

SW: A brand is a personality and DNA that differentiate you from the competition.

RY: What are the critical factors in building a strong and lasting brand?

SW: There are many criteria for success when building a strong brand, but I think the following three are key – competitive differentiation, relevance to consumers, and consistency in execution.

RY: How important is the "people" factor in brand-building? How do you build brands through "people"?

SW: People are key because you build your brands through people.

You have to align your internal team in the same direction and work with partners such as the advertising agency and the trade. Without a shared unique and clear belief, there is no chance to convey brand stories across the market.

Having a clear and well-defined brand makes it easier to reach alignment both internally and externally. You have to sell your brand to the team members within the organization before you sell it to the consumers! When I was the CEO of Carlsberg, the following were my principles for brand-building through people:

1. I had to deliver the vision of the company and brand essence to all the new senior management during orientation programs.
2. General managers in the region needed to be the key people conducting orientation programs for newcomers.
3. All new marketing programs needed to be presented to internal staff and business partners before the official campaign launched.

RY: Is the Carlsberg brand in China or Hong Kong different from the brand in the overseas market? Why so?

SW: Like many other multinational FMCG brands, Carlsberg is also moving towards one consistent brand around the world. With the Internet eliminating geographical borders, we are basically one global market. There are, of course, local differences in trade marketing, below-the-line activities, and price positioning. The bitterness level may slightly differ among Carlsberg beers in various markets. Yet the brand personality should be consistent across the world.

RY: After going through so many mergers and acquisitions, how can you maintain brand consistency across all companies in the same market?

SW: Though there are over 50 local breweries in China, most of the acquired breweries only focus on brewing and marketing locally acquired brands in their regions. Carlsberg's standard brand-building and marketing processes are used for local brand-building. Carlsberg beers can only be brewed in very selective plants where the production meets Carlsberg's unique standards. Whether it is Carlsberg or local, regional brands (like Dali Beer in Yunnan Province, Xixia Beer in Ningxia, and Wusu Beer in Xinjiang), we establish clear and well-documented guidelines on brand positioning and communicate extensively to relevant stake owners. At the same time, we need to set up an approval and control process to ensure compliance.

One key factor of Carlsberg's success in China is its decision to market each of the brands separately and hence create its own positioning in the mind of consumers. The brands are competitors on the surface but companions in retail outlets. One typical example is the collaboration between Asahi (we obtained the distribution rights in Hong Kong in 2010) and Carlsberg. In Hong Kong, Carlsberg expanded its distribution to Japanese restaurants while Asahi had the chance to enter other outlets. All this helped Carlsberg form a strong alignment against other premium brands. In early 2000, we successfully turned Carlsberg Greater China into multi-brand companies instead of purely a Carlsberg company.

Notes

1 Maslow, A. H. "A Theory of Human Motivation." *Psychological Review* 50, no. 4 (1943): 370–96. doi: org/10.1037/h0054346.
2 Carlsberg Group. "Who We Are." Accessed October 5, 2020. https://www.carlsber ggroup.com/who-we-are/about-the-carlsberg-group/our-rich-heritage/.

7

FROM MICRO TO MACRO ANALYSIS

FIGURE 7.1 Examining the functional aspect of a brand.

The bigger the organization, the more difficult and challenging it is to manage a brand. Yet if we look at some of the most successful disruptive brands, we see that the growth of their scale has not compromised their passion. They often start with a few like-minded individuals coming together to offer something new to the market. They establish a rapport by working seamlessly as a team with an aligned vision and future direction. Their workplace is the training ground for teamwork, and they figure out a way to complement and accept each other. Then when the entity grows bigger, the founders are conscious of implementing a system and work procedures without diluting the mindset and spirit of a startup. They are also able to bring in more professional managers to support the expansion of the company. To seize growing market opportunities, the product offerings will further evolve and become more structured and sophisticated. By leveraging technology and a sharing economy business model, they can expand quickly to become a global brand. They all share one common success factor – they have a robust corporate culture of which the brand is an integral part.

Most, if not all, brands aspire to become international one day. Even smaller brands that only focus on the domestic market will be compared against international standards by users. For instance, when consumers buy surgical masks for infection prevention during COVID-19, they will check whether the products meet the ASTM or European Standards, regardless of their place of origin. Consumers these days are very informed. They can access all the essential information online. Even if they do not actively surf the Internet, contacts within their social circle will share all the most current and relevant information with them. Depending on the nature of the product category, a brand must comply with both micro and macro operating environments. It is like getting a pass to enter the race – brand-owners must be aware of and factor in all these market fundamentals for the strategic planning of their businesses.

Corporate – brand is culture

Brand-building should always start from within the corporation. This is why the most critical decision that a corporation has to make is to hire the right people. These days, many companies still focus on hiring good people only in terms of their skills and experience. Granted, having the required skills and quality is a prerequisite. Yet a staff member who possesses the needed skills but does not fit the corporate culture will find it hard to perform. If a brand is a set of values, then the corporation should operate according to the philosophy behind the brand. Richard Branson has always emphasized putting employees above customers. I concur with his point, not because customers are less important, but because their experience will depend on how much the staff understands and embraces the brand vision. In other words, brand-building is not just the job of the marketing department. Anyone who bears the name card of the corporation is, by default, a brand ambassador because people will judge the corporate brand based on this individual's behavior. As mentioned in Chapter Three, under the section "personal branding," we all are ourselves a brand. If you follow this logic, you will understand why nurturing a corporate culture is so paramount. Strategically, the personal branding of the staff must synchronize with the corporate branding direction. If the quality, attitude, and working style of staff do not align with the brand, the work they do every day dilutes the equity of the brand. This is part of the *brand behavior* that we explained under the topic of *brand virtues*.

Disney Parks and Resorts are the largest theme park operator in the world. The way they successfully promote a Disney culture around the globe through their staff is incredible. Whether you are in Tokyo, Orlando, or Shanghai, their "cast members" will always greet you with a smile and open arms. In their park, you can only find "Imagineers," imaginative engineers responsible for the design and implementation of creative ideas. Staff members play a similarly important role at Starbucks. People working at Starbucks in black aprons are known as "Coffee Masters," trained baristas who are knowledgeable about all things coffee. They not only enjoy their work more, but also pass on their passion and love of coffee to the customers. Sometimes, a brand does not need a person to convey its brand culture. The famous rubber duck that sits by every bathtub in Conrad Hotels has reinforced the brand's dedication and attention to detail plus its commitment to making every guest's stay a pleasant and homey one. The small teddy bear that wears a Conrad T-shirt and leans on a big, soft pillow is a perfect take-home gift for the kid who misses his or her parent who has been away for a business trip. It is a fantastic way for Conrad to show that they care about the people the customers care about most.

Context – brand is trends

Disruptive brands can transform a market and redefine an industry because they are trend-setters. Consumers will follow the trends that make sense to them. In this digital era, consumers are the most powerful publisher. They are quick and direct in reporting the latest and coolest happenings in the market. Furthermore, because they are users themselves, their comments are credible. If a large number of consumers support a trend, it will soon become the new market norm. Empowered by social media that reaches every corner of the world, consumers can create a trend and turn it into a norm much faster than marketers can anticipate. Without the recognition and the vote of confidence from a big cheering crowd, disruptive brands would not have been able to reach the threshold so quickly and scale up to an influential position that no one can ignore.

A manufacturer may be immensely proud of its product and how it is made. But if it falls behind the market trends, it will be unlikely to make it in this increasingly competitive world. Big and traditional manufacturers must watch out for the smaller DTC (direct to customers) brands that are incredibly agile and can respond swiftly to the changing tastes and expectations of consumers. A substitute can turn into a major threat if it is in line with market trends because those are what the consumers want. No one will waste money or time considering old technologies or out-of-style products. The following are five megatrends that every marketer must be aware of to make sure their products and services are designed according to where the market is heading in the future. Depending on the type of industry, some of these trends are more relevant and critical to some brands than others:

Green total

"Green marketing" is nothing new, but the magnitude of its market adoption has magnified so much in recent years that it will disrupt a variety of industries. This manifestation is apparent in the automotive industry. Moving from petrol to alternative energy for fueling car engines has been on the agenda for all automobile manufacturers for decades. Much work has been done in the lab as far as research and development (R&D) is concerned. But the speed of rolling out newer types of vehicles has been slower than the market expected, possibly due to their fear of cannibalizing the existing "bread and butter" business. This paradigm shift may also be opening the market to new competitors who want to challenge the same batch of car brands that have dominated the global market for years. The tipping point comes when all three critical factors that determine an industry's future – the government, the industry, and the consumers – move towards the same direction.

According to France's ecology minister, who is determined to drive the green revolution, France is set to ban the sale of any car that uses petrol or diesel fuel by 2040.[1] There are countries such as Norway working on an even more aggressive timeline for prohibiting the sales of fossil fuel cars. Countries like China and Germany, which are both prominent car manufacturing nations, are selecting cities as forerunners to join this global transformation. Legislation has the most direct and immediate impact on business operations. Still, governments perceive a significant change of policies as a two-edged sword and will be extremely cautious when passing new laws. This movement, however, is a road of no return, and the action of one country will imply that of others, especially those that belong to the same geographical region.

Electric cars were never at the top of many car-owners' shopping lists until the arrival of Tesla. What makes Tesla an exceptional new market entrant is the man behind this brand, who is synonymous with the word "disruption": Elon Musk. From PayPal to Space X to SolarCity, Musk has never bored the market with his ideas for changing the world. Tesla has also openly announced its corporate strategy to first produce a small quantity of more pricey vehicles. Then, when both the production capacity and the users are ready, the business will be sustained with much more affordable models. As a brand, Tesla is more than electric cars. It holds a much larger symbolic meaning as a pioneer in leading change for good. Consumers are not only intrigued by the Tesla brand, they are also assured that the government's commitment to move towards a "greener environment" will ensure that the right infrastructure for supporting eco-friendly vehicles is put in place. When more car-owners open their minds to accept electric cars, mainstream manufacturers will be more inclined to move to "fifth gear" for the market transformation.

"Green Total" incorporates green marketing, sustainability, and more. It is a new undertaking that forms part of the fabric of forward-looking corporations. It is an orchestrated effort from the very beginning to the end of the entire business operation based on an ideology of respecting and embracing nature. It is not about pleasing specific market segments or meeting any compliance requirements set by the government or key clients. It is about a new mindset that revolves around a "greener" way of operating a business. Brand owners have to rethink and redesign their business process as going green is a megatrend that will shape the future of many industries. In short, a greener brand is a more preferred brand.

The other industry that has no choice but to confront "green total" is beverage manufacturers, particularly those that consume and create a substantial amount of plastic for producing bottled water. Now, almost all major brands of bottled water try to use less plastic or move towards using recycled plastic. Furthermore, most water bottles are collapsible and squeezable these days, so they occupy less space during the disposal or recycling process. Watsons Water is one of the pioneers that drives this change. It has set the benchmark for the industry by applying 100% rPET since 2015.[2] Nowadays, more and more manufacturers are following this practice. Watsons Water has stepped up its leadership role to deploy and manage a first-of-its-kind bottle recycling network. It has formed a cross-sector network of recycling partnerships, which includes various stakeholders from shopping malls, retail shops, schools, and stadiums to social enterprises across all prominent districts in Hong Kong (Image 7.1).

To normalize the concept of "commercialized sustainability," Watsons Water encourages consumers to participate in the movement through a combination of education and incentives. To make a real impact on the market, Watsons Water understands it takes more than just voluntary efforts from the users. By tapping its customer relationship management (CRM) program "Watsons Water Drops of Fun" and partnering with AlipayHK, it supports reverse vending machine (RVM) with a robust incentive mechanism. For every returned empty bottle of Watsons Water, the user will be rewarded with HKD 20 cents. If the user returns another brand of the plastic water bottle, they will be compensated with half the value.[3] The process is easy and almost self-explanatory.

IMAGE 7.1 Watsons Water launched the reverse vending machine (RVM) to take recycling to the next level. Credit: Watsons Water.

After opening the app and scanning the barcode printed on the bottle, all the user has to do is drop the bottle via the recycling entrance, and the machine will scan and recognize whether it is a plastic bottle (Images 7.2, 7.3 and 7.4). It will compress the bottle and prepare it to enter the next phase of recycling. Completing this step is an integral part of the whole logistics management process.

As the name implies, the cash rebate is not the main attraction; it is the "fun" and "feel good" element that motivates people to participate. The user can collect Watsons Water Recycling Green Points via the app for redeeming different prizes. The app also facilitates the collaboration between Watsons Water and various merchants, creating multiple-party interactions and increasing the appeal and stickiness of the app to users (Images 7.5, 7.6 and 7.7).

IMAGE 7.2 The "Watsons Water Drops of Fun" mobile app and RVM work as systems to engage and reward customers. Credit: Watsons Water.

Recycling Green Point Usage Guide ✕

3 Insert the empty plastic water bottle

4 Redeem gifts with Green Points earned instantly

IMAGE 7.3 The "Watsons Water Drops of Fun" mobile app and RVM work as systems to engage and reward customers. Credit: Watsons Water.

Health total

Consumers all over the world are becoming more health conscious. That is why almost all beverage brands have a "diet" version. Confectionery products have added vitamins as a selling point, catering businesses include lighter or more vegetarian dishes on the menu, and even smartphones automatically switch to "dark mode" in the evening to reduce eye strain. The other global phenomenon is the rise in the aging population due to lower fertility rates and longer life expectancy, especially in more developed countries and cities. For instance, according to government statistics, the elderly population (people aged 65 or above) in Hong Kong will almost double in size (2.44 million) and share (31.9%) between 2018 and 2038.[4] Insurance and wealth management industries have long been targeting this "silver grey" segment. Even for travel and leisure, special packages

IMAGE 7.4 The "Watsons Water Drops of Fun" mobile app and RVM work as systems to engage and reward customers. Credit: Watsons Water.

are developed to cater to this group of customers with less physically demanding itineraries. These changing demographics have urged brand-owners to continually review their product portfolio to ensure their offerings will be in line with the appetite of today's consumers.

The pandemic has further intensified the demand for infection control, a prerequisite for giving customers a peace of mind when they patronize a physical venue. Brand-owners may expand the scope of their quality assurance team, or even set up a new department dedicated to studying, implementing and monitoring a broad spectrum of health and hygiene-related issues. These issues can range from product development to business operation, which will all form part of the scorecard for brand performance.

Equality total

An enduring brand is one that is liked, respected, and trusted by people. To live up to this expectation, a brand has to be more than just competent. As we have

IMAGE 7.5 The app is an innovative way to track users' behavior and preferences, as well as a platform to promote multiple-party collaborations. Credit: Watsons Water.

seen, there have been numerous cases where a brand faces severe criticism or even a consumer boycott because its advertising contains messaging that directly or indirectly invokes social stigma.

Discrimination of any kind is not acceptable, especially among young and liberal consumers these days. This is particularly crucial for global brands that have a presence across various markets. They have to be all-encompassing as every country will have its specific sensitivities due to unique historical, cultural, or religious backgrounds.

This commitment to equality should be embedded in the workplace and gradually become part of corporate values. This will nurture a culture that genuinely looks after the interest of any minority groups, making it unlikely for the corporation to be in an unfavorable position. Individuals with any

IMAGE 7.6 The app is an innovative way to track users' behavior and preferences, as well as a platform to promote multiple-party collaborations. Credit: Watsons Water.

accessibility needs should also be considered so that their rights will be fully respected.

Connect total

The pandemic is a catalyst for the digitization of business operations around the globe. Consumers now expect most of their interactions with brands to be performed online with a mobile device, and door-to-door delivery is practically an expected service. "Connect Total" is more than just using marketing automation, shifting the business online, or adopting an omnichannel approach. These initiatives are mainly driven by intentions to improve operational efficiency or investment returns. By contrast, "Connect Total" is totally customer-centric and

IMAGE 7.7 The app is an innovative way to track users' behavior and preferences, as well as a platform to promote multiple-party collaborations. Credit: Watsons Water.

plans out the entire customer journey from the user's perspective. It is also about building an emotional connection with customers and anticipating their changing needs under different circumstances. It is through this value creation to the customers that the value of the business can be further enhanced.

Smart total

Smart homes and smart cities are becoming a reality. They are no longer marketing gimmicks, and they are not only within the reach of the privileged class. "Smart Total" is about making all walks of life safer, more convenient, and more satisfying. It is indeed a new way of living. The advancement of technology has created more intelligent ways to work, learn, and play. Hardware and equipment are becoming more accessible and better performing. They are also more compatible and connected in such a way that they will form a network to facilitate higher efficiency. Data-driven decision science can predict what we need before we even recognize our needs. The deployment of 5G has further reshaped the economy and shown that "what can be imagined can be achieved." Every brand has to reexamine its product design, features, customer interface, and total service delivery. When customers get smarter, they will expect brands to be smarter, too.

A brand-builder's perspective

Interview with TK Wong, Founder of TKMW Creative

Mr. TK Wong is a veteran in the creative industry. He has been managing his creative agency, TKMW, for over ten years. Before starting his agency, Mr. Wong was the Head of Creative for Brand Union in Hong Kong. He was involved in the creation of numerous iconic brands such as Hong Kong Post, HK Polytechnic University, Vocational Training Council, China Resources, China Oil and Foodstuffs Corporation, Jardines, and OCT.

Royce Yuen: What is a logomark? What is the relationship between the "logo" and the "brand"?

TK Wong: The logomark is the signature of a company. It can represent a company's name, vision, values, or founder.

When I approach a project, the first question I ask myself is – is this a "branding" or "design" issue? The problems we have to tackle differ depending on the nature of the project.

Branding and design can be separated in my view. A logo can exist without branding. It can simply be a nice design, like a badge you put up in your reception area.

Branding can also be fine without a logo per se, but it would work better with one.

A brand can exist without a strong visual component. Take General Electric, for example. You know what they do, but their name may not make consumers picture a particular visual, especially if they live outside the United States. They may have heard the name and great things about it in the news but may not have any visual registration. They are not designers or marketers. How they learn and what they want to know about a corporation is probably quite different from us.

But visual clues help with memory retention. All iconic brands may own a color within their product category (e.g., Starbucks is green, McDonald's is red, Oral B is blue, China Resources is yellow). And if you dig deeper, there is usually a story behind each logo. For instance, when I designed the logo for China Resources, a conglomerate that is engaged in real estate, retail, power, pharmaceutical, finance, etc., I started with an overall vision of the group rather than the graphic treatment. The logo of China Resources is made up of four characters that mean "people" since the group is committed to serving the people and adding values to their lives. Some people may not understand the symbolism right away, so we also communicate the backstory with them at appropriate times and through the right channels.

RY: What constitutes a great logo?

TKW: First of all, a great logo has to be distinctive so that it will stand out from the crowd and be easily recognized (e.g. Mickey ears = Disney, three strips = Adidas). Equally important is whether it can truly represent the company so that it is not just visually appealing, but also has a strong association with the brand.

That's why I always prefer to meet with the business owner or the senior management to understand how the business started. Usually, I am amazed by how these leaders have had a laser-sharp focus since the very beginning and built a sizable organization that is still centered on their original vision. My job is to translate all these wonderful stories into a visual language that connects people and invites them to learn more about the organization.

RY: Has the concept and/or expression of logo design changed in this digital era?

TKW: I always say that my work is about branding-design, not graphic design. As such, my role with organizations will continue no matter how the market has evolved.

The way to express ideas may be fancier with the use of digital technology, but the philosophy and principles behind logo design remain the same.

I do believe designers have to be more than designers these days. They have to look at things from the perspective of the business owner, to see how they can help solve problems or build bridges to the public.

A designer is like a visualizer who partners with the business owner to crop out unnecessary elements so that what matters will not be buried. That's why the design team and the brand-owners have to work together as a team.

RY: What is the challenge of logo design in this digital era?

TKW: In my opinion, we (as branding designers) are facing mounting challenges in this digital era, such that our job is becoming much more difficult than it used to be.

Firstly, due to advances in digital technology, everything, and I mean *everything*, seems to be accessible by a simple click, i.e., what you want to know, see, check, and search. This goes beyond the imagination of someone like me who came from the 1990s, a "stone age" where we needed to visit the public library just to dig up past annual reports of our clients. Now, every reference is less than a minute away from Google (or Baidu, depending on your location). As such, when a designer is working on a particular project (in any area), he can find whatever he needs via the Internet, and there are a few handy sites that can provide countless samples as reference or inspirations.

These sites may sound like a useful resource for designers. Yet they also create much harm at the same time; visual resemblance becomes a big issue when everything looks similar. We have a slang in our industry, "it looks very Pinterest." Even worse, it's not only designers who love going through these sites for inspiration (including myself), but also the clients. They may not be deliberately going to get some designs, but if they browse around some popular sites, they will see interesting content.

Moreover, I think this is an era where everyone can be a designer because almost everyone has a laptop. This has created another hurdle for us; if someone on Taobao can charge RMB100 (USD 15) for a whole set of the brand visual system with unlimited rounds of revisions, we as professional designers need to justify our professional charging system. The latest artificial intelligence (AI) technology has been employed in some overseas design sites; people can get their logo made quickly by answering a sequence of questions. After all, we're producing the same product visually by using a similar technique and similar ingredients such as colors, shapes, fonts, etc.

Sometimes, I remind my clients that I won't be able to show them any shape or color they haven't seen before. But what I promise them is that I can suggest a solution that means something to them.

That's why a proper and thorough discussion with the decision-maker of the company before the design process commences is key for me. There will be a slightly bigger chance to create something comparatively unique that comes originally from them. Nowadays, half the job (sometimes more than half) is not just designing, but visualizing the client's vision, value, and character (the company's character), and envisioning the agreed strategy or their business nature. Therefore, they will see part of "themselves" in the visual product we present at the end.

Human interaction is so inspiring and yet very unpredictable, which becomes a weapon we can use to win the battle of designing something both visually unique and meaningful at the same time.

According to my experience in branding design, my client always surprises me by giving me the inspiration for a seed of an idea during our conversation. The end result is quite often satisfactory. After all, communication is the root of design, although we sometimes easily overlook it.

Case study – China Resources
I always like to share the story of how we created the China Resources (CR) logo. The more I think about it, the more I believe it is a perfect case of logic meets magic. In meetings, the CEO kept saying that the brand will be all about "people" and how to improve people's lives. Of course, CR's main focus was on mainland China, not Hong Kong. Also, as one of the most crucial state-owned enterprises, they were tasked to implement policies from the central government. At the same time, he wanted CR to differ from typical traditional state-owned enterprises. Hence, he wanted a revolutionary approach to designing the logo; this is the logic part.

| Old logo of China Resources | The first character of China Resources is made up of four words of "people" | New logo of China Resources |

IMAGE 7.8 An illustration of the process of the creation of the China Resources logo.

Now here is the magic part; as my team was busy scribbling all sorts of ideas after I briefed them properly, I was casually flipping books with a cup of coffee in my hand one afternoon (see, I still can remember the scene that took place many years ago, in 2002) when I came across a Chinese calligraphy dictionary. There was no Google at the time, and I wanted to see if there were any interesting elements in the character *hua* that we could use, since it is part of CR's name and denotes "China." All of a sudden, I found a particular *hua* written by the famous ancient calligrapher Yan Zhenqing. The character that was peculiar because he wrote *hua* with four arrows inside, something that people would typically never do. However, each little arrow looked like the Chinese character for "people" to me. I found this wonderful, and then the biggest invisible light bulb lit up in my head. I walked back to my desk and carried out a straightforward yet modern rendering of what I saw within a small box. I made the box yellow, moved the four little arrows slightly towards the right, and removed the border lines (otherwise, the logo may look like the character for "prisoner") (Image 7.8). The whole process took less than 20 minutes. That layout later became the CR logo we know today. Seriously, this kind of "magic" has only happened once in my career.

Case study – Lee Kum Kee

A brand that never ages

Lee Kum Kee was established in 1888 when its founder Mr. Lee Kum Sheung invented oyster sauce in Nanshui, Guangdong. With a glorious history of over 100 years, Lee Kum Kee has become an international household name as well as a symbol of quality and trust. With "Promoting Chinese Cuisines Worldwide" as its mission, Lee Kum Kee provides over 200 sauces and condiments to over 100 countries and regions. The best-kept secret is often in the details – a simple, flavorful sauce can supply the magic behind any delightful meal. Lee Kum Kee is totally committed to ensuring high quality from farm to fork, bringing out the best in cooking and helping consumers serve up a sumptuous meal every time. Apart from focusing on condiments, Lee Kum Kee Group has also expanded to more businesses through LKK Health Products Group, turning the group into a modern enterprise with diversified business operations (Image 7.9).[5]

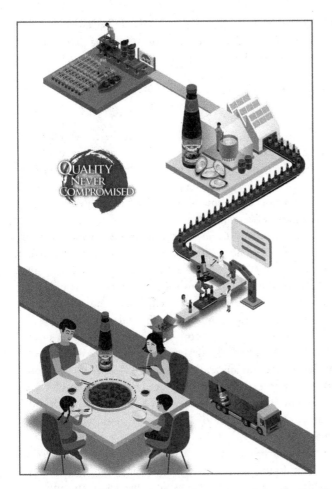

IMAGE 7.9 Lee Kum Kee is more than a sauce. It is a "taste of home." Credit: lkk.com.

Interview with David Lee, Chairman of Lee Kum Kee Family Foundation

Mr. David Lee started up the US operation of Lee Kum Kee Sauce Group in 1982 when he first joined the family business after graduation. He has served in various senior management positions at the Lee Kum Kee Sauce Group over the past 30 years, including as Managing Director overseeing the Worldwide Food Division, Chairman and CEO of Lee Kum Kee (USA) Inc., Lee Kum Kee (Europe). He took up the chairmanship of the Lee Kum Kee Sauce Group between 2009 and 2011. Mr. Lee also has extensive experience in building the family governance system for the Lee Kum Kee family. He has been a Family Council member since 2002, and previously took on chairmanship in the Family Office from 2012 to 2014 and the Family Learning and Development Centre from 2006 to 2008. Mr. Lee was reappointed to the position in 2017. Mr. Lee has served as Chairman of the

Lee Kum Kee Family Foundation since January 2013. He was awarded Chapter Honoree, Hong Kong Baptist University Chapter of Beta Gamma Sigma for his outstanding business and managerial leadership in 2014.

Royce Yuen: What makes Lee Kum Kee such as a special brand that can stand the test of time?

David Lee: Lee Kum Kee is a brand that has a very strong heritage and set of values. This is something that can be shared and felt by different stakeholders. Lee Kum Kee produces basic products, yet they are an essential part of everyday life. It is a genuine and non-flashy brand that enjoys an approachable image. At the same time, our dedication and commitment to quality have helped us uphold a premium position in the mind of consumers.

For a brand that is over 100 years old, the "trustworthiness" element is most critical. The users' own experience and positive word of mouth are what made the Lee Kum Kee brand what it is today. The whole product was created to give overseas Chinese the "taste of home" while most of them worked as unskilled laborers far from home, living a tough life. As such, the brand was actually imported back to this part of the world after it became popular overseas.

The brand obviously serves consumers in both the East and the West nowadays. Consumers around the world share one common interest, which is the desire for a tasty meal that is safe and authentic. Lee Kum Kee is the best companion for people cooking at home. It helps bring out the natural flavor of ingredients. The brand is synonymous with oyster sauce but has extended its product lines to cover hundreds of different kinds of condiments, making it a perfect complement to almost any dish.

Lee Kum Kee is a wholesome brand, and we are committed to giving back to the community. Our family foundation is dedicated to bringing happiness and harmony to families, which has been our mission since the very beginning.

RY: How can an established brand with more than a hundred years of history embrace different generations of consumers?

DL: Our brand helps people create stories of love and passes down virtues from one generation to another. This bond between people, especially between parents and children, will never go out of date. Our society may become more affluent, and there may be changes in lifestyle as time goes by, but the fundamental needs and desires of human beings remain the same. Nothing can replace the warmth and care of family members. Lee Kum Kee serves as the bridge that connects people and helps them to remember all these precious moments.

RY: People are cooking less at home and dining out more often. Would this limit the chance for the Lee Kum Kee brand to interact with the consumers?

DL: Our brand is very strong in the catering sector. Professional chefs and restaurants highly appreciate our products (Image 7.10). We also have products that are suitable for the different budget levels of restaurant operators. As a result,

IMAGE 7.10 The Executive Chinese Chef at Four Seasons Hotel (HK) is the first Chinese chef to gain three Michelin Stars through his delicately flavored Cantonese seafood dishes with a touch of French cuisine – truffles and foie gras. Credit: lkkprofessional.com.

we can maintain a close relationship with our customers. That said, we try to innovate and find new ways to convey our brand messages so that we will stay at the forefront of our consumers' minds. We treasure every encounter with our customers, and we understand it is the quality of each contact and not just the quantity of connections that counts. We will continue to hold on to our beliefs and principles, serve our customers with the best quality of products, and enrich people's lives in multi-dimensional ways – including, but not limited to, our corporate social responsibility initiatives. We will never take the "trust" that consumers have in us for granted. With the world coming together as one global village, one borderless market, we believe there is a lot of room for our brand to grow. The key is to stay cross-generational and cross-cultural by tapping the common soft spots of human nature. If we can do this, our brand can maintain its strong heritage but never age; it can continue to convey something meaningful for many generations to come.

Notes

1 "France Set to Ban Sale of Petrol and Diesel Vehicles by 2040." *BBC News*, July 6, 2017, sec. Europe. https://www.bbc.com/news/world-europe-40518293.
2 Watsons Water. "Viral Statistics." Accessed October 6, 2020. https://www.aswatson-careers.com/about-us/our-brands/watsons-water/.

3 MoneyBack. "Watsons Water Green Point Smart Water Bottle Reverse Vending Machine," 2019. https://www.moneyback.com.hk/en/about/corporate-social -responsibility/bottle-recycling.

4 Wong, Kelvin, and Matthew Yeung. "Population Ageing Trend in Hong Kong." The Government of Hong Kong Special Administrative Region, January 2019.

5 Lee Kum Kee. "Corporate Overview." Accessed October 6, 2020. https://usa.lkk .com/en/corporate/about-lkk/overview.

8

FROM STAYING IN TUNE TO STAYING IN TOUCH

FIGURE 8.1   Examining the aspirational aspect of a brand.

The Pepsi Challenge is an ongoing marketing campaign launched by PepsiCo in 1975 to challenge its competitor Coca-Cola as well as the taste buds of cola drinkers.[1] The challenge is a simple idea that is easy to execute and equally easy for consumers to understand. It is a blind taste test, where passers-by are asked to taste two different glasses of cola (with the logo hidden from view) and then pick the one they prefer. The campaign claims that most of the people who have taken challenges prefer Pepsi to Coke. The campaign returned again in the summer of 2019, featuring Pepsi Max in major European markets such as the UK. Aside from its ability to convert certain Coke drinkers to switch to Pepsi, the noise that the campaign generates has had an overwhelmingly positive impact on the Pepsi brand.

But some may ask: if the campaign is so successful, why does it have to continue for half a century? Wouldn't all Coke drinkers be Pepsi fans by now? This is an observation that shows how consumers may pick a drink (or any product in this regard) not purely because of its taste or physical attributes. Again, it reinforces the idea that consumer behavior is never totally rational. In fact, the strategy behind the Pepsi Challenge is not to ask people to buy what tastes better to them but to be more self-aware and avoid insensate conformity. Many young people in the 1980s preferred Pepsi not necessarily because of its taste but due to its rebellious, "challenger" image that was appealing to them – hence Pepsi's former slogan, "The Choice of a New Generation."

The Pepsi case affirms that finding a workable and engaging way to communicate, contact, and connect with consumers is absolutely critical for the successful acquisition and retention of customers. Any brand that fails to do so is alienating itself from its current and potential users and will never be recognized even if it has the best product offering in the market.

Connection – brand is meaning

Before a brand starts to approach its target customer, it must first pinpoint why people should be interested in it. Please take a moment to look at the following images (Image 8.1). Then, without overthinking, pick the brand from the list of logos underneath that you believe is best represented by these images. There is

IMAGE 8.1 Look at the collage above. Then, without over-analyzing, pick the brand underneath that you believe can best represent these images.

no right or wrong answer for this test, and it has nothing to do with your IQ, so feel free to pick any brand that you feel has the strongest association with these images.

This exercise reveals how we as consumers connect with a brand. Interestingly, this connection extends beyond the physical product, although the product is part of the mechanism that delivers the promise made by the brand. Throughout the day, consumers subconsciously pick up different clues or signals sent out by the brand. If these clues make sense to them and are somehow related to each other, consumers will assemble a mental collage and store this visual image in their brains. These images will be associated with certain needs or desires. Once this need arises or is triggered, consumers will look for the brand that has the strongest association with their particular desire. It is not uncommon for more than one brand within the same product category to try and own this association. Still, usually only one brand will stand out in the minds of consumers. Maybe because it was the first to step into this territory, or it has been repeatedly building this association, or perhaps it can show the consumers convincing evidence to justify its occupation of this position. If you chose Starbucks in the exercise above, you will be pleased to know that 99% of people who have tried this game also picked the same answer as you. I have conducted this experiment with my MBA classes multiple times, and they all arrive at the same conclusion. When students are asked to explain why they chose Starbucks, their usual answer is that the images convey a feeling of *relaxation* to them.

Starbucks' relaxing vibe may explain why it is so popular around the world, even though it was not the first store to sell coffee. In some Asian markets where coffee is an imported concept, Starbucks is even synonymous with coffee. Some people who are not regular coffee drinkers consider Starbucks one of their favorite brands, and think of it as a common meeting place for hanging out with colleagues during break time. This shows that people like Starbucks not because of its coffee or at least not the coffee alone. In fact, Starbucks probably realized this in 2011 when it dropped the words "Starbucks Coffee" from the outer ring of its original logo.[2] Now, the Starbucks logo only retains the firm's white and green image of a twin-tailed siren. This move makes perfect sense for Starbucks, given its global corporate strategy. Its future growth will rely on its market penetration into non-coffee-drinking countries outside the United States and Europe.

Consciously or subconsciously, consumers actively engage with brands all the time. While decoding different brands, they filter out those that are irrelevant or lack personal appeal. The brands that can build a lasting connection with consumers are the ones that relate to them somehow. In other words, *branding is not what you do. It is what you stand for.* In the case of Starbucks, its stands for relaxation. Generally, Starbucks stores have a comfortable environment and cozy ambiance. But most of them, with the exception of a few, have limited seating. If the feeling of relaxation is conveyed solely through the physical environment, the brand can only entertain 12 or maybe 15 people at one time. What is magical about branding is that the positive transformation it brings about can take place in a physical environment or in our mind. Even if I am just ordering a coffee to go, I somehow feel relaxed as long as I am holding the Starbucks coffee in my hand. To the users, the product holds tangible and symbolic meanings. Coffee contains the caffeine that give us the *physical* boost to stay awake. On top of this, Starbucks as a brand also provides *mental* refreshment. Because this transformation happens in our mind, the magnitude to which customers can feel satisfied with the brand is limitless. As such, people prefer to go to Starbucks even if they can get a cheaper coffee of similar quality elsewhere. To them, paying five US dollars for a black coffee maybe expensive, but it's a small price to pay in exchange for feeling relaxed and re-energized.

Iconic figures like Martin Luther King, James Dean, and Bruce Lee are great examples of "brands" with tremendous meaning. "I have a dream" is not only one of the most frequently cited quotes by today's politicians, it also captures a phenomenal meaning that resonates with almost anyone. "Rebel without a cause" is a sentiment that every young generation can relate to although they may interpret it differently over the years. "Be water" is a philosophy that emphasizes the importance of adaptability, a key skill in practicing martial arts or dealing with any challenge in life. What these legends represent are larger than who they are. Their values will last beyond their physical lifetimes.

The same goes for brands. If a brand can truly represent an important value to people, it will possess the quality to endure for generations. In a digital age where consumers have abundant choices, a brand cannot remain merely a concept. It must offer tangible values to the people it serves, or it will be easily replaced. Evian is not just premium bottled water from France. It represents vitality and youthfulness, which are essential elements that allow people to live their lives to the fullest. Water is a simple commodity if it is undifferentiated. As such, Evian uniquely positions its water both conceptually and very tangibly at the same time, saying that its water "gets its unique cool, crisp taste from its fifteen-year journey through the French Alps" and crediting nature for giving their water "everything it needs."[3]

Nothing is more precious than what mother nature has given us. That is why Evian is priced higher than most bottled water and is still well sought after by many people. People treasure the value that the brand represents and are assured by the quality of the product. To endure, *a brand must stand for a set of intangible values that can be translated into tangible meaning and have a lasting impact on people's lives.*

Communication – brand is dialogue

There are two pediatricians in my neighborhood. One clinic is always packed with patients while the other one is almost at least half-empty most of the time. The two clinics are within walking distance, but parents would rather wait for hours to see one pediatrician than allow their kids to be attended by the other pediatrician immediately. My curious nature has driven me to find out why.

The results of my investigation are very insightful. The two doctors graduated from the same medical school and have comparable years of work experience and credentials. They both served at the same public hospital before starting their private practices. And the fee they charge is almost identical, probably because they are quite close to each other. The only notable difference, as far as I can see, is the shape of the medicine bottle that they use. The pediatrician with an empty clinic uses normal medicine bottles while his counterpart gives away the medicine in bear-shaped bottles (Image 8.2). Apparently, this makes little difference to the kids (the consumers) as the content tastes the same no matter which container is used. But the bear-shape bottle can mean a lot to the moms (the customers) as they feel more assured by the pediatrician who is seemingly more caring and attentive to kids. The popular pediatrician may not be a better doctor, but he is certainly a better marketer. He manages to find a way to communicate with parents by promoting his brand (friendly, caring, and approachable) without doing any promotion. Once the parents have visited his clinic, which has the right atmosphere and lots of toys, plus a receptionist who always wears a smile, they have all the good reasons to stick to this doctor.

Speaking of bottles, Coca-Cola launched their "Share a Coke" campaign in Australia in 2011 and then rolled out globally.[4] The campaign prints popular names onto the wrapping paper of Coke bottles, such that you could buy a bottle with your own or your friend's name on it. The campaign has been a huge success around the world and has helped Coca-Cola connect with consumers using their local language, which is a fantastic way to localize a global brand and facilitate conversation among users. In markets like the US and Australia, you can even personalize your own Coke bottle (with your preferred flavor) to say,

IMAGE 8.2 A medicine bottle can say a lot about the doctor.

for example, "Share a Coke with Sonia" or "Share a Coke with Hillary." The online ordering process takes only a few clicks and your personalized Coke will be delivered to your destination in around one to two weeks. In this new age of marketing, even fast-moving consumer goods (FMCG) products must consider incorporating personalization into their campaigns.

In Chapter Three, we saw how the "Best Job in the World" campaign is one of the best examples of creative communication. The contest of applying for the dream job of being Queensland's island caretaker generated substantial media coverage over an extensive period of time. Another highly successful communication strategy built on a recruitment campaign is "The Toughest Job in the World."[5] The campaign started off with a recruitment ad that required candidates to attend a job interview online. All the candidates were completely shocked to learn during their interview that the job demanded an unbelievable level of commitment and sacrifice, with absolutely no pay at all. Only just before the interview was about to wrap up did they learn that this imaginary job is in fact practiced all over the world – by mothers. The viral campaign, created by American Greetings to promote Mother's Day, shows us that brand communication today is no longer just about image advertising. It commands a different way of storytelling. The traditional way of communicating a brand message is no longer able to cut through the clutter, partly because consumers are relying less on passive media to receive information. Pushing an ad by disrupting the audience's consumption of some other content rarely works these days. The only communication that works is the type of communication that the audience *wants* to interact with. If they like the content, they will voluntarily share it with their friends, which may lead to impressive results both in terms of reach and lead generation.

In the disruptive age, consumers are constantly bombarded by information and commercial messages that are directed to them based on their browsing history. To meet the changing expectations of their audience, brand-owners must adopt a new discipline in storytelling and design their communication campaigns according to the following Five As of Advertising:

Authenticity

Audiences today do not expect to see squeaky-clean characters in a story. Even animated films produced by Disney or DreamWorks no longer feature your typical Prince Charming, who is less appealing to today's audiences because he is not genuine. In Disney's *Tangled* (2010), the long-haired Rapunzel locked up in a tower is saved not by a prince, but a thief named Flynn. He is not a perfect guy, but has a good heart. Three years later, Disney released *Frozen*, a story about an ice princess named Elsa and her sister Anna. Although Anna initially believes that the seemingly charming Prince Hans will be her true love, she (and the audience) instead falls for Kristoff, a grumpy and clumsy person whose best friend is a reindeer. And if you are wondering whether one can make a hit movie with an unattractive protagonist, look no further than DreamWorks' *Shrek*, an animated comedy about an ogre who is ugly, selfish, and vulgar (smelly, too). However, his terrible appearance belies a warm character and no one knows this better than Princess Fiona, his soulmate. Ultimately, people identify themselves with characters and stories that are authentic. Some of the successful disruptive brands that we have cited in this book did not take off flawlessly. For example, both Airbnb and Uber had to change their brand identities several times within just a few years. Yet by being incredibly open and candid about their flaws and rebranding efforts, they projected authenticity and earned the support of their followers.

Affinity

The "Toughest Job in the World" is a perfect example of a story with a high level of affinity. No-one will doubt a mother's love, which is unconditional but often taken for granted. By drawing people's attention to this everyday yet powerful fact, American Greetings' campaign was able to win the audience's empathy and resonate with people of any nationality. What makes this piece of communication so powerful is that it allowed the audience to put themselves in the shoes of their mothers, and realize the incredible amount of unnoticed sacrifices made by moms over the years. There was also a strong call-to-action at the end, made possible with the product offered by the brand – a Mother's Day card. Yet it is not simply the product that the audience is grateful for, but also the "wake-up call" that the brand provided. The audience can associate American Greetings' campaign with an important internal feeling, which forms an excellent foundation for establishing trust.

Attainability

The younger generation chased dreams just like we did when we were at their age, but they now seek goals that are much more attainable. If something is too far away, they can feel the distance. There is no point in planning too long-term as no one can predict what the Internet world will be like in five or even three years. Therefore, young consumers prefer to opt for instant gratification. To them, a small reward that can be savored today is more palatable than a huge promise in the future. As mentioned in the last chapter, returning an empty bottle to Watsons' vending machine will only earn you a few cents but you can immediately see the money appear in your e-wallet. It is the instant encouragement, not the amount of cash, that draws people to participate in the recycling movement. As such, a brand must talk to consumers in their language and a context that is not out of range. We see fewer promotions these days that require consumers to wait a few months for a lucky draw result that only rewards one winner with a "grand prize" such as a car or a free stay in a resort. People not only do not bother to wait, but are also skeptical that such promotions are simply "bait" for enticing more sales.

Aspiration

Audiences today are spoiled – they do not have to think about what they want to watch because platforms like TikTok deploy sophisticated algorithms to push relevant content to each user based on previous search patterns and online behavior. As a result, tons of information and videos are continuously streamed to our smartphones throughout the day. To actively engage their audience, brands must carefully craft a story that has true stopping power. Out of all the content posted on social media every day, only the ones that are truly uplifting and motivational can go viral and receive substantial positive word of mouth (or mouse). Brands must therefore try to strike a balance when creating their content so that they are neither too heavy nor substanceless.

Artistry

The presentation style of communications today differs from the glamorous TV commercials of the past. Audiences do not tend to fixate on production quality too much when it comes to ads, but they do appreciate content that is well produced and has high entertainment value. Brands must learn how to amuse the audience while staying on course. There is only one rule for evaluating a piece of communication, which is to measure the extent to which it can achieve the objective it is supposed to accomplish. Amusement is the means, but not the end. Eventually, the communication has to convince the audience that the brand is a worthy choice.

The Five As show us that in this constantly changing market environment, we may have to find new and more accessible ways to tell stories. Volvo, as a brand, is synonymous with "safety." You rarely find a brand that can own a brand association so firmly and consistently across all markets. Volvo is also famous for its direct and hard-hitting advertising campaigns. One classic Volvo print advertisement shows an image of a car with its front and rear ends smashed alongside a headline that reads, "We design every Volvo to look like this." The ad copy then explains that the front and the rear parts of the car are designed to collapse in order to absorb the energy in the unlikely event of a car crash. The middle part of the car, on the other hand, is constructed like a safety cage to protect the passengers.

Since this advertisement is so successful, should Volvo just reuse it? In the past, it would have been logical to repeat tried-and-true procedures. Yet today, taking calculated risks is bold and admirable because it signals innovation. In other words, the so-called "safest" advertising move is actually the most unsafe one because it suggests complacency and resistance to change. Volvo still needs to maintain its "safety" association to satisfy its customers, but the way it achieves safety must advance with the pace of society. Volvo no longer shows smashed cars in its advertising. The audio script of one of its recent commercials reads, "there is no car in the accident because there was no accident." Needless to say, the safest scenario is to avoid accidents from happening. By shifting the focus from building a safety-cage to the advance accident-avoidance system, Volvo can assure car buyers even more. This shows how the *brand expression can change while the brand DNA remains the same.*

Many marketers concentrate on what they can do to build the brand. However, *brand communication is not just about what you do. It is also about what you do not do.* Offering discounts too often without a legitimate reason tells people that the brand is getting desperate, or it is trying to get rid of old stock. Entering unnecessary debates on social media can be seen as defensive and lacking gravitas. Pleasing new customers but neglecting existing ones suggests that you are only interested in the sales, not the relationship. Nowadays, working with key opinion leaders (KOLs) is a common marketing practice. It can be an exciting way to communicate your brand message as it is perfectly fine to find someone to tell the story on your behalf. Yet brand-owners need to bear in mind that working with KOLs is not about putting your brands in someone else's hands and letting them decide the fate of your most precious asset. After all, KOLs work with many other brands aside from you, and you have to maintain total accountability to make sure you are in control of your destiny.

Finally, communication is not restricted to traditional advertising. It can take any shape or form. Starbucks is known as a brand that never relies on advertising to connect with its customers. Its cozy ambiance, friendly service, and innovative seasonal drinks (its Pumpkin Spice Latte has become a cult favorite) are good enough reasons to drive customers to go back and check out this "third place" – the destination between home (first place) and office (second place). The third-place brand positioning is enforced with its extensive geographical coverage in every district and strategically selected locations. Its physical retail presence serves as a prominent outdoor advertising network. In Hong Kong's Starbucks, you can even order *Yuenyeung*, a popular local beverage that blends coffee and milk tea. This is a great way to communicate that Starbucks is a local and international brand that blends in with the local community while enriching it with international flavor.

Contact – brand is experience

In the past, a brand may have been built by perception, but now it is created by experience. The more tangible a brand is, the more people can involve and embrace it. There are many best practices around the world that show how brands have cleverly made contact with their customers through *sensory branding.*

Smell

In Chapter Five, we already saw how the fashion brand Abercrombie & Fitch used its Fierce cologne to jolt people's senses and draw them to its store. The way in which people immediately associate a smell with a place is also evidenced by Shangri-La, one of the first hospitality brands to own a unique scent. Regular customers will feel a sense of belonging as soon as they step inside the lobby of any Shangri-La hotel and detect "the Essence of Shangri-La." This distinctive scent does not just smell pleasant – the Shangri-La group spent six months perfecting their signature scent to evoke serenity and tranquility.[6] Of course, smell is also a key branding component for food and beverage companies. Seoul's Dunkin' Donuts installed special dispensers on buses that would transmit the aroma of coffee whenever the Dunkin' Donuts commercial played on the radio.[7] Dunkin' Donuts may not be the top-of-mind brand when it comes to coffee, since it primarily sells donuts. But once commuters associated the store with the smell of coffee, they couldn't wait to visit a Dunkin' Donuts once they got off the bus to grab a coffee, and in many cases, a donut as well.

Hearing

All food and beverage (F&B) outlets, Michelin Star restaurants, and fast-food chains alike play some kind of background music in their outlets. The right song can set the right mood for either a romantic candlelight dinner or a finger-lickin' good quick lunch. Another product category that utilizes "sound" to amplify its branding is the high-end sports car market. Ricardo, the UK company that builds McLaren's engines, not only chooses the engine parts but also helps create its rumbling, roaring sound.[8] One may not realize that the "vroom" sound of a supercar is not a natural by-product of its moving mechanical parts. In fact, a downside of adding a turbo charger to boost the power of a car is that it reduces the car's engine sound, which contributes 50% of the G-force – the thrill that people want to experience when driving a sports car, according to a study conducted by Ricardo. Although the turbo charger improves the performance of the car, it affects the *perceived* performance of the car that is created by its iconic sound. The famous ad copy David Ogilvy wrote for Rolls Royce will not work for a McLaren – "at sixty miles an hour, the loudest noise in the new Rolls-Royce comes from the electric clock." The task of Ricardo's acoustic technician is to design a McLaren that will sound as stunning as it looks.

Sight

While sound effects are crucial for a sports car, the visual impact that a product has is instrumental for premium fashion brands that want to project a desirable image. Not everyone has the privilege of attending fashion shows in Milan or Paris. As a way to recognize its VIP customers, Burberry organizes exclusive events in some Asian markets to allow people to visually experience the catwalk in real-time. Giant and top-quality LED screens project the models in life-size, showing every detail of the latest fashion trends and accessories. Customers can virtually join the extravagant fashion show and place their order on the spot. At the same time, they can indulge themselves by shopping at the local boutique in-person while being escorted by fashion consultants. Such a splendid brand experience is unmatched by online shopping.

Touch

FANCL, which we will discuss more in a case study at the end of this chapter, is a Japanese skincare and cosmetics brand that is built on the concept of "mutenka" (additive-free). FANCL products are made without preservatives or additives, giving users, particularly those with sensitive skin, peace of mind that nothing unnatural will come into contact with their skin. Customers are able to not simply imagine, but *feel* the mutenka effect at FANCL stores, which generously allow customers to touch and try out their products. Beauty consultants offer professional advice on how customers can choose the best combination of skincare products based on their different skin types. Quite frequently, customers are invited to try the product on one hand and observe how it compares with the other hand, such that the effect of the product's "touch" is even more palpable. Trying the product on your hand is worth a thousand words, if not more.

Taste

So far, we have reviewed how marketers successfully build their brands by appealing to what we smell, hear, see, and touch. But this section would be incomplete if we did not cite any example of how brands build themselves around "taste." Johnnie Walker, a brand that is built on 200 years of whiskey wisdom, has found a unique way to invite customers to enter its brand world through the Johnnie Walker House: a "blended" concept of gallery, lifestyle space, and museum all under one roof. There are four flagship Johnnie Walker Houses outside of Scotland – in Beijing, Shanghai, Chengdu, and Seoul.[9] Although each destination has its unique touch in terms of style, they all share the same philosophy of providing an exceptional and luxurious journey to learn, talk, exchange, and appreciate whiskey. Calling it a whiskey-tasting workshop would not be doing it justice. It is an embassy that welcomes whiskey lovers to savor "whiskey conversations" and feel connected with the brand alongside like-minded friends.

Branding as a discipline urges marketers to migrate from a transaction to a relationship mindset built on regular contact. Making contact is not about asking customers to buy more, although most of the emails that we receive every day are disguised sales pitches. *Selling is the outcome, not the purpose of branding.* Moreover, a lack of contact will widen the gap between the brand and the customers, but over-communicating can be irritating and push customers away. Try to respect the privacy of your members and only contact them when there is a need or valid reason. Otherwise, people will start to lose interest and stop opening your emails.

It is also important to communicate with sincerity instead of treating it as a routine. For the past two decades, I have been residing in properties developed by the same real estate company. They are kind enough to send me e-cards on my birthday, at Christmas, and on New Year's Day. Their original intention was good, but even after 20 years, they still only address me as "Dear Valued Customer." Apparently, I am just a serial number sitting in their customer database, and I bet all their members receive exactly the same e-card with the same message. This kind of contact does more harm than good to the relationship.

When customers see and feel the genuine values of the brand, they will not only use it for themselves, but refer it to their friends as well. Every customer has a unique brand journey based on his or her understanding, experience, and empathy with the brand. A contact strategy should guide customers throughout this journey by providing the most relevant information that they need at different stages and collecting feedback about their feelings towards the brand along the way. We must not underestimate the effect that the way we answer a customer inquiry or run a simple prize-redemption promotion can have. We need to ensure that those interested in our brand sustain their interest all the way, and convince those who prefer other brands to switch to our brand eventually. Above all, we must remember that *the brand experience at every touchpoint can reinforce or diminish a brand promise.* This is the importance of effective brand communication.

A brand-builder's perspective

Interview with Edward Bell, General Manager, Brand, Insights, and Marketing Communications, Cathay Pacific Airways

Mr. Edward Bell is a seasoned marketing professional with a background in psychology and a Master's of Marketing qualifications, with significant experience working on the frontlines of marketing in China and Asia, helping brands to find growth paths. He has worked for Adidas and several international advertising agencies in senior planning and management positions. Before joining Cathay Pacific, Mr. Bell was the CEO of FCB Greater China.

Royce Yuen: As an experienced brand-builder, can you name a few brands off the top of your head that have achieved exceptional results?

Edward Bell: The North Face is definitely one of my favorite brands, and I had the privilege to help to build this brand in Asia. Not only do I respect their dedication to producing top quality merchandise, I also like the meanings that the brand stands for. When people put on their North Face, they feel protected and more courageous to conquer the unknown. This brand involvement does not only have to happen when you are climbing the highest mountain; it works equally well when you are navigating the jungle of the complex business world.

Rolex is another brand that needs no introduction. It stands the test of time, and is so classic yet modern. It is a reliable performance watch that is endorsed by many professional athletes, while commanding a prestigious status. It is one of the very few brands that will never go out of fashion because it is more than just style. The quality of the watch movement is impeccable, complemented by an iconic look and feel.

Successful brands are not limited to the luxury sector. Quality brands exist in any category as long as they provide a good reason for people to follow them. Muji is an interesting company that is founded on an admirable philosophy, and it stays true to this belief by delivering a wide range of products. Muji's design philosophy is minimalist, and it is famous for not having a logo or even a brand. It's a brilliant case study that illustrates how "no-brand" can be a powerful brand. It has democratized good industrial design without asking people to pay a fortune for it.

RY: What is the biggest challenge for brand-building in this digital era?

EB: Digitalization has brought about severe market fragmentation that has never been seen before. The digital media has empowered both the users and marketers in many ways. You can start a business by leveraging the digital platforms offered by Google and Facebook without having to find a major investor. This has led to the influx of uncountable direct to customers (DTC) brands into the market.

While young brands without financial backup also stand a chance to compete, the flip side of digitalization is the proliferation of content, leading to a fragmentation of mentality.

It is harder to penetrate the mind of the audience these days. Even with a lot of marketing spending, there is no guarantee that one will receive the attention of the target audience. It is up to every individual at the receiving end to decide what to see and for how long, leading to hyper-segmentation.

The other trend is the emergence of tribalism within society, enabled by the technology platform. These tribes do not only live together geographically. They are digitally connected instead. When they share references and brand information, they nurture a self-reinforcing mechanism that relates to their own tribe. It is hard to penetrate the group as an outsider.

On the other hand, people do not have the time to view everything and respond to everything because of the information explosion. In reality, you may belong to a large network, but you may not have all the time to read and digest all the information available within the community. Due to the scarcity of time, you may only be able to respond to the people who are your friends. Brands have to understand how people are connecting and how the different circles overlap.

RY: Does the brand still matter when full information about corporations is available and accessible on the Internet?

EB: This idea is quite provocative and is something that marketers have to confront eventually. The truth is that an unintended consequence of digital media is the transformation of the relationship between the manufacturer and the consumer. It is now relatively easier to sell directly to consumers. Brands used to be the constructs used to sell products; manufacturers had to rely on brands to push the products out of the door. Nowadays, your brand is less important in the process of selling than it used to be. People look at the design they like, rather than the brand, and browse effortlessly. The role of brands in the past was to attract people to come to the store. This is less important today as a result of digital media.

This is very interesting because, in the future, the market will not be defined by manufacturing brands, but by the platforms that own the largest number of customers, such as Amazon, Facebook, Tmall and Tencent, etc. It will be the age of digital retail. The market used to be driven by brands like Walmart and Coca-Cola, which were powerful and could set the prices. But brands are becoming less critical to consumers. People are too scared to agree.

Technology is overtaking marketing to become the indisputable gateway to growth. Marketers do not have 100% ownership over the digital space where they sell goods and disseminate information. Corporations are confused on where and how to distribute their budgets. Typically, companies spend more on selling and less on marketing these days, by riding on their digital platforms. This is evidenced by the change of media investment by corporations such as P&G and Unilever over the years.

RY: Does this mean that the channels and platforms will be the ultimate winners, with e-tailers replacing traditional retailers as the gateway for selling to consumers?

EB: Marketers no longer talk about big ideas anymore. They are occupied by programmatic buy, real-time programming, and marketing automation. Sooner or later, everyone will have a data management platform (DMP) or access to a DMP that allows them to identify audience segments and to target specific users. Companies will rely more on platforms like JD.com or Tmall that provide end-to-end solutions for survival. These e-tailers have abundant real-time data about sellers and buyers and will be a dominating force in the new marketplace. They are far more potent than traditional retailers who mainly leverage their extensive geographical coverage.

What is compounding the problem is that companies are investing much less in brand-building than they used to be because they find it easier to sell on digital platforms. As a result, they are investing less in media and more in digital platforms because they believe they can achieve a higher return on investment (ROI).

The danger is that marketers may over-rely on these e-platforms, to the extent that they are losing their bargaining power. There may be counterfeit brands that are available on some of these platforms. They may look like the big brands but are much cheaper and, therefore, more likely to be listed on the front page. Brand-owners have to think three steps ahead to cope with the new market dynamics.

RY: Is it possible that things will be reorganized one day, ushering in a new world order?

EB: In the past, companies made things and then tried to convince people to buy what they made. They tried to persuade people through storytelling. To help people recall the brand, manufacturers would bombard the audience with campaigns containing catchy jingles and stunning visuals.

In the digital era, there may be people who do not genuinely understand marketing, but simply have the techniques that work in the digital space. They have not gone through any marketing training. Instead, they are technique-driven, and have one thing that works. They will become the "expert" in that area and thus play a part in the new eco-system.

Marketers have to figure out a way to tap all these different resources and connect the dots that will work for them by adhering to fundamental marketing principles. According to Cisco, 90% of the content on the Internet will eventually be videos, and most of them will be tailor-made to suit different segments or even specific individuals. Marketers have to convince consumers that they have the most suitable solution at the most reasonable price. All these reasons have to be evidence-based instead of perception-based. This will impact not only marketing communications but also the entire product development and management cycle. Not to mention that consumers will have no obligation to be loyal as it will be a "buyer's market" for many if not most of the categories. Consumers are becoming fully aware that the choice is theirs.

Case study – FANCL

Total marketing strategy for a beauty brand

In 1982, FANCL introduced its preservative-free skincare line in tiny, five-milliliter vials. Back then, most women in Japan suffered severe skin problems caused by the harsh ingredients in the beauty products they were using – chemicals such as parabens, sterilizers, and petroleum surfactants. Instead of enhancing their natural beauty, the products caused skin irritation and cell damage, and accelerated the aging of the skin.

As both a pioneer and continuous innovator in preservative-free skincare and cosmetics, FANCL is committed to eliminating these negatives and making skin healthier and, ultimately, more beautiful. The entire business of FANCL is built on this philosophy as well as the firm commitment that its products should give the skin only what it needs.

All FANCL products are formulated according to the highest standards. To guarantee their quality, they are packaged in small, hermetically sealed bottles and freshness-dated boxes. The innovative, touch-free caps are specially designed to keep out bacteria. Each bottle contains enough for a 30-day supply so that the products stay fresh through to the finish. This all takes place in FANCL's pharmaceutically sterile, state-of-the-art laboratories in Japan (Image 8.3).[10]

1982 1995 1998 2002 2005 2007 2012 2019

IMAGE 8.3 FANCL is a brand that is committed to producing skincare and cosmetics products that are 100% preservative-free. Credit: fancl.com.

Interview with Christopher Chan, Managing Director of FANCL

Mr. Christopher Chan is the Founder and Managing Director of Fantastic Natural Cosmetics Limited, the sole distributor of FANCL products in Asia, excluding Japan, as well as Gourmet Dining Group Limited and Nam Fai Woolen Spinning Factory Limited. Over the past two decades, Mr. Chan has applied his innovation and entrepreneurial acumen together with the operational experience he gained in other sectors to successfully expand the FANCL retail chain to over 240 outlets spanning Hong Kong, Mainland China, Taiwan, and Singapore. FANCL has become one of the most popular beauty and healthcare brands in the region, distributing a wide range of supplements and health–related products in addition to its skincare and cosmetics lines.

Mr. Chan is a Registered Professional Engineer and Registered Structural Engineer in Hong Kong, and a Chartered Civil Engineer and Chartered Structural Engineer in the UK. He holds a Master of Science Degree in Structural Engineering from the University of California at Berkeley and a Bachelor of Applied Science Degree in Civil Engineering from the University of Waterloo, Canada.

Royce Yuen: When you launched FANCL in Hong Kong, did you see the necessity of adopting a different way to build this brand due to the market and consumer differences in Hong Kong and Japan?

Christopher Chan: Consumers buy a product mainly because of two reasons: brand or price. The two are not mutually exclusive, but generally speaking, some people are willing to pay more to get the brand they desire while others prefer to buy something less costly with acceptable product quality.

FANCL Japan is very good at product development and production, but it is less marketing-driven as a corporation. We are building on the strength of

FANCL Japan in terms of its R&D and production capabilities, while at the same time implementing more strategic and bold marketing campaigns to build a brand that people trust.

When we introduced FANCL to the Hong Kong market more than 20 years ago, we had to start from ground zero. We needed to break through the clutter in a highly competitive market dominated by many international, well-established brands with substantial advertising budgets. Raising brand awareness was relatively easy; building a brand that people liked was difficult and complex.

As a new entrant and a young brand, we needed to find an angle that was strong enough to differentiate ourselves from the established players, one that was unique and could not be copied. It had to be something that could be substantiated and backed by strong evidence. The first objective was to "disrupt" people from their routine of buying skincare products. Curiosity is part of human nature. Once you get their attention, customers will voluntarily come to you to look for more information.

The most profound point of differentiation for FANCL is the fact that no preservatives are added to its products, such that every drop you put on your skin will be good for you. This is the concept of "mutenka," which means "additive-free." Mutenka gives FANCL strong stopping power as consumers are always looking for a safer and more natural product.

In the beginning, the consumers in Hong Kong may not have understood the concept right away. But after our continuous marketing investment, FANCL mutenka quickly registered in the minds of consumers. They equated mutenka with "no preservatives," which is a logical and attractive proposition to them. FANCL's track record in Japan also provided strong assurance to the consumers that mutenka products were proven safe. To sustain the market interest and to build an even stronger momentum, celebrity advertising was launched to project a clear image and further implant the concept of mutenka in the minds of consumers.

Even today, with the application of the latest production technology, FANCL products only come in small bottles (30 ml for lotion) to ensure product freshness. To ensure the optimal quality of the product before use, our distinctive container is designed to only open after customers first remove a ring and twist a cap with an inner cutter that breaks a seal. Free of preservatives and fragrances, FANCL cosmetics are perishable. Each product has an optimal period of use. The product will come with a "Freshness Period" sticker to remind the user of the date they opened the product. Instead of printing the expiration date, which is the common industry practice, the production date is printed on the packaging of all FANCL products so as to put the interests of the consumer above ours.

Building a sustainable business requires more than having a good product. It has to be complemented by good service. FANCL's retail presence serves as an essential bridge between our brand and the customers. With a network covering all strategic locations, we make store visits very convenient for our customers (Image 8.4).

IMAGE 8.4 A FANCL retail outlet is not just a point of sale. It serves as an interface with new and regular customers. Credit: fancl-hk.com.

Our well-trained beauty consultants offer friendly and professional advice to customers based on their needs (Image 8.5). Handy tools are used to understand different skin types so that the best product combination can be hand-picked for each customer. We take staff training very seriously, and we are committed to empowering our team to deliver first-class service to every customer who walks into our store. Our staff is fully equipped with product knowledge, and we also encourage them to use their common sense and look at things from the perspective of customers. Their task is to help to solve the problems faced by the customers; selling the goods is a natural outcome.

We fully understand the importance of content marketing, and we have applied this concept in our marketing campaign since the very beginning. We created and published an in-house magazine that customers receive for free with every purchase (Images 8.6 and 8.7). The magazine contains relevant, seasonal content, and also serves as a great medium for providing more product knowledge to our customers. It is a piece of leisure reading that they can keep at home or in the office, or pass to others. We also have a robust CRM (customer relationship management) program that allows customers to collect points for the redemption of FANCL items, other lifestyle products, or dining coupons.

Marketing is an ongoing commitment, and it requires the devotion of an entire team to deliver total customer satisfaction. We put a lot of effort into

IMAGE 8.5   Nothing is more reassuring than to be able to interact with someone who understands beauty and genuine consumer needs. Credit: fancl-hk.com.

managing the complete customer journey to make sure that the brand value is reinforced at every touchpoint.

RY: You have managed the FANCL brand for over two decades. Can you comment on the evolution of the FANCL brand, and how are you managing this change or evolution?

CC: FANCL is synonymous with mutenka. This will always be one of the strongest motivations for people to buy our products. This is our brand DNA. We believe our customers subscribe to our values, not just the efficacy of our products. Yet we try not to repeat the obvious and aim to find innovative ways to explain this philosophy. We recently launched a new campaign centered around "zero preservatives" to highlight the benefits of resetting and restoring your skin's glow for 100% Beauty (Image 8.8). To invite customers to take part in this campaign, we created the #0to100Beauty Community as a platform where consumers can discover 100% beauty with 0 preservatives.

While "0to100" is an effective tactical campaign that reinforces the mutenka concept, we recognize that we need to articulate our philosophy and brand equity in a way that extends beyond product attributes and appeals to a global audience. This is why "Less is More" was created, not only to act as a brand tagline, but also to serve as the beacon for driving our business forward. It can also facilitate our geographical expansion to non-Chinese speaking markets. "Less is More" conveys a broader meaning and has taken mutenka from product differentiation to the level of image differentiation. It challenges our traditional belief in life that "more is more"; on many occasions, actually "less is more." From a functional standpoint, after you have taken away the preservatives, you can have

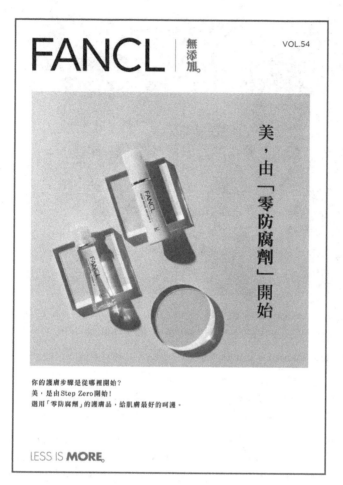

IMAGE 8.6 The FANCL publication provides the opportunity for consumers to learn more about the current topics on beauty and product information. Credit: fancl-hk.com.

more beauty. This logic also applies to other issues, such as environmental protection – "less pollution, more fresh air." The versatility of our tagline allows the brand to expand its sphere of influence while adhering to our core values.

Digitalization has become an integral part of our daily life. To follow the customers' footsteps and leverage technology to our advantage, we have migrated our loyalty program to a digital format. iFANCL was launched to serve as an effective way to collect data as well as interact with our members (Image 8.9). All the technical solutions are developed in-house as we want to lead on the

IMAGE 8.7   The FANCL publication provides the opportunity for consumers to learn more about the current topics on beauty and product information. Credit: fancl-hk.com.

IMAGE 8.8 "Zero preservative promises 100% beauty" is a new way of conveying the mutenka concept. Credit: fancl-sg.com.

IMAGE 8.9 The iFANCL app serves multiple purposes from higher efficiency to better customer experience. Credit: fancl-sg.com.

IMAGE 8.10 The crossover of FANCL and DALLOYAU is offering the customer a whole new experience right in the CBD. Credit: fancl-sg.com.

technology front, which will help us gain the upper hand in all areas, from operational management to customer management.

The mutenka concept is more than just skincare and cosmetic products. It can be extended to health supplements or even food. This allows us to gain a higher customer share and expand our customer base to include both genders. After all, the primary target customers for skincare products are female. However, health-related products can be consumed by any consumer regardless of their age and gender. This is also a great way to offer a total solution to our customers that embraces beauty inside and out.

To offer a different customer experience, we have unveiled the first-ever Hong Kong creative concept store that serves both beauty products and healthy dining (Image 8.10). This spacious, innovative store, located right in the heart of Central in Hong Kong, is designed to be stylish and modern, marrying shopping and café experiences. The contemporary design of the creative store reflects FANCL's brand personality – innovative with cutting-edge technology in its products and services.

Marketing is an ongoing learning process. We like to push the envelope and offer something new and exciting to our customers, from new products to new experiences. The expectation of consumers is continuously changing, and they have no obligation to stick to the same brand forever. It is up to us to decide how long the customers want to share the journey with us. Let's ask ourselves what we can give to the customers before we ask for their loyalty.

Notes

1 Little, Becky. "How the 'Blood Feud' between Coke and Pepsi Escalated during the 1980s Cola Wars." *History*, March 12, 2020. https://www.history.com/news/cola-wars-pepsi-new-coke-failure.
2 "Starbucks Drops Its Name and the Word Coffee from Logo." *BBC News*, January 6, 2011, sec. Business. https://www.bbc.com/news/business-12125440.
3 Evian. "Our Water." *Evian*. Accessed September 16, 2020. https://www.evian.com/en_us/what-is-spring-water/.
4 Coca-Cola Australia. "Local Idea Goes Global: Share a Coke," November 9, 2013. https://www.coca-colacompany.com/au/news/local-idea-goes-global-share-a-coke.
5 Richards, Katie. "A Look Back at a Masterpiece of 'Gotcha' Advertising that Was Both Prank and Tearjerker." *Adweek*, August 9, 2017. https://www.adweek.com/creativity/a-look-back-at-a-masterpiece-of-gotcha-advertising-that-was-both-prank-and-tearjerker/.
6 Hilton, James. "'Essence of Shangri-La' Greets Guests at Shangri-La Hotels and Resorts." *Hospitality Net*, September 13, 2006. https://www.hospitalitynet.org/news/4028813.html.
7 Evergreen, Inno. "Dunkin' Donuts Sprays the Smell of Coffee onto Buses to Increase Sales." *BostInno*, July 24, 2012. https://www.bizjournals.com/boston/inno/stories/news/2012/07/24/dunkin-donuts-sprays-the-smell-of-coffee-onto.html.
8 Crosse, Jesse. "The Sound of Electrical Power." *Ricardo Quarterly Review* (Q1 2018): 21–23.
9 Johnnie Walker. "Johnnie Walker House." Accessed October 6, 2020. https://www.johnniewalker.com/en-kr/the-world-of-johnnie-walker/johnnie-walker-house/.
10 Ikemori, Kenji. "Founder's Message." *FANCL*. Accessed September 16, 2020. https://www.fancl.com/shop/index.php.

9

FROM CUSTOMER TO COMPETITIVE ANALYSIS

FROM MICRO TO MACRO ANALYSIS	FROM STAYING IN TUNE TO STAYING IN TOUCH	FROM CUSTOMER TO COMPETITIVE ANALYSIS	FROM ROLE TO CUSTOMERS TO ROLE TO SOCIETY
CORPORATE Brand is culture	**CONNECTION** Brand is meaning	**CUSTOMER LIFESTYLE** Brand is a way of life	**CONVERGENCE** Brand is to play a role in the user's life
CONTEXT Brand is trends	**COMMUNICATION** Brand is dialogue	**COMPETITIVE ADVANTAGE** Brand is relative	**COMMUNITY** Brand is to play a role in the community
	CONTACT Brand is experience	**CUSTOMIZATION** Brand is fluid	

LIFESTYLE

FUNCTIONAL   ASPIRATIONAL   RESPONSIBLE

FIGURE 9.1   Examining the lifestyle aspect of a brand.

A brand is more likely to succeed if it can serve customers better than its competitors can. Unless you are a monopoly, consumers will always compare you with other brands from time to time. This is only normal. And this is particularly true for "high involvement categories" where consumers take a longer time to decide on their brand of choice. They tend to do their due diligence by researching online and consulting people they trust, including key opinion leaders (KOLs) or friends they regard as well-learned individuals in the respective category. They will also personally check out the products in the showroom and talk to sales staff to get their opinion. If there are any product catalogs or brochures available, these consumers will keep all of them to review all of the detailed information later.

A brand cannot stop its customers from checking out competitive offers. In many cases, it is the competitors who try to flirt with the customers. What a brand can do and should do, however, is to build a fruitful and ongoing relationship with its customers so that they are less inclined to switch to a competitive brand under any circumstance. For starters, the brand should try to understand the state of the relationship it has with each customer. Broadly speaking, there are four types of customers, depending on the relationship they have with a brand (Figure 9.2):

Regretfully trapped: Customers who are not satisfied with the brand performance and would stop using the brand if they had a choice. They are still with the brand, maybe because of some contractual obligation, or because there are no better options in the market yet.

Fake loyalists: Customers who seem to be satisfied but feel no obligation to use the brand. They do not complain about the brand, yet have no attachment to it either. The brand may fulfill their basic needs, but they are prepared to switch if a better alternative appears.

Bored lovers: Customers who are likely to continue using the brand but have a low level of satisfaction and engagement. The initial romance and excitement of using the brand are gone, and things now feel routine.

Die-hard fans: Customers who are not only satisfied with the brand but are also happy to stick with it. There is no strong reason for them to consider other competitive brands at this point.

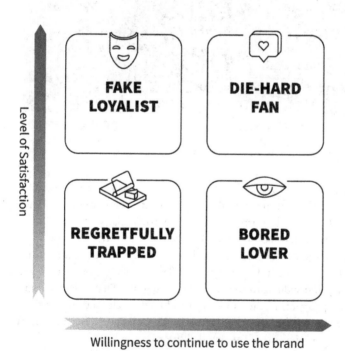

FIGURE 9.2 The different relationships between a customer and a brand.

A brand can gauge, either by conducting research or analyzing behavioral data, the percentage of their customers that belong to each category. Their goal is then to migrate the regretfully trapped, the fake loyalists, and the bored lovers to the category of die-hard fans. To achieve this goal, a brand must understand the different factors affecting the current relationship and figure out what must be done to improve customer engagement.

Customer lifestyle – brand is a way of life

The ultimate objective of any enterprise is to accomplish customer loyalty. Loyal customers cost less to serve as they are familiar with the brand's product and services. They will also voluntarily recommend the brand to other customers. Even when things are not going well, they are more accommodating and are willing to look at issues from the service provider's perspective. When customers are truly loyal to a brand, they do not switch to another brand purely because of lower costs. In other words, the brand does not have to compete on price and will therefore maintain a reasonable margin. This profit margin will enable the brand to reinvest in the necessary areas, such as strategic communications, to enhance its competitiveness.

Almost every enterprise has a loyalty or VIP program. Yet many of these so-called VIP programs are only mechanisms that encourage a higher level of spending by enticing customers with incentives or discounts. While the logic behind rewarding customers who contribute more is totally justified, merely relying on a point system may not promote genuine loyalty. In fact, such systems tend to train consumers to become loyal to points or incentives instead of the brand. For example, many credit card companies work with merchants to offer discounts to stimulate consumer spending. If customers use a particular credit card at designated restaurant outlets, they will enjoy a discount or a free dessert. This may sound simple, but such programs only encourage brand parity, which will eventually lead to price competition.

Loyalty has to be built on two-way relationships. To nurture an enduring relationship with the customer, a brand has to offer more than just functional benefits. A brand can hold a much stronger position in users' minds if it helps them enhance the ways they want to live. This impact will establish a special bond between a brand and its users. The stronger the bond, the less likely the chances of defection. Bonding can be constructed at three levels. *Transactional bonding* is the most basic level, and occurs when the brand meets the fundamental needs of the customers at a fair price. This is the prerequisite for any repurchase. The next level of bonding is *emotional bonding*, which takes place when customers develop a special attachment to the brand, usually through the staff responsible for the service delivery. A sense of mutual trust and respect will be established over time. Finally, the highest level is *structural bonding*, which is when the brand can effectively offer a viable solution to the customers based on its in-depth understanding of their needs. The brand can expertly pull together the resources required to assemble a workable proposition to help customers tackle the problem they face. When a brand possesses all three levels of bonding, it can build a substantial barrier to entry that fences off any intrusion from competitors.

A brand that has secured all three levels of bonding is Dyson, the household appliance brand. Dyson sells everyday appliances, but its popularity has shown that customers are willing to replace a typical functional product with a lifestyle brand, even if it means paying a hefty premium. Whether through a vacuum cleaner or hairdryer, Dyson has allowed its customers to turn the most routine and tedious chore into an act of style and perfection. Dyson products are not only slickly designed with superb performance, they also enable users to enjoy the lifestyle they desire that luxury brands have traditionally neglected. As such, the brand offers users an exceptional experience and secures an enduring bond.

Competitive advantage – brand is relative

Since consumers will compare the brand that they use or want to purchase with other brands in the market, the strengths of a brand are relative. Furthermore, this relativity can change following changes in the needs, lifestyle, budget, and life stage of the individual. Brand owners must understand this concept of relativity and not take the relationships they have with customers for granted. They have to aim at continuous improvement and "grow together" with the customers. In some cases, a brand loses the battle not because it has done anything wrong, but because it has not done enough to catch up with the consumers. This oversight may allow a competitive brand to surpass its performance ever so slightly.

Every consumer has a mental repertoire of brands for different categories, also known as a "consideration set." A brand has first to enter this league to be considered. Then, it has to emerge as the preferred choice by presenting consumers with a compelling and unrivaled argument, which usually consists of both rational and emotional reasons. Throughout this mental process, the consumer will compare the brand with other options from various perspectives. If the brand performs well along the dimension that the consumer emphasizes, it has a higher chance of standing out from the rest.

A brand should not blame competitors for its loss of business. Instead, it should ask itself why it was not able to fulfill the changing needs of the consumers or, in some cases, not even realize that consumers expected something different or better. Some brand owners never accept or admit that competitors pose a threat to them. In the film *Pretty Woman* (1990), there is a memorable scene where Edward Lewis (Richard Gere) has a severe argument with Vivian (Julia Roberts) in a hotel room. An egocentric, successful entrepreneur, Edward tells Vivian that she would never leave him because it's not as if she has better options. Edward's blind belief is the typical mentality of certain brand owners. They believe they "own" the customers just because they are the best in the market. To overcome this self-fulfilling fallacy, a brand has to objectively assess its relative performance against competitors from the consumer's perspective.

In the age of disruption, a consumer's consideration set can completely change when disruptive brands emerge to fulfill their needs in unconventional ways. These brands provide an eye-opening experience to consumers and may change their expectations and behavior forever.

Customization – brand is fluid

In the past, a brand was crafted to appeal to a tightly defined target audience. It was mainly an intangible image that drew people's attention and projected a unique personality for the product. Today, the role of a brand has expanded. Although the brand still has a specific group of target customers in mind, it realizes that *the market is always greater than the target.* In today's borderless market empowered by digital technology, a potential customer can be anyone from anywhere. To capture this explosive market opportunity, a brand should be expanding instead of restricting itself to serve only a confined market segment.

Helping a brand stay fluid and adaptive is not a new task for marketers. The classic growth strategy question has always been "how can we attract new customers while retaining the existing ones?" In Chapter Two, we saw from Chow Tai Fook how a century-old brand can stay vibrant by introducing trendier jewelry design, adopting new technology for customer interface, and revamping the in-store experience without compromising the trustworthiness of a well-established brand image. Chow Tai Fook also introduced a multi-brand strategy to cover a broad spectrum of customers with different lifestyles and attitudes towards jewelry, rather than compartmentalizing them demographically. Another brand that has successfully tapped different consumer markets is Toyota, the Japanese car manufacturer renowned for its practical and reliable family cars. In 1989, Toyota launched Lexus as a *flanker brand* to target the premium vehicle market. Nowadays, Lexus is regarded as a high-end car brand with a global coverage of over 70 countries.[1] Capturing a different market segment with another brand is a viable strategy, but it is not a foolproof solution. To succeed like Chow Tai Fook and Toyota have, brands must have total dedication and employ a unique approach with a team that commands the right mindset and skillset.

Previously, we mentioned that every consumer will have a different set of criteria when evaluating the various options in their consideration set. To effectively engage the different types of customers, a brand needs to possess profound *consumer insight: a rigorous understanding of what really matters to consumers.* By satisfying the primary motivation of the individual behind each purchase, the brand will come across as highly relevant and valuable. As such, a brand can have both identical and diverse connotations for different people based on their demographics, cultural backgrounds, and relationships with the brand.

In Chapter Five, we learned that "a brand is the set of values that it represents and the actual values that it can add to those who are involved with the brand." Indeed, a brand can uphold its core DNA while adapting its brand expression and execution according to the requirements of different situations. Tesla, for instance, is a fluid brand that people like and engage with for various reasons. It appeals to drivers who are environmentally conscious as well as those who are looking to save money on gas. Some people, on the other hand, may want to own a Tesla simply because of its hip and cutting-edge image. Regardless of the reasons it appeals to consumers, the concept of "being smart, not just different" will always remain an essential value that the Tesla brand represents.

While Tesla is a relatively young player in the auto industry, BMW is a brand with a long history and heritage. For many years, BMW only focused on three main product lines – the 3, 5, and 7 series. To thrive in a market with increasing competitive pressure and fragmentation, however, BMW now has the 1, 2, 3, 4, 5, 6, 7, and 8 series plus M, X, and i-series. Managing such a comprehensive product matrix has added massive complexity to the brand's business planning and manufacturing process. Yet the brand must go this extra mile to separately and effectively engage different types of buyers in a highly customized way. It is also common for the same customer to own more than one BMW, as different models provide different sensations. Even as it expands, BMW ensures that all its models share the core spirit of being "the ultimate driving machine."[2]

Throughout this book, we have seen how fashion brands engage different audiences with targeted marketing campaigns and products that are in the right style and price range. These strategies are highly motivated by strong consumer insight. Cartier is a brand that is well sought after by high society but may be too glamorous for the younger generation. To widen its brand appeal, Cartier launched a campaign in 2020 that featured Rami Malek, Maisie Williams, Willow Smith, Troye Sivan, and Jackson Wang, five performers who have a largely young fan base.[3] This group of young achievers represents a diverse array of talent, yet they are all known for being confident, expressive, and distinctive. Cartier also makes it iconic watches available in stainless steel models, which are not only more budget-friendly, but also more casual and sporty, which makes them suitable choices for younger customers. Similarly, sportswear and casual apparel brands such as Nike and Lululemon also have different product lines for different market segments. They can meet the needs of athletes who need the right gear for better performance, as well as everyday people who aspire to live an active lifestyle.

Consumers today also welcome brands that are dynamic and multi-dimensional by being luxurious, cute, classic, and modern at the same time. Louis Vuitton is famous for surprising its followers from time to time by collaborating with young and trendy designers to launch limited editions of merchandise. Since these are seasonal products with a novelty element, they do not erode the brand equity of Louis Vuitton. Instead, they inject some vitality into the brand, allowing it to resonate with the younger generation.

The importance of brand fluidity also applies to the business-to-business (B2B) sector. A company may start as a small to mid-size enterprise (SME), and its business may expand over time and eventually go public. The company will need a banking partner that can look after its needs at its different stages of development both in terms of financial support and strategic advice. The brand values that the bank represents can remain the same while it assembles different service teams and offers financial instruments to the company based on their evolving requirements. In a nutshell, successful brands can act "like water" and perform equally well in different contexts. They can also recruit new brand advocates while keeping existing ones without causing any image confusion.

A brand-builder's perspective

Interview with Ruthia Wong, former General Manager, Greater China eCommerce for Mead Johnson Nutrition, Reckitt Benckiser Group plc (RB)

Ms. Ruthia Wong is recognized as a sound strategist with a strong ability to translate high-level strategy into practical implementation. She has over 30 years of marketing experience with a proven track record to drive business and profit growth in the fast-changing and diverse Asian business environment. Ms. Wong was formerly the General Manager, Greater China (e-commerce) of Mead Johnson, RB. Before that, she was the General Manager of Mead Johnson Nutrition, responsible for managing its China and Hong Kong businesses for ten years.

Royce Yuen: Has your industry been "disrupted" by the digital revolution or e-commerce? In what ways?

Ruthia Wong: Definitely … the infant's nutrition market structure has gone through a major transformation following the boom of e-commerce and

IMAGE 9.1 The nutrition of children is always a key concern of parents. Credit: Shutterstock.

digitalization. Digital has become the key platform for reaching out, engaging, and finally closing the deal with the target audience. The business model, marketing, and selling approach inevitably have to evolve to be more digital-focused.

RY: Do you see any significant changes in terms of consumer expectations and behavior?

RW: Yes; nowadays, consumers do not just want to be the receivers of product and promotional information from the brand owners. They desire to be more "engaged" with the brand or even the innovation process, from product development to brand activation. They are much more vocal and expect their voices to be heard (Image 9.1).

RY: How is brand-building different right now as compared to ten or even five years ago?

RW: In my view, the most significant difference is that the "degree of consumer engagement" nowadays is much higher than before. Brand-building has become an "interactive and evolving" process to consumers. In other words, the way to do marketing is an act of marketing itself.

RY: What is the role of "brand" in this digital era? Has its role been diminished or expanded? Why?

RW: I think the role of "brand" has expanded. It now should go beyond just having a commercial relationship with the consumers. It is part of their lives.

RY: How does your brand tackle or embrace this digital revolution?

RW: We try to embrace change and be agile throughout the process. We learn, apply, relearn, and apply again.

Case study – Pizza Hut

Pursuit of excellence, not technology

Whether or not people in Asia would eat "cheese" was a big question mark 40 years ago, when cheese was not an element in most traditional Asian cuisines. In Hong Kong, the concept of "pizza" was introduced to the mass market in 1981 when the first Pizza Hut opened in Tsim Sha Tsui East, a district that people often visit for shopping and entertainment. Pizza Hut was so popular that people had to line up for more than two to three hours to get a table. Yet the question remained – were people crazy about pizza or cheese, or was there something else that "clicked" with local consumers?

In 1987, Jardine Matheson & Co. Ltd. took over the Hong Kong Pizza Hut franchise business. Since then, it has adopted "Customer Mania" as its corporate motto for serving customers with total dedication. They conducted comprehensive research to identify the magic of the Pizza Hut brand. The investigation revealed that "sharing" is an essential ritual in Asian society, and having a meal involves more than just eating. It is about relatives and friends getting together to see each other, especially during special occasions such as the Lunar New Year or other important festivals. And pizza was probably the biggest Western food concept at the time that was ideal for sharing among a group of people. Pizza Hut's famous cheese-pull also carried a significant symbolic meaning: "connection." Based on this insight, BBDO developed the very first brand tagline for Pizza Hut under Jardine – "Pizza Hut – We Bring People Together." The campaign was extremely successful, and more Pizza Hut outlets opened to meet growing market demand. Throughout the years, other pizza brands tried to enter the market, including Pizza Land and Domino's (limited to delivery), but none of these contenders was able to challenge the leadership position of Pizza Hut.

Pizza Hut is now the largest pizza and pasta chain restaurant in Hong Kong, with over 4,000 employees deployed to work in over 80 outlets throughout Hong Kong and Macau, including in takeaway and delivery services. Pizza Hut's vision is to become the leading casual dining restaurant chain in Hong Kong and Macau with a unique European feel, serving a wide range of relevant and delicious dishes with unsurpassed food quality and offering an environment where its customers can enjoy the European dining experience and a great time with friends and family on different occasions.[4]

Interview with Henry Yip, Chief Executive of the Jardine Restaurant Group

Mr. Henry Yip was formerly the Chief Executive of the Jardine Restaurant Group in Hong Kong and new markets. Under Mr. Yip's leadership, the Pizza Hut and KFC businesses have gained tremendous success both in terms of brand image as well as sales performance. The two brands have also won numerous marketing awards for their innovative ideas and operation efficiency. Mr. Yip is Chairperson of the Retail Training Advisory Committee and is dedicated to upgrading the industry standard and the quality of the talent.

Royce Yuen: Is the restaurant or catering business affected by disruption?

Henry Yip: Disruption happens all the time, and we witness this in food, service, ambiance, and decor. This will happen to mature or new markets but maybe in a different way. That's why every market needs a tailor-made strategy.

Every industry faces certain restrictions or parameters that are unique to its category, and the restaurant business is no exception. Typically, restaurants have to deal with rent, which puts much pressure on operating costs. Due to the increasing popularity of cooking and travel programs, consumers are not only more informed; they have also developed more demanding taste buds. Meeting their growing expectations is key to business survival. With the improvement of the quality of life in most countries, people are moving up the value chain, and they desire better things in life. This creates pressure on business operators because what works today may not work tomorrow. For instance, with consumers continually engaging themselves in social networks like Instagram and

Facebook, it's now the case that the "camera eats before the mouth" because people tend to take pictures of food before they start eating (Image 9.2). Restaurant owners, therefore, have to make sure the appearance and garnishing of their dishes are just as well-executed as the taste of the food.

The habit of sharing dining experience online has disrupted the restaurant business. We have to make sure dishes are dressed up to be visually stunning, and consumers are expecting more for every dollar they spend. People pick up new information every minute, and their exposure has driven expectations even higher. For example, they may expect to taste white truffles and not just black ones because they have learned about the difference between them on social media. Also, since news can be spread around the world instantly, any problem can be immediately magnified. Not too long ago, after a burger chain was confronted with some food safety issues in one market in Asia, consumers in surrounding countries and even globally became skeptical about the product. Although the root of the problem was caused by the meat suppliers, the restaurants had to be accountable ultimately for what they served to customers. Luckily, the chain took prompt action and tackled the problem quickly and effectively; otherwise, there could have been significant ramifications to its overall business worldwide.

RY: How do you tackle disruption caused by technology?

HY: It is the culture that makes a corporation stand out from the rest, and it is the people that create the culture. People are the "heart" of any organization. They are equally, if not more, important than technology. Managing people and having good people is key to long-term success. If we want a business to be

IMAGE 9.2 Feeding the cameras before feeding the mouth is a common ritual around the world. Credit: Shutterstock.

sustainable, we need good people, not just the latest technology. The people will sort out the technology required. For instance, our mobile app and online ordering service offer more flexibility to our customers on how they want to engage with us, while not compromising our commitment to excellent service.

As leaders, we have to strive for non-stop improvement in an overall sense. Companies that care for people, especially their staff and customers, can usually sustain regardless of the different waves of change in the market.

RY: How do you define branding in the modern context? And how should brands connect with millennials?

HY: A brand consists of its own identity, clear image, and brand "personality." In the restaurant industry, 360-degree packaging is required to build a distinctive brand. It requires holistic management of all the five senses down to the very detail, including the genre of music you play in your restaurant. They all contribute to the formulation of your brand. The same goes for the staff uniform, which sends out a signal to your customers and hints at the experience they can expect.

One thing for sure is that branding is more than advertising. It is the summation of all the work devoted to telling people who you are. It takes continuous hard work and investment to build an endurable brand.

Any generation, including millennials, look for the same things when they patronize a restaurant – great taste and excellent service. However, millennials will emphasize the aesthetic value more – the restaurant's 3-D look, feel, color palette, etc., on top of its value for money. One distinct characteristic of millennials is that they lack loyalty. They want to try new things every now and then, so restaurants have to think about how to deliver the "novelty" element as part of the total package. The Maxim's Group, which is a prominent player in the catering business, has implemented a multi-brand strategy for years. The key is not to have too many branches under one brand (e.g. Simply Life), but to have a more diverse portfolio of brands. At Pizza Hut, we always try to strike a balance between pleasing the younger audience and retaining our core brand equity. A good example is Pizza Hut Express, which offers more convenience and value through venues that prioritize takeaway and provide no seating. We also try to introduce new beverage items on the menu, so that there is always something new for customers to try when they visit us. There are six windows each year for product innovation, which has become an essential part of our business strategy. We now offer many dessert items such as ice-cream waffles and chocolate fondant, which are very popular among the younger customers who have a sweet tooth. We need to motivate people to drive all these innovations, which again reinforces the importance of having and managing good people.

We talked about the location of the restaurant earlier, which is an important component of its business. You have to work with the malls, which also have high expectations for their tenants. They do not want too many similar types of food outlets in their location. They also want restaurant brands to be in line with the positioning of the mall and appeal to their target audience. We have adapted ourselves to compete in a highly fragmented market by stepping into the breakfast and tea-time segments. By doing that, we stretch our operation hours throughout the day, which in turn can justify the high rental cost.

RY: Pandemics like COVID-19 may disrupt the market quite severely or even put some companies out of business. How can a brand be more resilient in coping with a dramatic setback like that?

HY: To be more prepared is always better than just reacting to any challenge. A pandemic can put a halt to many business activities. If people are staying home and not going out, it will undoubtedly be detrimental to traditional restaurant operators who solely rely on customers' patronization to their physical outlets. With two brands and three channels in our portfolio, we can adjust the ratio of sales contributions to our total business according to different market operating conditions. Besides our core brand Pizza Hut, we have another brand, PHD, which focuses more on the delivery and takeaway businesses. We roll out these two brands strategically according to different geographic locations to fulfill the different primary needs of the customers. The fact that we offer dine-in, takeaway, and delivery (the three channels) also gives our customers the freedom to pick the most desirable way to enjoy a mouth-watering, piping hot pizza. We have proven time after time that we can withstand tough operating environments caused by unexpected circumstances. The key is to managing all these different units with different, specific skillsets while being able to find good business synergies.

Notes

1 Forbes. "Lexus," July 27, 2020. https://www.forbes.com/companies/lexus/.
2 Mokau, Thato. "The Secret Origin of BMW's 'Ultimate Driving Machine' Slogan." *HotCars*, July 4, 2020. https://www.hotcars.com/secret-origin-bmws-ultimate-driving-machine-slogan/.
3 Tanwar, Shanai. "Rami Malek, Willow Smith, Maisie Williams, Troye Sivan and Jackson Wang Star in Cartier's New Campaign." *Harper's Bazaar Arabia*, September 4, 2020. https://www.harpersbazaararabia.com/featured-news/cartier-unveils-latest-watch-campaign-featuring-willow-smith-troye-sivan-and-other-talents.
4 https://www.pizzahut.com.hk/corp/en/aboutus/hk_macau

10

FROM ROLE TO CUSTOMER TO ROLE TO SOCIETY

FROM MICRO TO MACRO ANALYSIS	FROM STAYING IN TUNE TO STAYING IN TOUCH	FROM CUSTOMER TO COMPETITIVE ANALYSIS	FROM ROLE TO CUSTOMERS TO ROLE TO SOCIETY
CORPORATE Brand is culture	**CONNECTION** Brand is meaning	**CUSTOMER LIFESTYLE** Brand is a way of life	**CONVERGENCE** Brand is to play a role in the user's life
CONTEXT Brand is trends	**COMMUNICATION** Brand is dialogue	**COMPETITIVE ADVANTAGE** Brand is relative	**COMMUNITY** Brand is to play a role in the community
	CONTACT Brand is experience	**CUSTOMIZATION** Brand is fluid	

RESPONSIBLE

FUNCTIONAL   **ASPIRATIONAL**   **LIFESTYLE**

FIGURE 10.1   Examining the responsible aspect of a brand.

In the last chapter, we discussed the relationship between a brand and its users extensively. All kinds of relationships that we experience will go through four stages; the relationship between the brand and its users is no exception (Figure 10.2). First of all, users have to be *aware* of the brand. They may have read about the brand on social media in the form of a product review. Or they may have been exposed to its advertising. It is also possible that the brand was referred to them by their peers. Once the brand is on users' radar, they will pay more attention to it and be more receptive to learn about what it is, what it can do, and how it differs from other brands that they know within the same category. We are bombarded by loads of information every day, or should I say every minute. Our minds work remarkably to help us process information and make meaning out of it. Without having to think, we use *selective attention* to spend time only on issues that concern us. Throughout the process of digesting and filtering information, we employ *selective retention* to keep information that appears relevant and useful. Then, based on our previous experience or perception, we use *selective interpretation* to extract the meaning we have distilled from the information. Our branding message will have to go through this scrutiny, and in the end, maybe only a fraction of it will remain in the mind of the target audience.

If users are curious about the brand and have some initial interest in it, they may proactively search for the brand online or even visit the physical outlet to check it out. After they have learned more about the brand's uniqueness and selling points, they may start to *like* it. Physical interaction with the brand will provide needed assurance, as users will be more certain about the product's quality and ease of use. Some may want to try the brand to get firsthand experience while others may wait further before making a purchase. How quickly they decide will depend on the urgency of their need and the level of investment required. The positive progression of the relationship will lead users to *identify* themselves with the brand. This will usually require a deeper understanding of the value that the brand represents. At this stage, users are likely to see the brand

FIGURE 10.2 Any relationship (including the one between the brand and its users) will go through four stages of development.

as a preferred choice and have sufficient justification for making the final purchase. After the users have been involved with the brand for a while and see that it can consistently deliver the promises it makes, they will finally *trust* the brand and rely on it to cope with the related issues they encounter. Once users trust the brand, they will have faith in it and may not have to go through the same reasoning process again to be further involved with the brand. Yet this commitment and confidence in choosing the brand are not easy to achieve, and there is no guarantee that the relationship will remain the same perpetually.

Convergence – brand is to play a role in the user's life

Consumers will identify with a brand if it aligns with their values. They will also trust the brand if they can benefit from the added values it delivers. This brings out one of the most profound branding principles – *a brand exists because it has a role to play in people's lives*. Indeed, a brand is meant to remove the obstacles users face or improve their quality of life. The more prominent the role of the brand in users' lives, the more important it is and the less likely it is to be replaced. Kirin is a leading beer brand in Japan. It holds a strong position in the lives of its loyal drinkers. Yet a beer brand will only have a role to play after hours when friends meet up in pubs or restaurants. In other words, in the morning and throughout office hours, Kirin will not be on the users' radar. It is a brand out of sight and mind during this significant portion of the day. By introducing Kirin coffee, which can be easily purchased in a vending machine or convenience store near the office, the Kirin brand's total presence will span almost the entire day by serving the users what they need during different times. What is interesting, from a strategic perspective, is that coffee and beer are two different kinds of beverages yet serve quite similar roles. They both can be regarded as "social lubricants" that facilitate conversations among friends or customers. Coffee contains caffeine that refreshes our mind, and beer has alcohol that helps us relax. When our body and spirit unwind, we can have a more enjoyable or fruitful discussion with others. Kirin's case is an act of *brand extension*; it extended a brand's footprint from its core business to another product category.

One of the most successful examples of brand extension is Montblanc. Founded in Germany in 1906, the brand was dedicated to producing premium writing instruments. After decades of just selling pens, Montblanc took a bold move and stepped into the leather goods business. It was a logical move for the brand as the first leather good it produced was a pen pouch for protecting its precious fountain pens. After receiving positive feedback from the market, Montblanc extended its product line to include a wallet, cardholder, briefcase, and leather belt. Gradually, the brand was perceived as serving customers well in men's accessories, so it was able to market other products such as cufflinks, rings, spectacles, and timepieces. Over the years, Montblanc has evolved from purely "a writing instrument" to a brand for empowering people to "write their own success stories." It is still a masterclass in producing sophisticated writing instruments, but the role the brand plays has expanded substantially to support businessmen (and businesswomen) to perform in an environment where both substance and style matter.

In some cases, users' lives will improve significantly when a major obstacle that bothers them is removed. Nano was a compact, inexpensive car launched by Tata, the Indian car manufacturer, during the global financial crisis of 2008. The car was sold at USD 2,500 and positioned as a replacement for motorcycles and scooters.[1] This was more than a lifestyle upgrade; many families relied upon motorcycles for their daily commutes from home to schools and offices. It was quite common for an entire family of four to share a ride on the bike during the busiest times of the day; parents would use it to drop kids off at school before going to work or running errands. Nano aimed to help families feel more comfortable and safer going from one place to another. Although the project came to a halt after a decade due to different reasons, the brand's intended role was a noble one and would inspire other brands to follow.

Community – brand is to play a role in the community

A brand will be treasured and appreciated by its users if it plays a substantial and positive role in their lives. So, if a brand can go beyond its commercial boundaries and play a role in the community, it will naturally be seen as an admirable brand. As mentioned previously, *branding is not just about what you do. It is also about what you do not do.* Doing good may generate goodwill that leads to opportunities for a corporation to do well. Yet it is important to reiterate that serving the community must not simply be done to generate more business or gain positive publicity; otherwise, it will backfire and harm the corporate reputation.

We have discussed brands that are good, bad, and ugly. Good brands are the ones that are distinctive, consistent, and relevant, "relevant" being the most critical attribute of the three. A corporation can be highly profitable and incredibly sizable with market dominance. And yet, it may not be relevant to the society at large, except maybe during tax season. *Branding is not about what you can do or how good you are. It is about the positive difference that you can make.* A responsible brand does not have to compromise profitable opportunities. To be accountable, it must look after its shareholders and staff members' interests while remaining fully aware and committed to playing a role in society. This is more than making a cash donation or sponsoring a big social event. It is about leveraging its expertise and influence to add value to the community. It should consist of a plan with lasting impact rather than an ad hoc idea. It demands a vision, strategy, clear roadmap, and action plan with an objective measure of success. A company of any size can be a responsible corporate citizen. Even a relatively small player can be the initiator of a great campaign that draws upon government resources, social and private sectors to collectively focus on some meaningful causes. Towards the end of this chapter, we will use Green Monday as a case study to see how a big idea may start small but end up as a massive movement. Real leadership is not just about how strong or intelligent the individual is, but about how they can mobilize other people to put in effort and accomplish a common target together. As we have established in our discussion of the new market equilibrium, value creation can be beneficial to all parties concerned. A healthy society will generate demand for all kinds of goods and services.

McDonald's has always prided itself as a place for families to have a wonderful time together. I still keep a faded Polaroid picture of the time my wife and I celebrated our twin daughters' third birthday at McDonald's. These sweet memories are priceless, and last for a lifetime. McDonald's is a brand that is conscious about adding value to families during good times and when their support is needed the most.

Ronald McDonald House Charities (RMHC) was established in 1996 with Ronald McDonald House as its cornerstone project. Ronald McDonald House aims to provide a "home away from home" – accommodation for families so they can stay close to their children who are in need of hospitalization. When a child is hospitalized, family love and support are the best prescription. By providing a comfortable and caring environment, RMHC allows families to stay together during extremely stressful times.

The first Ronald McDonald House opened in Philadelphia in 1974 through the efforts of Fred Hill, a Philadelphia Eagles football player. When his daughter was diagnosed with leukemia, Hill and his wife camped out on hospital chairs and benches and got by on food from vending machines.

They saw others suffering as they did and wondered how they could provide temporary housing for families with seriously ill children. With considerable help from local McDonald's franchises, they established the very first Ronald McDonald House. Today, over 300 Ronald McDonald Houses worldwide provide thousands of rooms for families each night in dozens of countries and regions.

Established in 1996, The House for Hong Kong is the first Ronald McDonald House in Asia. The 2,000-square-meter site is a four-minute walk from the Prince of Wales Hospital in Sha Tin, and the 23-bedroom house gives occupants the privacy of their own air-conditioned, bathroom-equipped bedrooms. Among the house's previous occupants was 15-year-old Yan Yi, suffering from Down Syndrome. When Yan Yi was only two months old, she had heart surgery because of an atrial septal defect and continued to suffer numerous illnesses throughout her childhood. But things took an upturn when a social worker referred her to Ronald McDonald House, where Yi and her family received all-round support from staff and healthcare workers. Yan Yi transformed from a sickly child into a competitive swimmer. She won a gold and a silver medal and broke seven Asian records in the Down's Syndrome World Swimming Championships in Canada in 2018.

Yi's story is just one of many that shows how McDonald's nurtures a corporate culture centered around serving customers' needs sincerely and thoughtfully. This genuine commitment can be a rallying cry that unites the team together to be proud of what they do. And this heartfelt sincerity will naturally be felt in the daily work, which is an important touchpoint between McDonald's and its customers.

A brand-builder's perspective

Interview with Dr. Michael Chan, Honorary Chairman of the Hong Kong Institute of Marketing

Dr. Michael Chan is currently a non-executive director of Café de Coral Holdings, which operates over 580 restaurant units around the world covering territories in the United States, Canada, Hong Kong, and China. He has been the Executive Chairman of the group for 25 years. Dr. Chan is the Honorary Chairman of the Hong Kong Institute of Marketing and is active in the business sector and public services, and also serves as independent director of six other public companies in Hong Kong. With his distinguished management leadership, Dr. Chan is the recipient of various awards, namely the Stars of Asia Award, the Executive of the Year Award, the Bauhinia Cup Outstanding Entrepreneur Award, the Director of the Year Award, and the Ernst & Young Entrepreneur of the Year.

Royce Yuen: Generally speaking, do business owners understand and appreciate the value of brands?

Dr. Michael Chan: Business owners do recognize the importance of brand-building. However, most owners only understand branding on the face value of its name, logo, and slogan, whereas only a few appreciate the value of the brand as a reflection of the company vision and mission. Furthermore, business operators of multi-national corporations (MNC) adopt a longer-term perspective on brand image for sustainable growth purposes, while small and medium-sized enterprises (SMEs) place much emphasis on the immediate benefits derived from their brand value.

RY: Do they see brand-building as an investment or expense?

MC: In the early stages of corporate development, most business owners see brand-building as only a necessary marketing expense to enhance their competitive edge. As for when the company matures, branding is considered as a long-term investment for customer loyalty and market territory expansion.

RY: Are business-owners investing enough time and resources in building their brands? Why?

MC: Most business owners are operation driven, thereby spending most of their energy in the tangible aspects of their businesses, such as operation logistics. As such, they do not dedicate enough resources and attention to the intangibles of brand-building. Rather than leaving branding as a sole mandate for the marketing department, corporations should allocate resources with top-down commitment. The brand should even be a personification of the CEO, as a corporate brand does not only project a personality for the company, but also reflects its beliefs, philosophy, vision, and mission.

RY: What are the biggest challenges faced by marketers these days during the process of brand-building?

MC: Brand-building these days is no longer solely consumer-centric but also community-centric. The process of branding involves engagement with a multitude of stakeholders, including customers, employees, suppliers, interest groups, politicians, and the community at large. The challenges are further exacerbated by the onslaught of social media, putting brand equity at constant risk under public scrutiny.

RY: What is the role of "brand" in the practice of marketing? Has it changed over time?

MC: The role of branding has undoubtedly transformed over time from being product-centric to consumer-centric and to the present human-centric era of the millennials. Brands have to appeal to the inner emotion and aspiration of all stakeholders to make the world a better place, including in areas like environmental concerns and social justice.

RY: What are the common characteristics of great and successful brands?

MC: Great and successful brands usually embody the company's own corporate vision and mission, their business beliefs and philosophy, their commitment to quality and sustainability, and their accountability to all stakeholders, which will ultimately stand the test of time.

Case study – Green Monday

Starting a movement with global impact

Green Monday is a social startup that aims to tackle climate change and global food insecurity by making low-carbon and sustainable living simple, viral, and actionable. Its innovative platform, which consists of public advocacy, impact investing, corporate consulting, and specialized retail, provides holistic and versatile solutions that empower corporations, academic institutions, and the general public globally to build a sustainable and responsible economy (Image 10.1).[2]

In 2015, Green Monday opened its very first plant-based concept store – Green Common – to bring Food 2.0 and a revolutionized food mindset to the mass market, with the mission to normalize eating in a way that is good for ourselves, good for others, and good for the planet. Green Common is where common good becomes common sense. In addition to the retail business, Green Common is also a wholesaler and distributor of vegetarian, vegan, organic, and natural foods. Its expertise on vegetarian and vegan products enables the company to offer expert advice on nutrition and food service for green menu planning.

IMAGE 10.1   Green Monday has started a movement that is now embraced by many like-minded people around the world. Credit: Green Monday.

Interview with Mr. David Yeung, founder and CEO of Green Monday

Mr. David Yeung is the founder and CEO of Green Monday, a multi-faceted social venture with a mission to take on the world's most pressing crises: climate change, food insecurity, and public health (Image 10.2). He has pioneered the global sustainability movement Green Monday; the market-transforming, plant-based, retail, dining, and distribution network Green Common; and the revolutionary food technology innovations Right Treat and Omnipork. His one-of-a-kind integrated platform engages and empowers millions of people, along with public and private sectors, towards green awareness, action and economy. His work has earned him the "Social Entrepreneur of the Year" award by the World Economic Forum and Schwab Foundation. Other honors and recognitions include "Ten Outstanding Young Persons Hong Kong," "50 Most Innovative Companies," and "Idea of the Year."

As a noted environmentalist and entrepreneur, Mr. Yeung has spoken at the World Economic Forum, Milken Institute Summit, and TEDx, as well as financial and academic institutions such as Credit Suisse, UBS, and UCLA. International media coverage of Green Monday and Mr. Yeung has appeared in CNN, CNBC, Bloomberg, and Forbes.

Royce Yuen: You have successfully started a movement that is gaining momentum globally. What are the critical success factors for starting a movement?

IMAGE 10.2   Founder of Green Monday, David Yeung, photographed at the storefront of Green Common. Credit: Green Monday.

David Yeung: The pace of change happens so rapidly these days. The cycle of business planning and new product introduction has been drastically condensed. The smartphone has only been on the market for slightly over a decade and it has already completely disrupted the usual way of doing business.

The traditional way of crafting a message for a defined group of the target audience no longer works as the consumer's expectation is continuously changing. Your message can be easily outdated if you do not keep up with the pace of the consumers.

Marketing today is about "authenticity" – people can relate to key opinion leaders (KOLs) and YouTubers. These people may not have the resources of a huge entertainment company, but they can become stars because they appeal to tens or even hundreds of thousands of fans – this is true disruption.

The same applies to my idea. I preach what I believe. Climate change and environmental protection are topics that touch the lives and hearts of many people around the world. They share the same concerns as I do. Transparency is key when connecting with people. The cruelty and inhuman practice of factory farming is also a fact. I will let the people judge and draw their own conclusion. Manufacturers can't brainwash people with advertising anymore – people look at product labels and do all the fact-finding about how and where the product was made. People subscribe to the idea of "wholesomeness," and will voluntarily follow brands that share the same belief.

When we first started Green Monday, even the most enthusiastic supporters were skeptical because we were going against the norm. Now, Green Monday has become a global movement, and not because of us. It is driven by the people themselves, as they identify with the Green Monday brand, which stands for "authenticity," "trustworthiness," and "integrity." We need to bear in mind that looks and taste are subjective, but integrity is objective (Image 10.3).

Thanks to our persistent effort and the positive word of mouth spread by people, stakeholders such as restaurants and schools have joined the cause, too (Image 10.4). This is how disruption happens in our case.

We do not come across as confrontational, arrogant, or snobbish. We take a humble approach because it is the action and results that count.

RY: What is the most effective way to "motivate" and "engage" consumers these days?

DY: In addition to what we offer, it is also what we do not offer that explains who we are and what we do. People can tell whether you are profit or mission-driven. Once you get their attention, you will be on their radar.

Of course, we will have to present ourselves in a relevant way so that people can see why we do what we do. For instance, people are becoming more interested in health and wellness. Many people engage in running, yoga, or other kinds of sports regularly, and dieting goes hand in hand with living a healthier lifestyle. In fact, traditional diet culture is lagging behind. There is a

IMAGE 10.3 Launching Green Monday in Thailand. Credit: Green Monday.

IMAGE 10.4 VeggieLicious is a veggie promotional event co-organized with Green Monday and supported by PolyU. Credit: Green Monday.

latent demand for a more proper and healthy diet, which opens up a window of opportunity for us.

I have been a vegetarian myself for 18 years. I understand some people crave vegetables for different reasons (health, religion, etc.) but they have been underserved for years. We are also turning a vegetarian diet from being seen as making a sacrifice to a trendy lifestyle. The Beyond Burger now accounts for 15% of the sales of the Butcher's Club, and is one of the hottest-selling items that is gaining more and more popularity (Image 10.5).

From an environmental standpoint, things are getting so bad that the consciousness level of people will only go up as the adverse effect of global warming and climate change has caused so many natural disasters around the world in recent years. People can no longer pretend that these terrible things are not happening.

Timing is also an important factor. We have seen disruption in transportation, office space, hotels, communications, music, and entertainment; food happens to be the last frontier that hasn't been disrupted. FoodTech is now a hot topic in Silicon Valley. Aside from innovative entrepreneurs and venture capitalists, iconic figures like Bill Gates, Richard Branson, Leonardo DiCaprio, James Cameron, and Li Ka-Shing are showing increasing interest and backing up the research and development in this area. Food innovation is offering more choices to the market. For example, vegetarian burgers made with natural ingredients provide people with the sizzling sensation that is rich in protein and iron, yet

IMAGE 10.5 Selling at US$5.4 for a 230-gram bag, Omnipork is a novelty choice for both vegetarians and meat-lovers. Credit: Green Monday.

they are free from cholesterol, GMO, antibiotics, and hormones. It differs from fake meat, which is extremely unhealthy.

Green Monday is not trying to sell anything. We are simply offering a new way of living. The market has the urge and need; we are just acting as the catalyst.

RY: How do you turn your staff into your "brand advocate"?

DY: We have created a workplace and career disruption in a positive way. Of our staff, 20% proactively approached us because their life values and passion align with our brand vision, while 50% of them came to us after reading our stories on Facebook or after visiting our physical stores. There was a reporter who wanted to join our team after interviewing me. Again, we never force people to act. We just have to keep our doors open and be honest about what we do.

RY: How do you define a "brand"? What role does your "brand" play in this movement, and what is its contribution to your business?

DY: A brand comes with a reputation. It is a combination of credibility, responsibility, good quality, track record, and authenticity. Spending money to build a brand is already contradictory. We should be spending our best effort, not money, to build brands by providing added value to the people that we serve. We believe doing good and doing well can co-exist. Of course, there is a certain degree of difficulty in doing good before doing well because the rules of the game do not always allow that. Once you have overcome the initial hurdle, the "do good" portion of the initial period can become an intangible asset for advancing your business forward because you are gaining goodwill in the market.

Notes

1 Chandran, Rina. "Tata Unveils the Nano, World's Cheapest Car." *Reuters*, January 10, 2008. https://www.reuters.com/article/idINIndia-31331120080110.
2 Green Monday. "About Green Monday Foundation." Accessed October 6, 2020. https://greenmonday.org/en/green-monday-foundation/.

11

THE 4E BRAND MANAGEMENT PROCESS

The 10 Cs of Sustainable Branding discussed in the last few chapters provide a complete checklist for brand owners to ascertain how well their brands perform against meaningful dimensions. This chapter will introduce a framework for how to build and manage a brand step by step. *The 4E Brand Management Process (4E-BMP)* is a logical approach that can unleash a brand's potential and keep it competitive in today's constantly changing marketplace (Figure 11.1).

Building a viable brand requires more than marketing investment. *Your brand is like your child. It bears your DNA.* Naturally, you will have certain expectations of your child, and you may recognize their inborn qualities and talents. It is your responsibility to provide the care, guidance, and resources for your child to grow up healthy. But in most cases, your child may outgrow your expectations; after all, they are constantly absorbing nutrients and inspirations from the outside world. Their interactions with peers and other people surrounding them will also mold their future. Our job as parents is to steer our children and nurture them throughout the good and bad times. We must also keep an open mind and welcome other people to provide them with more knowledge and coaching.

Most importantly, we want our children to uphold the right value system, possess an adorable personality, and behave. In the end, we want them to do well and do good, be a useful person, and add value to our society. In one of the corporate training sessions I conducted for a sizable corporation that possesses its own brands and acts as the sole distributor of various reputable global brands in Asia, I was once asked the following question: how should we treat the brands that we do not own when we are just the custodians? I used the above analogy to explain my answer. Although these brands are like our adopted children and may return to their biological parents one day, it does not mean that we should love them less. We took these infants under our wing because others believed we had the competence, resources, patience, and commitment to help them grow

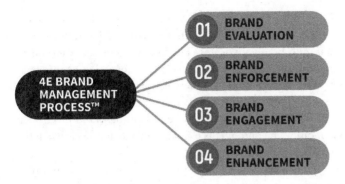

FIGURE 11.1 The 4E Brand Management Process is a step-by-step approach for building a viable and enduring brand.

and shine. The process can be tremendously rewarding, and no one can claim the
achievement and pride we feel from nurturing such outstanding individuals with
great characters and promising futures.

The 4E-BMP is like a blueprint for building a massive architecture that has
both practical and aesthetic values. Brands that are built with solid foundations
have the potential to become a permanent landmark. Like the Empire State
Building in New York, the Shanghai Financial Tower, or the Burj Khalifa in
Dubai, these buildings bear important symbolic meanings and are icons in their
respective cities.

The 4E-BMP involves four interlinked steps that this chapter will first briefly
summarize below, then illustrate in more detail:

Brand evaluation – The first step of 4E-BMP is to find out where the brand
currently stands in the market and in consumers' minds. It warrants the
interrogation of the brand's position from all angles, including the brand's
performance from the user's perspective, how it compares with the main
competition, lost business opportunities, how well it is represented by staff
at all the contact points, etc. This will ensure that we derive an objective,
professional, and complete evaluation that can lead to the successful formulation of the most viable brand strategy.

Brand enforcement – After gathering all the relevant information and strategic
insights, the next step is to consolidate all the inputs to articulate your
brand promise in a compelling way that your target customers cannot
resist. Brand transformation involves more than just launching a new
advertising campaign. It may require fundamental changes to the product
design or how the service is delivered. In a nutshell, the focus of brand
enforcement is to identify an enduring and viable positioning for the brand
so that it answers customers' needs better than the competition can in a
highly differentiating way.

Brand engagement – The third step of the 4E–BMP is to map out an integrated approach to effectively engage the brand's different stakeholders to the extent of converting them into brand advocates. The branding messages should be customized so that the various segments receive the most relevant information throughout the different stages of their involvement with the brand. All the above-the-line and below-the-line communication work should be reviewed thoroughly to assess whether they reinforce the brand promise at every single touchpoint. The outcome is to maintain a dialogue between the brand and its stakeholders to contribute to strong bonding.

Brand enhancement – A strong brand may enable the corporation to step into new territory that has synergy with its core business. By doing so, the corporation can leverage its established brand equity through brand extension, new segment penetration, a global expansion strategy, and more means.

Brand evaluation

The first step of 4E–BMP is an extension of the 10 Cs of Sustainable Branding. It is a consolidation of the brand's biggest strengths and limitations. The purpose of brand evaluation is not to simply obtain a scorecard or glorify the brand's exceptional achievements. Instead, it is about objectively discovering "what is not working" and going to the root of "why it is not working." To properly complete the first step, the corporation's management needs to be prepared to face some potentially brutal facts about their organization's fundamental problems. That said, brand evaluation is not about fault-finding or finger-pointing either. It is a professional and fair investigation of the brand's current performance. It may not be a pleasant process, but it is like doing a thorough health checkup. Identifying alarming news during a checkup may be a good thing because it allows us to promptly take the necessary actions to set our bodies on the track of recovery as soon as possible. If we avoid finding out or confronting the problem, the problem may worsen to a point of no return.

A regular health checkup may be done for the sake of being prudent. Or there may be irregular symptoms or certain malfunctions that trigger a special examination of the situation. Either way, the 10 Cs provide a useful assessment that can lead to fruitful conclusions:

Corporate
- Do the team members (from the management to operation level) understand and embrace the brand values?
- Are they able to uphold the brand values in their work, both internally and externally?
- Are their values aligned, or do they have different interpretations of the brand?

Context

- To what extent is the brand keeping up with industry and global trends throughout its product and service delivery?
- Is the brand a trend-setter, follower, or laggard?
- Does the brand have any major innovations and breakthroughs in product design or service fulfillment?

Connection

- What are the brand's most profound values?
- Is the meaning represented by the brand relevant to stakeholders today, and how?
- Can these values and meanings be tangibly substantiated?

Communication

- Does the brand maintain an optimum level of dialogue with its stakeholders in terms of frequency and intensity?
- What is the quality and variety of these dialogues?
- Does the brand structurally receive any feedback from the market and take these comments into account?

Contact

- Does the brand provide a thorough and consistent experience to its stakeholders?
- Is the brand experience effectively and seamlessly disseminated through the line?
- Do the brand ambassadors provide the desired "moment-of-truth" at different touchpoints?

Customer lifestyle

- To what extent is the brand empowering the consumers to live the way they want?
- Does the brand meet the consumers' different levels of needs and expectations?
- Does the brand utilize all the relevant and useful elements to deliver the desired consumer lifestyle?

Competitive advantage

- How is the brand better than its competitors in serving the needs of the customers?
- What can be learned from the competition?
- Is the brand leveraging its full potential and all the available resources to lead the market?

Customization

- Does the brand delight different customer groups while maintaining its core brand proposition?
- Is the brand dynamic enough to seize current and future business opportunities?
- How innovative and creative is the brand in presenting its selling points to the users?

Convergence

- What is the positive difference that the brand has brought to the lives of its users?
- Is the role played by the brand getting more or less prominent over time?
- What can be done to strengthen the bond between the brand and its users?

Community

- What is the positive difference that the brand has brought to the community?
- Is the role played by the brand getting more or less prominent over time?
- What can be done to expand and spread the positive influence led by the brand?

The above points may be summarized by a simple three-point roadmap: find out where we stand, identify where we want to go, and define the best way to reach the desired destination. Brand evaluation is a fact-finding process that lays out all the facts and findings of the investigation. Its strategic implications explain why the brand and the business achieve the current performance and customer satisfaction level. A robust process will involve both quantitative and qualitative efforts, plus an interrogation of all the available and relevant sales, market, and customer data. It is recommended to conduct the same process periodically or when there are any unusual factors that may change the market dynamics so as to keep track of the brand performance.

Brand enforcement

After completing a thorough diagnosis, the next step is to resolve the branding issues identified according to the corporation's priorities. This may require refining the product design, boosting certain product features, or reconfiguring the service delivery. Furthermore, there may be miscommunication or a lack of contact and understanding from either side during the engagement process. This is an area that we will discuss in the next section. At the same time, it makes sense to further reinforce leadership in areas where the brand is performing exceptionally well.

Whether the corporation aims to tackle an image or operational issue or strengthen its leading edge, the outcome should contribute to a clear articulation of the most viable *brand proposition*.

Every brand can be special because of its unique DNA. Thus, it is logical to revisit or, in some cases, dig up the original corporate mission from the brand's inception. Obviously, the corporation may have evolved over the years, and the scope of its services and product range may have expanded quite substantially. Still, the original purpose of the brand creation will always remain the common factor that brings the team together. For example, the status of women today vastly differs from how they were perceived in 1910, the year that Coco Chanel opened her first shop on Paris's Rue Cambon.[1] Yet the spirit of Chanel's devotion to "style" and not just "fashion" is evergreen. Likewise, there was no Internet or digital technology when David Ogilvy founded his agency in 1948. Still, the agency's commitment to the interminable pursuit of creative ideas for positive business transformation remains the core motivation for the stunning work it produces for clients around the world today.

The focus of brand enforcement is to anchor the brand strategically based on the findings and insights distilled from step one. A brand is the total impression that our stakeholders have of us in their minds and in their hearts. Hence, the key is to translate the brand DNA into something that emotionally resonates with the consumers and offers tangible benefits that can be seen and felt every time they encounter the brand. A concrete depiction of the *brand values* will connect the brand with like-minded people and attract them to join the brand world, be it as coworkers or consumers. An enduring brand is evidence-based and makes good sense to its stakeholders.

Clearly defining the *brand personality* with a list of carefully curated brand attributes will create a mental picture of what the brand is and is not. This will guide the corporation in crafting content with an appropriate tone and formulating marketing activities that synchronize strategically with their overall brand direction.

Brand guidelines can be developed to provide a clear briefing on brand expression and ensure there is a unified understanding of the brand proposition. Brand guidelines are not meant to create rigid boundaries for people. In fact, they are meant to produce the opposite effect. By referencing a set of clearly defined guidelines, concerned parties can be assured that they are projecting a consistent image according to the right principles and communicating with the appropriate visual language. As such, they will have more flexibility in executing their programs.

Brand engagement

Brand-building does not happen inside the board room. After we identify a viable and potent brand proposition, the next step is to reach out to stakeholders and engage them proactively. *One universal truth about marketing is that there are no unlimited resources.* The expected brand strategy these days is to outsmart, and not to outspend, the competition. Not to mention that we are not just competing with our head-on competition but also all the other information out there that takes up the time and attention of our target audience. Corporations should map out a year-long schedule that details how they will communicate and engage with different stakeholders on an ongoing basis using the most sensible budget. This contact strategy should be reviewed and updated as needed to ensure the maximum impact is created with a lasting impression.

A brand promise can be reinforced or diminished based on the brand experience at every touchpoint. A well-orchestrated message architecture is critical for ensuring that the branded content will be consistent without being redundant or repetitive. Communication is about storytelling. Effective storytelling involves the right storytellers and includes a compelling way of telling the story on top of the story itself. Message architecture is a matrix that outlines key messages through the appropriate corresponding media. The four types of media (paid, earned, owned, and shared) discussed in Chapter Two should be tactfully deployed in the most desirable permutations so that stakeholders can be supplied with the most relevant information during their entire journey with the brand. Media has also evolved to be much more than a messenger. To maximize the value of each media, corporations must thoroughly understand its characteristics and capitalize on its strengths.

In this new age of stakeholder involvement, communication is only part of the big picture. Stakeholders prefer more active engagement with the opportunity to interact, provide feedback, and co-create. Brand owners should carefully plan the outcome of each encounter so that a positive loop can be ignited to generate desired results. After all, the relationships between a brand and its different stakeholders do not exist in a silo but rather as a network of constant exchange. An example of this positive loop is the "Dumb Ways to Die" campaign that Melbourne's Metro Trains rolled out in 2012. Every city is concerned with public transportation safety, but railway safety education is not always effective. "Dumb Ways to Die," a public service announcement disguised as a catchy song, got almost 200 million views on YouTube.[2] It replaced the usual "parent's lecture" with fun and memorable lyrics that could effectively promote the campaign's safety message to any audience. Later on, online games, storybooks, and roadshows featuring the characters that appeared in the music video magnified the campaign's positive indoctrination by targeting different age groups in the community.

Brand engagement is also about sending out an invitation to the target audience or arousing their curiosity so that they will proactively search for the brand themselves based on personal needs and interests. Therefore, a brand must be searchable online and present the right level of information that is adequately organized both in terms of depth and breadth, making it accessible to any searcher.

Brand enhancement

The best way to counteract market disruption is to reset your own agenda. This reinvention can range from the modest introduction of a new brand experience to an astonishing revolution through which the brand steps into totally new territory. The most common ways to add novelty and excitement to existing customers include introducing seasonal products for a limited period of time, extending the product line, or adding a new product line. A brand can extend to any new form of brand manifestation as long as it retains its core brand values. Following a sensible and successful brand extension, a brand can play a more extensive role in users' lives. It can also expand its customer base without alienating its regular and loyal users. As mentioned in Chapter Ten, Montblanc is a classic example of a brand that successfully stretched into various dimensions. Its collection of writing instruments consists of regular editions, special editions, and limited editions. It provides customers with legitimate reasons to own a variety of its products, even though they all perform the same functionality.

While Montblanc retained the same brand while expanding its business scope, Armani adopted a different strategy by introducing a portfolio of sub-brands to cater to different categories. Aside from Giorgio Armani, which is its flagship brand, it has Armani Collezioni, Emporio Armani, Armani Jeans, EA7, A|X Armani Exchange, and Armani Juniors to serve different market segments. The brand has also extended its footprint to other business sectors by introducing Armani Beauty, Armani Casa, and Armani/Privé.

Brand innovation is not limited to product development. Alibaba experiences exponential growth by tirelessly experimenting with "new retail" business models and aggressively bridging its online and offline arenas. Aside from its core business in e-commerce, the group now consists of cloud computing, mobile media and entertainment, and other innovative initiatives such as healthcare and insurance. Its brand DNA of "unlimited possibilities enabled by technology" is a common thread that links its different businesses under the same roof.

Likewise, if Amazon had not meticulously enhanced its brand, it might still only be an online retailer for books. Brand-building is an ongoing commitment. It takes tremendous discipline, effort, investment, and courage to cultivate an immense horizon. Observing and exercising the branding principles such as the ones cited in this book can shorten a corporation's soul-searching path and increase their chances of success.

A brand-builder's perspective

Interview with Dr. William Leung, SBS, JP, Chairman of Legal Aid Services Council

Dr. William Leung has served as Executive Director of Hang Seng Bank, CEO of Sun Hung Kai Financial, and CEO of WeLab Bank. He has also held key positions in major financial institutions in Hong Kong and Australia, including

American Express, Standard Chartered Bank, Visa International, and Mastercard International.

Dr. Leung serves a spectrum of community and public organizations. He is Chairman of the Legal Aid Services Council, Chairman of the Estate Agent Authority, Chairman of the Hong Kong Creative Arts Centre, Emeritus Chairman of the Hong Kong Dance Company, Vice Chairman of the Hong Kong Heart Foundation, and an adviser of the Our Hong Kong Foundation, just to name a few.

In view of his distinguished services, HKBU awarded him an Honorary University Fellowship in 2013 and a Distinguished Alumni Award in 2013–14. For the same reason, HKU Space conferred upon him a Distinguished Alumni Fellowship in 2010, and VTC granted him an Honorary Fellowship in 2016. In October 2017, he received an Honorary Doctorate from the Hong Kong Academy for Performing Arts and an Honorary Fellowship from HKU Space.

The Government of the HKSAR appointed Dr. Leung as Justice of the Peace in 2005 and honored him with a Bronze Bauhinia Star and a Silver Bauhinia Star in 2009 and 2016, respectively.

Royce Yuen: What is the impact of technology on managing a business and a brand?

Dr. William Leung: Technology is used in business for a lot of different purposes. Some businesses use it for economic reasons, some for speed of service, others for control and for improvement of customer experience, etc. Adopting the right technology projects a positive image on the business because it is generally believed that a strong technological foundation enables further service improvement and product enhancement. So, the use of technology in business is a must and not just an option nowadays.

RY: What is the biggest difference between a physical and a virtual bank?

WL: The answer to your question differs from market to market because of different local regulations. But broadly speaking, the biggest difference lies within the use of bank branches. Virtual banks that do not serve customers with manned branches obviously have to adopt more technology to narrow the otherwise present service gaps.

RY: How do you convince people to put money in a virtual bank?

WL: Some people are dissatisfied with traditional bank branch services and find them very unfriendly. This group would need no encouragement to switch to a virtual bank. They would voluntarily sign up to try out the service of a virtual bank. As for the others, more effort would be required to attract and interest them. They would need to be convinced by appeals such as bank image, financial stability, pricing, user experience, etc.

RY: What is the changing consumer expectation when it comes to wealth management?

WL: Customers interested in wealth management have just one unique expectation, and that is to earn good returns on their investments. This statement, however, is only true for those who are eligible and experienced. There is a big group of potential customers who have not started to invest yet because of inadequate capital or lack of investment knowledge. This is an expectation yet to be met by financial houses.

RY: How do you manage customers across different generations?

WL: In a traditional bank, customers are not managed by generations but by life stages. A young person would need a bank account for receiving payrolls and savings, a credit card for shopping and entertainment. When a young man gets married, he will need a mortgage. When his baby is born, he will need insurance, and so on. In the end, he will need investments for his retirement. Businesses used to segregate the tech-savvy from the tech-illiterate by generations, but this concept is out-of-date. Seniors in their 70s are now capable of surfing the web with their mobile phones and fulfilling their needs on the Internet.

RY: What are the key principles for building a strong and enduring wealth management brand?

WL: Financial houses are entrusted with clients' hard-earned money. Clients expect financial houses to look after their money with care and professionalism. That is my personal belief as a veteran banker. So, when I had the chance to design the branding strategy for the company where I served as CEO, the advertising headline I used was "Putting Customers' Interests First." We pledged to take good care of their money as opposed to maximizing the company's profit. Once we won their trust, we could win their hearts and, additionally, their customer referrals.

Case study – SmarTone

Be smart when serving customers

Interview with Dr. Anna Yip, CEO of SmarTone

Dr. Anna Yip is the CEO of SmarTone, a leading mobile operator in Hong Kong known for its powerful network, superior customer service, and digital innovations. Entering the 5G era, SmarTone is blazing the trail for the new technology and Smart City development in Hong Kong (Image 11.1).

Before she joined SmarTone, Dr. Yip was Head of Hong Kong and Macau for MasterCard Asia/Pacific and Managing Director for Strategy and Planning at the United Overseas Bank. Prior to that, she was a partner with McKinsey & Company in Greater China where she was a co-leader of the Asia Financial Institutional Group and led the Asia Payments practice.

IMAGE 11.1   SmarTone is a leading telecommunications company providing voice, multimedia, and mobile broadband services, as well as fixed fiber broadband services for the consumer and corporate markets. Credit: smartone .com.

Dr. Yip is an independent non-executive director and Head of the Risk Committee of Bupa (Asia) Limited. She is also active in public service. Dr. Yip is an appointed lay member by the HKSAR Government at the Joint Committee on Student Finance, and a member of the Civil Court Users' Committee of the Judiciary of the HKSAR Government. Concurrently, Dr. Yip is the Vice Chairman of the Women Executives Club of the Hong Kong General Chamber of Commerce, and a member of the Advisory Board of MBA Programs of the Chinese University of Hong Kong. She was formerly an appointed council member of the Open University of Hong Kong, and chairperson of the Audit Committee.

Dr. Yip earned both MPhil and DPhil degrees in Management Studies from the University of Oxford and her undergraduate degree from the Chinese University of Hong Kong with First Class honors.

Royce Yuen: Has your market been "disrupted" by the digital revolution? In what ways?

Anna Yip: Yes, although more in terms of customer engagement than in transactions. Many customers still prefer the traditional mode of going to the shop or talking to customer service agents for transacting their service needs. At SmarTone, we are optimizing customers' touch points with digitalization and offering seamless O2O (online to offline) experiences.

RY: Do you see any significant changes in terms of consumer expectations and behavior?

AY: In the telco industry, digital engagement is changing some of the customers' expectations and behaviors. In light of that, we introduced the first all-digital self-service mobile brand in Hong Kong in 2017. "Birdie," which was specifically designed for millennials and tech-savvy customers, provides simple and easy service and onboarding through its online platform. Customers have access to various innovative features including the Birdie Farm (a popular proprietary online game developed for the brand).

RY: *How is brand-building now different compared to what it was ten or even five years ago?*

AY: Traditional media is still important, but digital media plays an increasingly important role, even though it is not displacing traditional ones yet. In other words, TV advertising is still important, but it is appearing in different forms beyond traditional terrestrial TV, like over-the-top (OTT) streaming services.

RY: *What is the role of "brands" in this digital era? Has its role been diminished or expanded? Why?*

AY: The role of brands is of paramount importance in an age of tremendous "noise" and information overload. An average consumer is bombarded with so much news and data that brand-building becomes ever more critical yet challenging. Authentic brand differentiation is the key.

RY: *How does your brand tackle or embrace this digital revolution?*

AY: We believe that relentless focus on the customer experience is required for success in the digital age; brands should literally be obsessed with the customer experience in every way. We still have much to learn and improve on that front. Every time I use our own app or visit a store, I find something that may be improved to drive a better experience. I often draw on my experience as a product manager working in the consumer product industry; one should be constantly, totally immersed in the development and improvement of one's products to drive the best results on an ongoing basis.

Notes

1 Inside Chanel. "1910." Accessed October 6, 2020. http://inside.chanel.com/en/timeline/1883_birth-of-gabrielle-chanel.
2 McCann Australia. "Metro Trains: Dumb Ways to Die." Accessed October 5, 2020. https://mccann.com.au/work/dumb-ways-to-die/.

CONCLUSION

The magic and logic of branding

There is no better way to wrap up our discussion on branding than by reviewing both the "magical" and the "logical" sides of it. This concludes our rigorous journey of *Decoding Branding* and reveals the harmonious fusion of its seemingly paradoxical interpretations. It also urges us to adopt a holistic approach to understand and manage our brands so that they can flourish to their full potential.

Values + added values

One of the focal points of this book is to refine or redefine the concept of branding in the age of disruption. To persevere in today's highly unpredictable marketplace, a brand has to stand for a set of values that appeals to our conscience as citizens of a global village. This is what makes a brand great and admirable and leads people to identify with it. Simultaneously, it must provide added values to remove people's problems or improve the quality of their lives. As such, a brand has both magical and logical reasons to exist.

Tangible + intangible

A brand has an intangible nature because it exists in our minds, and is so dynamic that it cannot be contained by any physical boundaries. Yet it is more than just a concept. It is the most important asset of any organization. People are willing to pay a premium to enjoy the tangible benefits a brand delivers through its superior products, services, and experiences. A responsible brand plays a prominent role in our community and can make a positive difference that touches the lives of many.

Mind + heart

People make decisions in life for both rational and emotional reasons. This applies to the purchase of any product, either for self-consumption or as a gift for others. To be likable and trustworthy, a brand must speak to both the minds and hearts of consumers. In this digital era, consumers have full access to all critical information, and they possess the power and influence to cause the success or failure of any corporation. A brand must provide proof and evidence to justify any consumer action and build an emotional connection beyond reasoning.

Incentives + reasons

In today's borderless world, consumers can buy anything, anytime, anywhere. A brand must offer sufficient incentives to reward consumers and stay competitive when technologies substantially narrow the gap among different players. Size is no longer a guarantee of any long-term prosperity. A product leader today can be surpassed by any form of competition or substitute tomorrow, to the extent where the entire industry can be completely disrupted. However, offering incentives alone is not enough. To win the loyalty of the most profitable customers, which is the ultimate goal of any corporation, a brand must provide the reasons for people to continue having a relationship with it that gives rise to strong bonding between them both emotionally and structurally.

Feel good + feel right

A brand can delight a customer and fulfill their dreams. This "feel good" element is priceless and is what makes a product aspire to be a brand. This assurance and peace of mind come from value creation and a promise of a brighter future for people who are engaged with the brand. As consumers become more discerning and sophisticated, they subscribe to brands with a more profound undertaking for a sustainable world. Only the brands that can make people "feel right," not just "feel good," will be the true winners in the end.

Science + art

The deployment of data science and analytics has changed the practice of brand management and overall marketing from planning to implementation. This is a megatrend, and more advanced tools and techniques empowered by artificial intelligence (AI) will be made available to business operators. When campaign results are precisely measurable, marketers become more accountable. Marketing spending can be planned according to the increasingly accurate indication of the return on investment (ROI) that different forms of communication generate. As data becomes more accessible and abundant, brands that deploy a genuine understanding of consumer psychology to entice and engage consumers creatively will gain a competitive advantage.

Instant + lasting

A wholesome brand can add magic to people's lives in an instant. Consumers never analyze as marketers do, but they can feel the difference right away. This is how a brand can stay relevant to the people it serves. Obviously, making this spontaneous connection and magical transformation requires substantial planning and investment that must be logically justified. As long as brands can stay relevant to changing consumer lifestyles and expectations, they can be enduring icons that set the industry standard.

Left brain + right brain

Knowing that branding is a combination of science and art, business owners must assemble a team that consists of both the logical "left brain" and the creative "right brain." With this configuration, the team can work seamlessly as one to effectively understand, strategize, innovate, and create product ideas and marketing programs that will contribute to the building of brands with a sustainable future.

Beginning + discovery

We are approaching the end of this book, but it is by no means the end of our discussion and exchange on the topic of branding. The purpose of this book is to form the basis for further academic research, to test some of the hypotheses introduced here, and to trigger business owners and operators to pay more attention to branding. A website has been set up to facilitate ongoing exchange about the latest branding developments to enrich our collective understanding of this domain. I hope reading this book has increased your interest in branding and allowed you to see its relevance to you and your work. Your comments and inputs are welcome and highly appreciated. I will continue my journey of learning and investigating the evolution of branding, a subject that will only increase in value and importance as we venture into the future.

Appendix I
LIST OF KEY BRANDING PRINCIPLES

Branding is a dynamic concept. The same brand can mean different things to different people, depending on their relationship with the brand. A brand may therefore manifest itself in different ways and play different roles in the user's life.

A lifestyle brand is a brand that matches our life philosophy. We do not carry these brands to project a certain image. We identify with them because they allow us to pursue the style of living we desire.

A responsible brand is concerned with more than just its own commercial interest. It will not compromise on its ethical values during its pursuit of profit.

A brand stands for absolute quality and implies a more satisfying experience. A trusted brand gives people assurance and peace of mind. As such, people engage in brands they believe in. The brand becomes a promise, and it nurtures relationships based on this promise.

Your brand exists before you start to promote or advertise it.

If you do not actively manage your brand and guide people on how to appreciate it, you are leaving it to the audience to define your brand.

A loyal customer is not necessarily someone who buys your brand regularly but one who promotes your brand and defends your brand voluntarily.

There is no trade-off between building a brand and building sales. They complement each other due to the simple fact that a well-crafted brand will attract buyers, and the more that people use the product, the more they appreciate what the brand can do for them.

Premium pricing has to be justified by superior quality and product performance, or else the brand will not last long in the market.

A brand can be low-cost but not low-end.

To merit the ongoing support of their users, brands must maintain the following qualities:

- Experience: to satisfy the users and enrich their lives in a tangible way;
- Entertainment: to engage the users with exceptional sensations;
- Collaboration: to involve the users in manifesting the values of the brand;
- Technology: to enhance the delivery system and infrastructure;
- Newsiness: to offer upgrades and surprises that are in line with the brand proposition.

Your brand can be regarded as your most valuable asset. It is the result of all the hard work you have put into your business and the market reputation that you have earned over the years.

A brand will draw the consumers to focus on the value they can get rather than the price they have to pay.

A product becomes a brand when it has a personality.

Building a brand is different from selling a product because it is not just about what you do as a corporation, but also how and why you do it.

In the age of disruption, companies that continue to produce a standard product will fade away, but those who possess strong and enduring brands will persevere.

A brand is unique because of its brand DNA.

A brand is defined by the people who relate to it rather than the brand-owner itself.

Branding is not about making but delivering the promise.

Building a brand is like playing chess. You need to understand your opponents, then work out a viable strategy and plan a few steps ahead before you make any move.

Regardless of its age, a brand will start to age when it loses its relevance to the users.

To revitalize a brand is to make it relevant again by reconnecting with the consumers of today.

Brands can stretch their life cycle by keeping abreast of the latest market and consumer trends or introducing new variants guided by their brand DNA.

The concept of branding applies not only to commercial products but also to cities, countries, non-governmental organizations (NGOs), and people.

Brand-building is not only about what we do, but also what we don't do.

A brand with a long history can also be modern and cutting-edge. There is no tradeoff between heritage and innovation.

Branding provides rational reasons for consumers to behave irrationally.

Brands only exist when humans appreciate them; they do not exist by themselves.

In the digital and interactive world, branding is a collective experience, and everyone can play a part that will either reinforce or diminish the brand experience and its reputation.

People can see your behavior, feel your personality, and sense your values. Together, they represent the totality of who you are and what you stand for in the eyes of those interacting with your brand.

A brand is the set of values that it represents and the actual values that it can add to those who are involved with the brand.

A great brand does not only add value to its users; it also radiates positive energy that brings opportunities and possibilities to anyone who is involved with the brand.

People are connected to the values of the brand, attracted by its personality, and impacted by its behavior.

Users will regularly appraise their relationships with different brands, and there is no obligation for them to stick to the same brand for any category.

It is critical to ensure that the brand is properly understood and embraced by the team whose task is to promote the brand to the outside world. If they are not convinced about the values of the brand themselves, there is no way that they can convince others.

A brand is worthless if it is not appreciated by the people it serves.

A brand can only blame itself for any customer defection, for being good is no longer good enough.

A brand exists because it has a role to play in people's lives.

A truly respected and admired brand extends its positive influence from the industry to the community.

A sustainable brand is one that understands and can meet changing expectations by offering the most appealing and up-to-date merchandise according to "customer lifestyle."

Brand-building should always start from within the corporation. This is why the most critical decision that a corporation has to make is to hire the right people.

The user's experience will depend on how much the staff understands and embraces the brand vision.

Disruptive brands can transform a market and redefine an industry because they are trend-setters.

Branding is not what you do. It is what you stand for.

If a brand can truly represent an important value to people, it will possess the quality to endure for generations.

In a digital age where consumers have abundant choices, a brand cannot remain merely a concept. It must offer tangible values to the people it serves, or it will be easily replaced.

A brand must stand for a set of intangible values that can be translated into tangible meaning and have a lasting impact on people's lives.

Selling is the outcome, not the purpose, of branding.

The brand experience at every touchpoint can reinforce or diminish a brand promise.

A brand is more likely to succeed if it can serve customers better than its competitors can.

A brand cannot stop its customers from checking out competitive offers. What a brand can do and should do, however, is to build a fruitful and ongoing relationship with its customers so that they are less inclined to switch to a competitive brand under any circumstance.

Every consumer has a mental repertoire of brands for different categories, also known as a "consideration set." A brand has first to enter this league to be considered. Then, it has to emerge as the preferred choice by presenting consumers with a compelling and unrivaled argument, which usually consists of both rational and emotional reasons.

A brand should not blame competitors for its loss of business. Instead, it should ask itself why it was not able to fulfill the changing needs of the consumers or, in some cases, did not even realize that consumers expected something different or better.

In the age of disruption, a consumer's consideration set can completely change when disruptive brands emerge to fulfill their needs in unconventional ways. These brands provide an eye-opening experience to consumers and may change their expectations and behavior forever.

Consumers today welcome brands that are dynamic and multi-dimensional by being luxurious, cute, classic, and modern at the same time.

Branding is not about what you can do or how good you are. It is about the positive difference that you can make.

Your brand is like your child. It bears your DNA.

Brand engagement is about sending out an invitation to the target audience or arousing their curiosity so that they will proactively search for the brand themselves based on personal needs and interests. Therefore, a brand must be searchable online and present the right level of information that is adequately organized both in terms of depth and breadth, making it accessible to any searcher.

The best way to counteract market disruption is to reset your own agenda. This reinvention can range from the modest introduction of a new brand experience to an astonishing revolution through which the brand steps into totally new territory.

A brand can extend to any new form of brand manifestation as long as it retains its core brand values.

A brand must provide proof and evidence to justify any consumer action and build an emotional connection beyond reasoning.

To win the loyalty of the most profitable customers, which is the ultimate goal of any corporation, a brand must provide the reasons for people to continue having a relationship with it that gives rise to strong bonding between them both emotionally and structurally.

Only the brands that can make people "feel right," not just "feel good," will be the true winners at the end.

INDEX

Page numbers in *italic* denote figures.